TRIPOLI

TRIPOLI

THE UNITED STATES'
FIRST WAR ON TERROR

DAVID SMETHURST

BALLANTINE BOOKS • NEW YORK

A Presidio Press Mass Market Original

Copyright © 2006 by David Smethurst

Published in the United States by Presidio Press, an imprint of The Random House Publishing Group, a division of Random House, Inc., New York.

PRESIDIO PRESS and colophon are trademarks of Random House, Inc.

ISBN 978-0-89141-859-7

Cover design: Carl D. Galian
Cover illustration: © Jim Griffin

Printed in the United States of America

www.presidiopress.com

OPM 9 8 7 6 5 4 3 2 1

"If the President, the Congress and the Navy—above all, the Navy—will take my advice, the United States will win the greatest victory in her history, and the pirate states of North Africa will be totally defeated, never to rise against us or other civilized nations again."

—WILLIAM EATON in a letter
to Secretary of State James Madison,
October 1804

CONTENTS

viii CONTENTS

PROLOGUE

The year is 1799. The United States is a new nation, barely twenty-two years old. After defeating the British in the Revolutionary War, America has set out to build on her hard-won freedom. American merchantmen ply the oceans, selling American goods abroad and bringing back capital to build the new nation.

America is expanding, not only through trade and commerce, but also in size. Kentucky and Vermont have joined the union, and two stripes and two stars have been added to the flag's original thirteen. However, America realizes that maintaining her independence is based on her ability to freely conduct commerce with other nations. If she can trade freely, she will be able to maintain her independence; if not, she could slip back into colonial status as a dependent of either of the two major powers, Britain and France. As a result, the Marine Corps is established and the U.S. government orders American shipyards to build a fleet of powerful warships to protect American interests abroad. The clang of hammers and the rasp of saws resonate from the shipyards of Philadelphia, New York, Boston, Norfolk, Portsmouth, and Baltimore, where oak skeletons begin to take on the graceful lines of warships. Once these ships are ready, the first of America's newest fighting force, the Marine Corps, which consists of twenty-five officers and fifty-eight enlisted men, will sail on them to protect American trade.

The United States is threatened from two quarters: France and the Barbary States of North Africa. The French monarchy, which helped the United States during the War of Independence with money, military assistance, and matériel, has been overthrown and the revolutionaries, led by Napoléon Bonaparte, have conquered much of Europe. Because the United States sided with the monarchy, France has broken off diplomatic relations and is waging an undeclared war on American shipping. Throughout the oceans of the world, French privateers stalk American merchantmen; at any moment the conflict threatens to break out into open hostilities.

Meanwhile, America is also threatened by the Barbary States of Morocco, Tripoli, Algiers, and Tunis. These states, located on the shore of North Africa, have for centuries demanded an annual tribute to allow Christian vessels to trade unmolested in the Mediterranean. Since the young nation is no longer covered by the annual tribute paid by Britain, President John Adams signs peace treaties with each of the states, and grudgingly agrees to pay annual tributes. The peace, however, is fragile, and the Barbary States continue to increase their demands for military stores and gold, and threaten to declare war if their demands are not met.

Because the United States lacks a strong army and navy, President Adams appoints four consuls to maintain the fragile peace. One of them is William Eaton, a thirty-four-year-old soldier-diplomat and the personification of the young nation—independent-minded and aggressive. This is his story.

I

THE THIN BLUE LINE

Musket balls whizzed overhead like angry bees while chunks of lead kicked up stones and dirt as they slammed into the ground nearby. William Eaton stood beside Marine lieutenant Presley O'Bannon and studied the enemy rampart that blocked their path while his men, strung out on either side of him, fired back. They were pinned down on a hillside overlooking their objective, the pirate fortress of Derna. To get into the town, they would have to cross the Wadi Derna, which lay below them, and then overcome the Arab defenders who had formed a defensive position on the opposite bank of the river by piercing the walls of houses with loopholes, from which they kept up a steady fire on Eaton's men.

Eaton shifted his gaze from the fortifications and looked beyond them, where he spied their main objective: the fortress of Raz el Matariz, guarding the seaward approaches to Derna with eight nine-pound guns. Eaton snapped shut his glass and cursed. They were pinned down within sight of their objective; unless they somehow overran the parapet that lay before them, they would go home defeated, or worse.

It was April 27, 1805, and Eaton and his ragtag army had journeyed from Alexandria, Egypt, across more than five hundred miles of desert, to reach this town and wrest it from Yusuf Karamanli, the ruler of Tripoli. Their avowed purpose was to install his brother, Hamet, in Yusuf's stead. Eaton hoped that once Derna fell, the other major towns of Benghazi and Tripoli would follow suit, Tripolitans would flock to Hamet's banner, and Yusuf would be forced to flee into exile. But first they had to find some way of taking Derna.

As fire from the ramparts increased, Eaton glanced at his men. Six blue-jacketed U.S. Marines, directed by their sergeant, carefully aimed their long rifles at the Arab defenders, squeezing off shots whenever an enemy appeared too long in their sights. On their flank, forty Greek mercenaries, veterans of numerous European wars, were firing on the ramparts as well, directed by Captain Luco Ulovix and Lieutenant Constantine. Lastly, Eaton heard the steady boom of their supporting fieldpiece, manned by twenty-eight cannoniers and led by Selim Comb, his janissary and translator, and Lieutenants Connant and Rocco.

In all, Eaton had seventy-four men strung out on the barren hillside. He estimated that they were facing ten times that number, judging from the rate of fire and the steady whine and slap of the musket balls that peppered the slope. But more important, Eaton realized he was losing momentum and that the assault on Derna was in jeopardy. The next few moments would determine the outcome of four years of careful planning. If he and his men succeeded, Yusuf would be forced to sue for peace and free the more than three hundred American sailors imprisoned in a squalid dungeon in the capital city. If Eaton's attack was successful, Derna would fall, Tripolitans would flock to Hamet's banner, and Yusuf would be removed from power, something America, using only the conventional arms of the U.S. Navy, had been unable to do for the past four years. Yet in a few minutes, if Eaton did not get his men to move and take the ramparts, their dreams of victory would be dashed, American power and prestige in the Mediterranean would ebb, and all that had been fought for would be lost.

Eaton grimaced, swung his telescope to the left, and scanned the open ground to the south of town, where the rest of his force, a mixed contingent of Arab cavalry and foot soldiers led by Hamet, were flanking the town, securing the two districts that were most loyal to Hamet. They could hold the approaches to town, but Eaton knew they would not take it unless he and his small force cracked the defenses that lay in front of them, routed the defenders, and then took the battery at Raz el Matariz, whose guns could easily be turned on Eaton's army. Eaton swung his telescope toward the blue-green ocean, shimmering in the afternoon sun, and saw that Isaac Hull, commanding the American squadron, was doing his part. Jets of flame and smoke erupted from the gun ports of the *Nautilus, Hornet,* and *Argus* as they fired on the battery, keeping the enemy gunners within the battery pinned down.

Eaton knew something had to be done, and quick, to save his army from defeat. He conferred with O'Bannon, who had stood with him through uncertainty, mutiny, hunger, and disaster over the past five months. The twenty-nine-year-old lieutenant nodded grimly as Eaton told him what he intended to do. Eaton signaled to the bugler as O'Bannon ran along the thin blue line of marines, telling them to ready themselves. The bugler put the instrument to his lips, and the shrill, wailing notes rose above the whistle and crack of musket balls. As the bugler sounded the charge, Eaton raised his scimitar and roared as marines, Greeks, and cannoniers rose from the dusty ground and began to run through a hail of lead toward the ramparts.

They surged downhill, the Stars and Stripes rippling in the breeze. As Eaton's force raced forward, the ramparts erupted in smoke and stabs of flame as the defenders redoubled their fire. Suddenly, a blue-jacketed marine stumbled and fell, facefirst into the North African soil. The remaining men closed ranks, screaming at the top of their lungs and surging forward to determine the outcome of the United States' five-year-long war with Tripoli, and map out the young nation's place in the world.

II

CONSUL TO TUNIS

William Eaton took hold of the taffrail to steady himself as the *Sophia* plunged through the Mediterranean swell and gazed intently at Algiers, the capital city of the most powerful of the Barbary States. His stepson, Eli Danielson, and James Leander Cathcart, the American consul appointed to Tripoli, stood next to him, their feet firmly planted on the newly washed oak deck.

After a passage of thirty-three days from Delaware, they had arrived at this strange port on the North African coast. The date was February 9, 1799. Before them was a city of white, square-roofed houses, interspersed with minarets and the domes of mosques, that hugged the rugged hills shadowing a large, crescent-shaped bay. At the top of the highest hill was the Dey's palace fortress, called the Kasba, which was adorned by minarets. The anchorage was a poor one, with no natural mooring. It was, however, well defended. A pier extended from the walled city into the Mediterranean on which was built a large mole covered by batteries and a castle, all supplemented by shore batteries. Fortresses guarded the landward approaches to the city.

William Eaton, a thirty-four-year-old former captain of the U.S. Army, was one of three consuls selected by President John Adams to ensure that America maintained friendly relations with the Barbary States, with which the United States had concluded peace treaties—Morocco in 1786, Algiers in 1795, and Tripoli and Tunis in 1797. Eaton stood five feet, eight inches tall, and his blue eyes, set in a ruddy face, expressed energy, authority, and intelligence. Eaton was passionate, perceptive, bold, and independent, qualities Secretary of State Timothy Pickering believed would make an impression with the Barbary States.

Eaton was born in Woodstock, Connecticut, on February 23, 1764, the second son of a farmer. In 1780, at the age of sixteen, he left home and joined a battalion of Connecticut troops during the Revolutionary War. The start of his military career had been undistinguished: He served as a dishwasher and waiter in the officers' mess. After a year, he returned home, but grew bored and reenlisted. By the time he was discharged in 1783, he had made the rank of sergeant.

After the war, Eaton studied at Dartmouth, then taught school in Vermont. But army life still beckoned, and with the help of a senator from Vermont, he gained a captain's commission and made his way to Pittsburgh to join General Anthony Wayne, who was fighting Indians on the Northwest frontier in the Ohio Territory. After the conclusion of the campaign, Eaton made his way to Savannah, Georgia, where he clashed with his commanding officer and was court-martialed. Pickering, though, had taken a liking to the pugnacious, independent-minded young officer, and appointed him consul to Tunis. It was the perfect assignment for Eaton. Brusque, outspoken, and strong-headed, Eaton was the least likely choice for a diplomatic post, but in negotiations with the Barbary corsairs, Adams wanted men of strong character to ensure that peace was maintained.

The safest anchorage was to the right of the pier, where breakwaters formed a harbor. Eaton peered at the port in disgust and recognized the three American ships that now rode at anchor and were "gifts" to the Dey. Those ships, along with the *Sophia,* had departed together from Delaware a little more than a month before and were destined to join the Algerian navy. The *Hassan Bashaw* was a 275-ton brig carrying eight six-pounder cannons, the *Skjoldabrand* was a 250-ton schooner the U.S. government had purchased from Sweden armed with sixteen four-pounder guns, and the *El Eisha* was a 150-ton schooner carrying fourteen four-pounder guns. A fourth ship, not to be handed over, the *Hero,* was some distance behind. She was a slow sailor, loaded with naval stores for the Dey as part of America's treaty obligation. Eaton shifted his gaze from these gifts to the pirate galleys that bobbed at anchor. This was his first glimpse of these peculiar warships. The vessels had sails, but for additional speed, Christian slaves chained to benches rowed the ship under the lash of their Algerian guards.

The "gifts" were demanded after the United States had defaulted on its treaty payments. Under the treaty of 1795, the United States had agreed to pay Algiers $642,000 and provide the Dey with an annual tribute in naval stores, including powder, lead, iron, bullets, bombshells, masts, poles, and yards, at a value of 12,000 gold sequins or approximately $21,000. The payment was late, and the Dey had used the threat of war to demand three new ships to augment his navy.

Eaton was a pragmatist and knew America had few options. Even though three new warships had been launched in 1797— including the forty-four-gun *United States,* the forty-four-gun *Constitution,* and the thirty-eight-gun *Constellation*—and three more were being built, America did not yet possess a navy capable of tackling the Barbary pirates. For now, America needed to buy time.

Eaton was also well aware of the history of the Barbary pirates and Europe's long accommodation with them. Washed by the Mediterranean and bounded on the east by Egypt, on the west by the Atlantic, and to the south by the vastness of the Sahara desert, the four Barbary States—Morocco, Algiers, Tunis, and Tripoli—had been a scourge on seaborne commerce for centuries.

During the Crusades, from 1095 to 1295, Muslim pirates, operating from bases in North Africa, plundered ships carrying Christian soldiers and pilgrims, selling many into slavery. Two hundred years later, as Spain and the Ottoman Turks struggled for supremacy in the Mediterranean, an Algerian adventurer named Khair ad Din, called Barbarossa ("red beard"), fought with Turkey to secure the Maghrib (Northwest Africa) from the formidable Spanish armada. For his troubles, Barbarossa was appointed the Ottoman sultan's regent over this territory; "Barbary" was derived from his name.

In the seventeenth century, Barbary pirates plundered ships at will, grabbing sailors and soldiers to be sold into slavery or held as hostages. The corsairs sometimes also raided coastal settlements in Britain, Ireland, Andalusia, Calabria, and Sicily, running their craft onto unguarded beaches, then creeping up on villages in the dark to snatch their victims and retreat before the alarm could be sounded.

Eaton knew the Europeans could easily beat them into submission. Yet they paid them off. Yearly tributes from Britain, Spain, Italy, France, the Dutch, and the Germans ran into the hundreds of thousands from each nation. A portion of the money was paid to ransom slaves, although many of these unfortunates languished in captivity for decades while the ransom money was spent to further trade. It was not the most heroic of systems, but it did put up a convenient trade barrier to those nations that would not, or could not, pay such tribute.

The United States had little choice but to do as the Europeans had done—pay off the pirates. In the ten years prior to signing the peace treaties, she had suffered losses of both ships and men. More than a dozen ships and over a hundred sailors had been interred in Barbary dungeons, including Cathcart. As a result, American commerce, and prestige, had suffered.

Eaton understood Adams's motives. The president was a realist; he believed that the young nation should buy peace to save her commerce. After all, compared to the benefit, the price was small: Each year, more than a hundred ships carried tons of salted fish, flour, lumber, and sugar to the Mediterranean, and returned with lemons, oranges, figs, olive oil, opium, and wine. Furthermore, American commerce was growing briskly in the Mediterranean, and a war might interrupt that growth. In addition, Adams felt that the United States was just that, a collection of people who identified themselves as New Yorkers or Virginians, Green Mountain Boys or Georgians, and was unable to fight such a foe. And so, Eaton knew, he had been posted to Tunis to maintain the peace, while Cathcart had been sent to maintain good relations with Yusuf Karamanli, the Bashaw of Tripoli.

But Eaton didn't like it, and found himself siding with Jefferson's views of dealing with the pirates. When Thomas Jefferson had been secretary of state to George Washington, he had urged Congress to wage war on the Barbary pirates and "repel force by force." That, Eaton thought, is what America should do, not post diplomats to keep the peace. The United States was taking a businesslike approach instead of being forceful and taking on the barbarians.

Eaton gazed at the harbor and felt a sense of adventure and excitement mixed with some small trepidation. In a few moments, Richard O'Brien, who had arrived ahead of them and was consul to Algiers, would greet them. Both O'Brien and Cathcart were old hands. Eaton, on the other hand, had no experience with the Barbary pirates. Cathcart had been a prisoner in Algiers since 1785, and had used those years to his advantage, working his way up to serve as the clerk to Prime Minister Hassan, who became the Dey of Algiers. He had an entrepreneurial spirit, and during his captivity he had opened three taverns to serve local Christians, using the money from their sale to purchase a bark upon his release. O'Brien had commanded a privateer during the Revolutionary War. He had also been a slave of the Algerians and had skillfully assisted during the treaty negotiations between Algiers and the United States.

As two bells rang in the afternoon watch, signaling the hour of one p.m., the *Sophia* dropped her anchor and Eaton, Danielson, and Cathcart made their way to shore. Richard O'Brien greeted them and described the situation: The Dey, Bobba Mustapha, was angry about the delay in receiving money and stores from the United States and had refused to see him. O'Brien also told the men that Bobba Mustapha was making life difficult for him, refusing to allow him to hire Algerian servants. For that reason, O'Brien explained, pointing to the hills above town where the American house was located, they would have to carry their own luggage. The sailors manning the jolly boat quickly picked up the consuls' dunnage and began to carry it up the steep, winding streets of the town.

The lanes were narrow and so steep in places that they resembled a long series of steps. The streets were little more than alleys, so constricted that three men could not walk abreast. The upper floors of the houses projected over the street on wooden struts, their walls sometimes joining to form a tunnel. To Eaton's surprise, crowds of Algerian men stood along their route, cursing them. Would he receive the same treatment when he reached Tunis?

They waited three days for an audience with the Dey. During that time, Eaton learned that the French had taken Naples and that Napoléon Bonaparte had taken possession of Egypt. Eaton wondered if Bonaparte would now turn his attention to the Barbary States and complete his conquest of North Africa.

Finally, seventy-two hours after their arrival, the Dey sent word that he would receive them. On the afternoon of February 12, the consuls and the captains of the four American ships in harbor trudged from the American house to the Kasba. At the main gate, armed guards instructed them to remove their swords and then searched them for concealed weapons including daggers and pistols. Once they had finished with their search, the sentries stood back and the captain of the guards motioned for the Americans to enter the palace. They walked through a large, arched doorway and found themselves in a courtyard. There they were instructed to take off their hats; they were then led through a hallway and up five flights of stairs. At the top, they found themselves in a dark, narrow passage. At the end of the passageway, their escort told them to remove their shoes. Eaton did so, and they entered a small room approximately eight feet by twelve. The room was dark, the only illumination coming from small iron-barred windows set high in the walls.

As Eaton's eyes adjusted to the light, he spied a huge, shaggy beast sitting on a low bench. He reminded Eaton of a bear. As they approached, the beast reached out with his forepaw and Richard O'Brien kissed the offered hand; Eaton and the rest of the entourage followed suit. Eaton watched as the beast remained seated and listened to O'Brien's description of the ships, delivered in compensation for failing to meet the treaty obligations. The Dey nodded, accepting the gifts, and declared that the treaty between the United States and Algiers was in effect again and that relations had been restored.

The Dey ordered refreshments, honey cakes and strong coffee. Eaton surprised the Dey by eating the cakes with his right hand, as was the custom in Muslim countries. He surprised the Dey even more when, ignoring the interpreter, he addressed the Dey in Arabic. His accent was atrocious, but he made himself understood, and impressed not only the Dey but also Cathcart and O'Brien.

When the audience was over, the consuls retraced their steps to the palace gates. Eaton blinked in the bright afternoon sun, like a man coming out of a dream. He could hardly believe what he had just witnessed, America reduced to the role of supplicant to a half-educated savage in a country where Christians were spit upon and cursed. The brute had seven kings of Europe, two republics, and a continent paying tribute to him, yet he possessed a naval force that could be whipped by two line-of-battle ships. Still, what concerned Eaton even more was that the European consuls he had met claimed that the Dey was more civilized than either the Bey of Tunis or the Bashaw of Tripoli. It was a rude yet eye-opening introduction to the power of the Barbary pirates.

On March 14, after a twelve-day passage from Algiers, the *Sophia* rounded Point Farina, a hooked point of land that shoaled well out into the sea, and entered the Gulf of Tunis. Eaton, Danielson, and Cathcart stood on the quarterdeck and gazed at the landscape that came into view. Ahead of them, the Plomb Mountains rose above the ochre-colored shore. The *Sophia* cut through the wind-ruffled waters, heading to the southern end of the gulf where there was a bay, bracketed

by Cape Tortas to port and Cape Carthage to starboard. As
Eaton gazed toward Carthage, he could see the ruins of what
looked like an ancient castle along with several houses. Beyond Carthage, Eaton knew, was the plain where Hannibal
and Scipio Africanus had fought. The *Sophia* passed into the
bay, and a large fortress came into view, which Eaton surmised from his studies was the Goulette. The battery guarded
the opening of a smaller bay, to starboard, that led to the city
of Tunis some six miles distant. As they approached the battery, the *Sophia*'s anchors slashed the surface of the bay, settling into the soft mud off the Goulette. Now, thought Eaton,
his real work would begin.

As the cutter crew's powerful strokes propelled them
through the narrow passage that separated the Gulf of Tunis
from the smaller bay separating the Goulette and Tunis,
Eaton reviewed the instructions he had received from Pickering almost three months earlier. On December 18, Pickering
had handed him a set of orders, as well as a warning. His immediate objective was to negotiate changes to the treaty between the United States and Tunis that the government found
objectionable.

Joseph Etienne Famin, a Frenchman who had been em-
ployed by Joel Barlow, the American consul to Algiers and
Tunis, had negotiated the treaty. Barlow, based in Algiers,
had engaged Famin, an influential person who was a French-
protected subject of the Dey of Algiers, to act as the American consular agent to Tunis. He had been doing so since
1797, and it was three articles of the treaty Famin had negotiated that Pickering wanted to change.

Article fourteen of the treaty concerned custom duties.
The treaty allowed Tunisian merchants, under any flag, to
carry merchandise to the United States and pay three percent
duty. Pickering told Eaton this was a dangerous precedent
and could be ruinous to the United States, which derived
most of its revenue from imported goods; the duties levied
generally exceeded ten percent. If the United States government were to ratify this treaty, the duty charged on all foreign
goods would have to be reduced to three percent. Pickering

felt that this article had been slipped into the treaty through the influence of a few European merchants in Tunis who alone would benefit. The article itself would offer no benefit to the Bey or any of his subjects. Pickering instructed Eaton to negotiate the removal of this article from the treaty.

He further instructed Eaton to modify articles eleven and twelve. Article eleven stipulated that whenever either an American or a Tunisian warship entered the port of the other country, the shore batteries would salute the vessel by firing one gun for each gun fired by the warship. What Pickering found objectionable was the stipulation that the visiting ship would pay one barrel of gunpowder for each gun fired by the shore battery. Since it was unlikely that Tunisian warships would ever visit the United States, this article, Pickering felt, was merely a thinly disguised levy of naval stores. Pickering wanted the required payment of one barrel of gunpowder removed and a limit of fifteen gun-for-gun salutes.

Finally, article twelve allowed the Bey of Tunis to requisition American ships for his own use. Pickering wanted Eaton to remove a clause of the article that would permit the Bey to compel an American ship's captain to allow the Bey to use his vessel at a rate determined by the Bey. This could lead to any Tunisian merchant who had influence in court asking the Bey to seize an American ship for his own use and decide on the compensation. Pickering also wanted language added to ensure that no ship that was previously engaged could be requisitioned.

To effect these changes, Eaton had been given cash, with payments for each modification spelled out. Lastly, Eaton was authorized to spend up to $100,000 in place of delivering the agreed-to naval stores, which were worth $35,000. This would save America both time and money in collecting the stores, and would deny the Barbary States the war matériel needed to fight a war.

As the cutter approached the bustling wharf of the Goulette, Eaton also recalled Pickering's private instructions and words of advice. In particular, Eaton remembered two sections of Pickering's letter:

To account for the extraordinary stipulation in the 14th article of
the treaty, it is to be noted, That the negotiator, Mr. Famin, is a
French merchant residing at Tunis, and much in favor with one
or more of the influential officers of that government. Mr. Barlow asserts that neither this stipulation nor that of the eleventh
article nor the one the last paragraph in the twelfth was compre-
hended in the first project of the treaty transmitted to him by
Mr. Famin in April 1798: and he can account for the insertion of
the fourteenth article only on the ground that Mr. Famin, being a
merchant, might expect to derive great commercial advantages
from the direct trade he might carry on to the United States.

It is farther to be considered that the hostile measures and
designs of France against the United States were well known
to Mr. Famin before the conclusion of the treaty; and that as
Mr. Herculais the principal French Agent in the Barbary who
recommended Mr. Famin to Mr. Barlow, as well as all the other
agents of that nation at Algiers, Tunis or Tripoli, were thwarting
the interests of the United States, so Mr. Famin might be willing to
join his countrymen, with the like national view. He and Mr. Herculais, nevertheless, reproach each other and perhaps very justly.
The result of this negotiation demonstrates that neither deserves
the confidence of the United States.

It is to be remembered that as the policy of the Barbary Powers constantly leads them to make war on some of the christian
nations, so the agents of these nations respectively endeavour to
ward off the mischief; and thus are, in some sort, in a state of
hostility among themselves. Whenever therefore the interests of
the United States are in question, you must chiefly rely on your
own means to secure them.

As Eaton clambered out of the boat and onto the wharf, he
knew that his first mission was to assess Famin and determine
whether he was friend or foe. He knew that Barlow had
promised Famin the consulate at Tunis if he succeeded in negotiating a treaty with Tunis. Famin might view Eaton as
usurping the post he could rightly claim he had earned. Furthermore, Famin was an influential personage, whom Eaton
would have to treat with respect. But based on Pickering's
admonishments, Famin might not be trustworthy. Eaton
would have to look the man in the eye and assess his charac-

ter for himself. If he was an enemy, then it was up to Eaton alone to negotiate a revised peace treaty with the Bey of Tunis.

After they had unloaded their baggage, they hired carts and made their way toward Tunis. Eaton spied a town of dun-colored walls topped by the spires of minarets. The wheels of the coach clattered against the cobblestones as they entered the city through an arched gate. Once inside, they navigated a warren of streets, or souks as they were referred to, heading for the diplomatic district where Famin's house and those of the other consuls were located.

Eaton noted that each souk seemed to be devoted to a trade. There was a shoemaker souk, a leather-worker souk, a coppersmith souk, and a souk for weavers. Along the way, they also passed the Djama Zitouna, or mosque of the olive tree, an important center of learning. Finally, they reached the diplomatic quarter, and Eaton saw that all the consular houses were decked out in bunting in honor of his arrival, and that one of the houses flew the American flag.

As the coach came to a halt, Famin stepped out of the house and greeted them, ordering servants to take their bags. After they had settled in, Famin welcomed Eaton and told him that he had arranged a party to honor their arrival. Eaton told Famin that before joining the party, he would like to re-quest an audience with the Bey, and the message was duly sent. With this important business out of the way, Eaton began to relax. Refreshments were served, and Eaton was in-troduced to the various consuls who lived in the city, as well as fourteen Americans who resided there.

Famin was a good host, but perhaps too good, Eaton thought, as he realized that the man was on hand whenever he met any of the Americans or consular agents. The British consular agent, Major Magre, must have noticed as well, for when Famin became engaged in conversation with Cathcart, Magre quickly steered Eaton away from the Frenchman and told him that contrary to appearances, Famin was extremely angry that Eaton had arrived and would do everything in his power to undermine him.

He told Eaton that his situation was peculiarly critical, that snares were set for him on many sides, and that the utmost vigilance might not save him from falling into some of them. Magre advised Eaton to move with caution but firmness in the business of his negotiations, and said the Bey was a man of acute discernment, and generally of fair dealing, but that he was vain and avaricious. Famin had been making money on the side, selling trading "rights" to captains of American merchant vessels. Eaton's arrival would end this source of income and decrease his power with the Bey. The British consul also told Eaton to be wary of the French consul, Maurice Herculais.

Eaton thanked him as Famin, seeing the two conversing, walked over and introduced the French consul, who was openly hostile toward Eaton. It was a refreshing change; at least it was out in the open that France and the United States were not friends. The two countries were at that moment fighting a war on the high seas. French privateers were attacking American merchant ships, and the American government had responded by sending a squadron to the Caribbean.

Eaton had no idea that France was already reeling from a major defeat. On February 9, 1799, Commodore Thomas Truxtun, commanding the *Constellation,* had defeated *L'Insurgent* off the island of Nevis in the Caribbean. Yet in the war that now consumed Europe, France was faring much better. Napoléon had conquered Egypt the previous summer, and although his fleet had been defeated at the Battle of the Nile, France remained in control of Egypt. Furthermore, France had conquered Belgium, Holland, the Rhineland, and much of northern Italy.

Eaton knew that his role was to remain neutral insofar as the war in Europe was concerned, maintaining American trade and commerce in the Mediterranean. While France had been weakened on the seas by its defeat in the Battle of the Nile, the French were almost impregnable in North Africa. And so, Eaton knew he would have to be extraordinarily careful.

*   *   *

The following afternoon, Eaton received a reply to his message: He and Cathcart were expected at the Kasba at eight o'clock the following morning.

The next day, they set off in a carriage drawn by two mules. The palace was four miles from the city, and the trip took an hour. As they clambered out of the coach, Eaton asked several of the Bey's sentries to assist him with a sack that was stowed in the carriage. In it was a gift for the Bey, a gift that Eaton hoped would ensure tranquil relations with Tunis, especially since America was late delivering the naval stores stipulated by the peace treaty. The sack contained ten thousand silver dollars, and was so heavy that it took three soldiers to lift it out of the carriage and place it into a wheelbarrow.

Once inside, they were ushered into the audience chamber, where Eaton saw a man seated on a sofa with his legs tucked beneath him like a tailor. Eaton bowed and presented his gifts to the Bey Ahmed Pasha, whom he was grateful to see was quite the opposite of the Dey of Algiers, in appearance at least. The Bey was tall and elegant, and in no way resembled the shaggy beast Eaton had met in Algiers. He was seated on a sofa covered in velvet and embroidered with gold. Wearing a turban on his head, with a rich surplice over his shoulder, he offered Eaton a seat on his right. Eaton noted that his chief minister, who was referred to as the Sapitapa, or Keeper of the Seals, sat on the Bey's left.

After Eaton sat down, he addressed the Bey in Arabic. The Bey was pleased with Eaton's use of his native language and the two quickly hit it off. Eaton also learned that they both spoke Greek. After the introductions, three Christian slaves entered the chamber bringing a salver of coffee and beautiful china cups set in gold and richly ornamented with diamonds. Sipping his coffee, Eaton told the Bey that he had been instructed to secure modifications to the treaty between the two countries. The conversation quickly moved to article eleven, which required American warships entering Tunisian waters to salute the shore battery by firing a gun-for-gun salute, and to deliver a barrel of powder for each battery fired by the shore battery.

"Is your vessel a vessel of war?" asked the Bey.

"Yes," replied Eaton.

"Why was I not duly informed of it, that you might have been saluted, as is customary?" responded the Bey.

"We were unacquainted with the customs," replied Eaton.

The Bey changed the subject, informing Eaton that the basis for peace between Tunis and the United States was the timely delivery of stores promised by the treaty. Those stores had been due a year before. If the treaty stores were not delivered soon, said the Bey, there would be war. The Bey was especially angry that the Dey of Algiers had received supplies as well as warships, while he had received nothing.

Eaton offered the Bey a compromise. He told the Bey that he was authorized to pay an equivalent amount of money in lieu of the stores. The Bey responded that he had cash to spare, but stores were what he needed, gunpowder and shot, spars and timber, which, the Bey told Eaton, he understood the Dey of Algiers had just received.

Eaton responded by saying that the cruisers provided to Algiers had been paid for with cash, and that since they were armed, provided the means of safeguarding the treaty stores delivered to Algiers. Eaton told the Bey that since the United States and France were virtually at war, it was dangerous to send supplies to Tunis aboard an unarmed American merchantman, which was another reason why he had been authorized to offer cash.

Eaton explained that the American government had only received the treaty eight months before, when plague had raged through Philadelphia, and the government offices had been closed as a result. And then winter had arrived and the harbors had iced over, thus delaying the shipment. Eaton also explained that the Senate had objected to three articles in the treaty and that when those were altered the stores would be sent.

The Bey turned to Famin, who had remained silent during the audience, and asked why, if the treaty had not been ratified, had he hoisted the American flag?

Famin responded that he had received orders from the American government.

Eaton and Cathcart told the Bey that no such order had been given, nor would be until the three articles had been modified.

"It cost you but little to have your flag hoisted," the Bey responded. "It will cost you less to have it taken down." Eaton picked up on the threat: The Barbary pirates declared war by chopping down the flagpole of their enemy.

Eaton again pressed the Bey to compromise. The United States would offer the Bey a cruiser in exchange for the stores. The Bey responded angrily that he would expect the stores as well as a cruiser, as a present.

Eaton told the Bey that he was not authorized to provide a cruiser, gratis, to the Bey. The U.S. Navy was currently battling French privateers and needed every ship it could spare. At that, the Bey dismissed Eaton and Cathcart. However, as they left the audience room, the Sapitapa told Eaton that the Bey would receive him again on Monday, just two days later.

After the audience, Cathcart made his way to the Goulette in an attempt to sail for Tripoli. He had seen to Eaton's safe arrival, and after watching him during the audience, Cathcart knew Eaton could handle himself and America's business with Tunis. But upon his arrival at the Goulette, he was detained and not allowed to board his ship. As he whiled away the evening with an old engineer who worked for the Bey, Cathcart again heard what the diplomatic community had told him and Eaton: Famin was not trustworthy. The engineer told Cathcart that all of the consuls believed Famin was actually a spy in the employ of the Bey, providing reasons for the Bey to demand fresh tributes. For his services, claimed the engineer, Famin received a commission. The next day, Cathcart made his way back to Tunis. If he couldn't leave, he would at least help Eaton renegotiate a more favorable treaty.

Over the course of the next two days, Eaton and Cathcart negotiated with the Bey over the three objectionable articles of the treaty. The Bey was particularly intractable on article eleven, which specified that whenever a U.S. ship arrived in

Tunis, it had to pay one barrel of gunpowder for each gun fired by the shore battery. "Strike out the barrel of powder for each gun, and reduce the number to fifteen," Eaton requested.

The Bey declined, stating that he would allow the article to apply to Tunisian vessels visiting American ports.

Eaton replied that this was already implied in the phrasing, and that he could not agree to it, because although the expense was small, the demand was humiliating to the United States and not honorable for him.

"However trifling it may appear to you, to me it is important," said the Bey. "Fifteen barrels of powder will furnish a cruiser that may capture a prize and net me $100,000."

Eaton remained firm and told the Bey that both justice and honor would forbid the United States from agreeing to this demand.

"You consult your honor, I my interest," replied the Bey. "But if you wish to save your honor in this instance, give me fifty barrels of powder annually and I will consent to the alteration."

Eaton and Cathcart remained firm and told the Bey this they could not do. The Bey turned to the Sapitapa and said: "These people are Cheribeenas [Persian merchants]. They are so hard there is no dealing with them."

The Bey rose from his sofa to signal that the audience was over. He told Eaton and Cathcart, "You will call the day after tomorrow."

The negotiations continued for several weeks. Finally, as March ended, the Bey agreed to modify the three articles. With regard to article twelve, in which American ships could be impressed into the service of Tunis, Eaton compromised and agreed to the article provided that the ship owners were compensated. Regarding article eleven, which specified that a barrel of gunpowder would be paid for each Tripolitan gun fired in salute of an American warship, the Bey agreed to modify the article so that a salute would only occur if an American vessel demanded it. Finally, with regard to article fourteen, which would have allowed Tunisian merchants to pay lower tariffs in America than American merchants would have to pay in Tunis, the Bey agreed to make the tariffs equal.

After the Bey and his ministers had signed the treaty, Eaton received a note from the Sapitapa indicating that the Bey expected something "a little better" than the standard presents required on the occasion of hoisting the flag.

On April 2, the Bey allowed Cathcart to sail for Tripoli. Meanwhile, Eaton arrived at the Kasba bearing chests containing presents for the Bey and his ministers. For the Bey, Eaton brought linen, two caftan brocades, a diamond watch and chain set, a gold snuffbox set in diamonds, and a diamond ring. For the Sapitapa, Eaton brought a number of gifts, including a gold watch and chain, a ring, and two caftan brocades. When Eaton presented the presents, the Bey asked Eaton if he had not received his note indicating that he had requested something a little better, a present similar in value to what he had received from Spain on the occasion of hoisting that nation's flag?

Eaton replied that the presents he had brought with him were valued at more than $6,000.

The Bey picked up the gold snuffbox, turned it over in his hands, then put it down. He told Eaton that while the presents were fine, he insisted on a handsome present of gold-and-diamond jewelry similar to what the Spanish consul had given him. He suggested that the present contain an emerald the size of a seagull egg.

Eaton told him that if that was the case he would have to consult his government.

The Bey responded, "If you will not agree to it, you may go home, and consider void all that has been done."

Eaton replied that if there was no other alternative then he would indeed leave.

"Very well," replied the Bey. "I give you ten days to consider the subject; if you continue in your present resolution, you may embark in the brig, on her return from Tripoli, and go home."

With that, the Bey stood and left in a rage. After he left,

the Sapitapa reaffirmed the importance of the present. "The Bey must have his present; it is indispensable," he told Eaton.

Eaton told him that the sort of present the Bey wanted would be difficult to procure, which left war as the only alternative. Eaton begged the Sapitapa to persuade the Bey to drop his demand.

As Eaton left he wondered why, at this late stage, the Bey had demanded a more handsome present than he would rightly have come to expect. The value of such a present was easily in the neighborhood of $41,000. This was a vast sum. As he walked home through the souks, he found himself thinking of Famin. The man had treated him well on a personal level and had acted with what Eaton believed was true friendship, but everyone he had met had denounced the Frenchman as a perfidious scoundrel. Could Famin have whispered in the Bey's ear, asking him to make this request? Famin would know that Eaton would have a difficult, nay impossible, time obtaining such a present. And if Eaton was therefore unable to procure such a gift, would not the Bey expel him from the country, and thereby restore Famin to his place as consul to Tunis? Yet Famin had done nothing overt, and as a result, Eaton dropped the idea. He would keep an eye on Famin, but in case he was still angry over his reduced role, Eaton would soften the blow and pay him two years' salary and two years' house rent. Eaton hoped that would assuage his feelings and keep Famin on his side.

The next day, Eaton again appeared before the Sapitapa. The minister was in a much more agreeable mood, but he still insisted upon a handsome present for the Bey.

Eaton again replied that the gold and diamonds requested were not available in America, nor were the craftsmen to work them.

"What are you, a parcel of countrymen, shepherds, and rustics?" asked the Sapitapa.

"Very much so," replied Eaton.

"But you build ships," retorted the Sapitapa.

"Yes," agreed Eaton.

"Well, suppose you agree to make the Bey a present of a small, handsome cruiser?"

Eaton said he would consider this request and left the audience chamber. That night, Eaton sat at his writing desk and opened his journal. He dipped the nib of his pen into the inkwell and poured out his frustration:

> It is hard to negotiate, where the terms are wholly ex parte. The Barbary courts are indulged in the habit of dictating their own terms of negotiation. Even the English, as the consul himself informed me, on his arrival and reception here, had furnished him a present in cash and other articles, valued in England at seventeen thousand pounds sterling. But Tunis trembles at the voice of England. This, then, must be a political intrigue of England, to embarrass the other mercantile Christian nations; and it has the effect. To the United States, they believe they can dictate terms. Why should they not? Or why should they believe it will ever be otherwise? They have seen nothing in America to controvert this opinion. And all our talk of resistance and reprisal, they view as the swaggering of a braggadocio. They are at present seriously concerned, through fear that the English and Americans are in offensive and defensive alliance. The report is current, and I have taken occasion to cherish it, by being seen frequently with the British consul, dining with him, and holding secret intercourse. But, whatever stratagem may be used to aid our measures, it is certain, that there is no access to the permanent friendship of these States, without paving the way with gold or cannon balls; and the proper question is, Which method is preferable? So long as they hold their own terms, no estimate can be made of the expense of maintaining a peace. They are under no restraint of honor or honesty. There is not a scoundrel among them, from the prince to the muleteer, who will not beg and steal. Yet when I proposed to the Sapitapa, to-day, to substitute money in lieu of a present, he said the Bey had too high a sense of honor to receive a bribe; he would receive a present, but it would affront him to offer him money.

America, Eaton knew, wished for peace in the Mediterranean so she could expand her trade while France and Britain were at war. Eaton also knew that America was about to formally declare war on France, which was one reason the British consul had been so friendly of late. And so, in the short term, all he could do was appease the Barbary tyrants and wait until his government decided to use cannon balls instead of gold to build a long-term relationship with the Barbary pirates.

Eaton soon realized, however, that the demands for money, presents, and bribes would never end. On April 6, the prime minister, Mustapha Hogea, returned his present, claiming that it was inferior to the present Eaton had given the Sapitapa, who was the second minister. Hogea demanded presents of higher value. Eaton boiled with inner rage, but took back the presents. On the next day, the admiral of the Tunisian navy sent Eaton a note, demanding a gold watch and chain, and twelve picks of cloth. Later that day, Eaton received another note, this from the Aga of the Goulette, asking for a gift customarily given when the first vessel of war of a nation at peace with Tunis arrived in the bay.

These demands, Eaton knew, were all part of the way of life in the Barbary States, where every official was a beggar and a thief. The revenue of the United States, Eaton realized, was inadequate to satisfy these scoundrels' every demand. He would have to provide an additional present to Hogea, but as for the Aga, he jotted a quick note telling him he would provide the man with a copy of the treaty as a gift. Paper was less expensive than cloth, gold watches, and jewels. As Eaton sat back, satisfied that he had at least thwarted one of the beggars, a note arrived from Famin, indicating that in addition to the sum of money Eaton had given him, which included two years' salary, he required $1,918.21 for repairs, alterations (paper hanging, etc.), nine months' additional house rent, and furniture. Eaton fumed and decided he would not answer Famin's fresh demand for money.

After sending home a packet of letters and the modifications of the treaty to Pickering, Eaton turned his attention to securing a house for himself and Eli. Famin was alarmed to hear that Eaton was moving out, and offered to provide Eaton with a servant. Eaton refused, preferring to hire his own. He needed a man he could trust, someone who would not spy on him as any servant offered by Famin would likely do, and found just the man he was looking for. Aletti had been born in Gibraltar and came with a checkered past. He was a convict in Ireland, was well traveled in Europe and the Barbary, and had a gift for languages. Eaton liked him immensely and hired him as his major domo.

With the treaty negotiations concluded, Eaton returned to the Kasba on April 14 to address the continued delay of the annual tribute. After coffee was served, the Sapitapa told Eaton that he had discussed Eaton's offer of a cruiser in lieu of stores, but the Bey would not hear of it.

Eaton responded by asking if the Bey would accept a payment in cash in place of the stores, and offered him $50,000.

The Sapitapa answered that military and naval stores were very much in demand at this time. Because France and England were at war, they were very hard to come by. Should Eaton offer $250,000 in lieu of the stores, the Bey would decline it. On this, the Sapitapa told Eaton, the Bey was firm.

Eaton argued again that it was difficult to get the stores to Tunis in an unarmed American merchant ship while French and British fleets fought throughout the Mediterranean.

The Sapitapa was unmoved, stating that the stores were required, as was a present for the Bey. And furthermore, stated the Sapitapa, the Bey requested two additional presents: a double-barreled gun and a gold watch-chain.

Eaton could not believe the impudence of the man, and found he could not hold his temper in check. He told the minister that sending stores and public presents, and now receiving requests for private presents, the United States might find it more economical to send a squadron of warships to the Mediterranean to defend its commerce rather than accede to these demands. The Sapitapa listened to Eaton's angry response and then excused himself.

A short time later, he returned and bade Eaton to the Bey's apartment. There, Eaton found the Bey in a foul mood, angered, no doubt, by Eaton's outburst. He let Eaton know his displeasure and then walked toward the door. Just as he was about to leave, he turned and addressed Eaton. "Consult your government. I give them six months to give me an answer, and to send the presents. If they come in that time, well; if not, take down your flag and go home."

Eaton left the audience and realized that the only way to preserve the peace was to send the stipulated stores before six months were up. But he also realized that such an unequal relationship could not continue forever. Force rather than diplomacy would soon have to be used to deal with these scoundrels. That night, he sat at his writing desk and penned a note to Richard O'Brien laying out his feelings. He wrote that the United States should fit out a fleet, send it to the Mediterranean, and sink every corsair they could find, "and let the Bashaws wreak their vengence on the consuls— if they pleased, eat them."

Yet Eaton did not give up on diplomacy. He knew that America had cash, but her ships were currently fighting the French in the Caribbean and could not be dispatched to the Mediterranean. Therefore, Eaton made another attempt to get the Sapitapa to agree to a cash payment instead of stores. He offered the Sapitapa $90,000 in lieu of stores, and promised him $10,000 in consideration of his assistance. The Sapitapa told Eaton he would think on it.

While Eaton waited to see if his bribe had any effect, he donned Arab dress and set off into the countryside, getting to know Tunisia and gathering intelligence about Tunis's navy and commerce. Back in December, when Pickering had issued him with his instructions, the secretary of state had emphasized that in addition to negotiating modifications to the three articles, Eaton should also gather intelligence about commerce to assist American merchantmen, and report on the strength of the Tunisian naval forces, should war break out. Eaton spent weeks touring the countryside. What he found was that there was a strong demand for muslin, fine clothes, iron, coffee, sugar, pepper, spices, bleached wax candles, cochineal, dried fish, and lumber. All of these articles, Eaton estimated, would fetch more than three hundred percent what they would in the United States.

About Tunis's navy, Eaton also prepared detailed reports. He noted that Tunis had a hundred and twenty cruisers—most of them small with mounted guns ranging in size from four- to nine-pounders. Eaton also noted that on average, pirate vessels made five cruises per month, chiefly to the cruising grounds of Corsica; Sardinia; Sicily; along the Italian coast of Genoa, Tuscany, Naples, and Calabria; and as far as Venice. However, since these coasts had come under the protection of France and Britain, the Tunisian cruisers had to look elsewhere for prey. Venice had come under control of Napoléon, and was allied with the sultan of Turkey. The remaining Italian states were allied with either France or England. Furthermore, other nations threatened by the Barbary pirates sent ships in a display of force. Denmark and Sweden both sent frigates, which appeared regularly off Tunis. Eaton also studied their tactics:

> Their long latteen yards drop on board the enemy and afford a safe and easy conveyance for the men who man them for this purpose. But being always crouded with men, they throw them in from all points of the rigging and from all quarters of the decks, having their sabers grasped between their teeth and their loaded pistols in their belts, that they may have the free use of their hands in scaling the gunnels or netting of their enemy. In this mode of attack they are very active and very desperate. Taught by revelations that war with the Christians will guarantee the salvation of their souls, and finding so great secular advantages in the observance of this religious duty their inducements to desperate fighting are very powerful.

Eaton had heard just how vicious an enemy the Barbary pirates were from the British consul, who had described a raid that took place in Sardinia the previous September. Five corsairs carrying almost one thousand men had captured seven hundred women and children and two hundred and twenty men. The prisoners were crammed into the ships' holds and brought to Tunis, where they were goaded through the streets, some without clothes, driven to the auction square, and sold into slavery. The Bey demanded $640,000 for their release, but the king of Sardinia could not find the funds to pay for them. Eaton had seen some of the wretched Sardinians, and had given one hundred dollars to feed and clothe them.

Under the pretext of sightseeing, Eaton visited Carthage, and sketched the surrounding countryside from a military point of view. He also made his way to Bizerte and reported that the defenses there were weak. Eaton admired the quaint old castle, but noted that there was no garrison, only an old caretaker. Strolling along the seawall, he counted seventy soldiers commanded by a Turk, and saw that they were ragged-looking and poorly equipped. Eaton wrote a report indicating that an invasion force of eight battalions could take and hold the town, and in doing so flank the more extensive seaward defenses of Tunis.

Besides these visits, Eaton also made a detailed survey of the winds and weather, harbors, fortifications, and garrisons along the entire Tunisian coast. As Eaton gathered information, he grew more and more angry at the Bey and the Barbary pirates, as well as the impotence of his position. He was also angry at America's feeble policy of buying off the pirates in light of his own intelligence indicating that the forces of Tunis were weak and could be destroyed by a small force of Americans. He wrote O'Brien and asked why the United States had not sent even a frigate into the Mediterranean to send a message that America had muscle to back up diplomacy. "If Congress do not consent that the government shall send a force into these seas, at least to check the insolence of these scoundrels and to render themselves respectable, I hope they will resolve at their next session to wrest the quiver of arrows from the left talon of the eagle, in their arms, and substitute a fiddle bow or a segar in lieu."

On June 28, the Sapitapa held a dinner at his home. Once coffee had been served, the Sapitapa announced that Eaton's proposal of a cash payment in lieu of stores was not feasible. Even now, reported the Sapitapa, the Bey had sent vessels to Trieste, Mahon, and Spain for maritime and military stores to replace those he had expected from the United States. The

Sapitapa told Eaton he was authorized to declare that no sum of money would be considered as a replacement for the requested presents.

Eaton was now becoming wise to the ways of the Barbary. He was convinced that the Bey and the Sapitapa had made demands for additional presents and a cruiser to find a pretext for war. Later that night, after the guests had finished, Eaton's suspicions were confirmed. A body of Turks came into the garden where the diners were enjoying coffee and dessert and demanded money from the Sapitapa, claiming that since Tunis was at peace with everyone, they had been reduced to famine. Eaton understood that in order for the regime to survive, the Bey had to let his navy loose on someone, and realized that if the promised stores and presents did not arrive by February, the Bey would send out his cruisers to sweep up American merchantmen.

On the following day, Eaton grew even more alarmed at the precarious position of the United States when he learned that the Portuguese and Sicilian ambassadors had left Tunis, having signed peace treaties with the Bey. Eaton decided to ask for an audience with the Bey in one final effort to pay cash in lieu of the promised supplies and alleviate the threat of war, rather than let the situation smolder until the arrival of an American store ship. On July 4, Eaton visited the Bey and asked what sum of money would satisfy his claims and cancel his demands for stores.

"No sum whatever," replied the Bey. "You need not think more of it."

The Bey told Eaton that he had already heard Eaton's proposals on the subject, and had instructed his ministers to provide Eaton with his response, which he had just done again. Eaton left the audience fearful that if the stores did not arrive in time, the Bey would declare war on the United States.

Eaton was also convinced that American policy toward the Barbary pirates needed to change. As the heat of the day crept in through the shutters of his home, Eaton sat down to write a letter to William Smith, the U.S. minister to Lisbon, and lay out his thoughts on American policy:

"I have earnestly insisted on the necessity of showing a force in this sea.—The arguments advanced in favour of the measure accompany this in two letters to Colonel Pickering." Eaton continued, writing about the Bey's repeated demands for jewels. "We must at some point dare begin to resist demands of this nature.—Why should further sacrifices be made before we try the experiment of resistance? Humility invites insult. The greater our concessions the more accumulated will be the demands upon us. Nothing can be more absurd than to expect by presents to satisfy the demands of these marauding and beggarly courts, who have no sense of gratitude, no sentiments of honour, no respect for justice, no restraint from fear, and whose avarice is as insatiable as death."

Eaton continued: "I am more and more convinced that the mode of our negociation with these regencies must be so reformed as to remove the impressions that weakness and fear have dictated the measures to which we have hitherto yielded."

He noted that already he had spent $100,000 in negotiating with Tunis, and peace had still not been secured. The Bey wanted additional stores and presents that would bring the total to almost $200,000. Eaton's pen scratched against the paper as he concluded his letter. "America must shew a force in this sea. National interest, honour, safety demand it. The appearance of a few frigates would produce what the whole revenue of a country would not. They would produce impressions of terror and respect. Without force we are neither safe nor respectable here. Does not good policy dictate this caution against aggression before we shall be compelled to the measure to chastise outrage?"

Toward the end of the month, the Bey invited all of the consuls of tributary nations to the Kasba. In the audience chamber, the Bey demanded that each nation immediately send him military and naval supplies. Turning to Eaton, he demanded that he charter an American ship and send for the supplies. Eaton spent the next three days in the palace, haggling with the Bey until he finally agreed to drop the demand

and wait for the store ship's arrival. The Bey, Eaton thought, was, for the most part, reasonable, but the same could not be said for the Sapitapa, who owned corsairs, and Famin, who Eaton believed was in league with him.

Meanwhile, Eaton continued to take trips throughout Tunisia, gathering military intelligence. In late September, he asked the Bey if he could go to the seaside for his health, and spent two nights lodged with the governor of Porto Farina, Tunis's principal naval port, located twenty-five miles north-northwest of Tunis, just to the east of Bizerte. While ostensibly recuperating by the seaside, Eaton climbed to the top of the watchtower and sketched the town and its surroundings. He noted that the town could be taken by a three-pronged attack. One force would attack from the northwest and flank the seaward fortifications, while the other forces would attack the town from the rear, descending through the mountains using one of five passes. Eaton estimated three regiments would do the job, while frigates could blockade the harbor and prevent any vessels from escaping. Such an attack, he surmised, eyeing the town and the harbor, would put almost the entire Tunisian navy out of commission and force Tunis to sue for peace.

By October, Eaton grew increasingly worried that Tunis would break the treaty and declare war on the United States unless the treaty ship carrying the stores arrived by January 1, 1800. In addition, the Bey kept up his demand for a gift of jewels, which he now required three months after the arrival of the military stores. Eaton continued to try and buy off the Bey and provide him with a gift of ten thousand dollars in articles he should choose from England in lieu of the requested presents, but again the Bey told Eaton he did not know the value of the presents, only that he had requested them and again reaffirmed his interest.

Eaton wrote to Pickering, outlining the present situation and then, unsure as to whether the military and naval stores would arrive in time, he took up pen and paper and wrote the following circular that he would distribute to American ships in the Mediterranean:

Caution against Barbary Pirates—

> The Bashaw of the kingdom of Tunis having limited the period
> of his forbearance with the United States for the delivery of the
> regalia, stipulated by treaty, to the first of January next and hav-
> ing menaced us with war in case of a failure of said delivery, It
> results from my duty to communicate as well to the owners and
> masters of American vessels, which navigate the Mediterranean
> as the government of the United States this state of affairs, that
> suitable precautions may be used to save their property from
> Capture and our citizens from Slavery in case that any thing
> should operate to impede, beyond the limited period, the dis-
> charge of said stipulated obligation—It is also to be noted that
> the kingdom of Tunis has a truce with Her Most Faithful
> Majesty, the Queen of Portugal, during the present war with Eu-
> rope, which admits the corsairs of the former into the Atlantic—

Finished with this dispatch, he placed it, along with letters
to the secretary of state, in a parcel and wrapped the entire
contents in oilskin. A moment later there was a knock at the
door and Danielson ushered John Shaw, ship's doctor on the
Sophia, into the room. Eaton had persuaded Shaw to remain
in Tunis as his vice-consul. He had hoped Shaw would work
out, but he had fallen in love with a Tunisian woman. To
avoid further complications, Eaton was sending him home.

Eaton bade Shaw to sit down and handed him the packet
of dispatches, and instructed him to carry them to England.
There, he was to consult with Rufus King, the American
minister, and deliver to him the Bey's demand for jewels. He
instructed Shaw to procure the jewels at the lowest price.
After he had delivered the letter to King, Eaton instructed
Dr. Shaw to proceed with the dispatches to Philadelphia.

Shaw left on October 17 and Eaton noticed an immediate
improvement in relations between himself and the Sapitapa.
Eaton attributed the change in relations to three factors.
First, by sending Shaw to the United States he had sent a
message to the Bey that America was serious about her relations with Tunis. Second, he had told the Bey that the Quasi-
War was over and that there would be peace again between

France and the United States. And that, Eaton told the Bey, would mean that American warships would be free to protect American commerce in the Mediterranean. Finally, Eaton used his remaining available funds, as well as promises of riches resulting from increasing commercial trade, to win over the Sapitapa. In meetings with the minister, Eaton used the Sapitapa's interest in expanding the already extensive commerce between Tunis and Spain to his advantage by pointing out that American ships could easily transport Tunisian goods to Spain and were the best carriers given the war between France and England, which had tied up much of the Mediterranean's merchant fleet. Eaton stated, however, that American ships would only stop in at Tunis if the treaty was favorable to them. Once Eaton had informed his government that this was the case, a flood of ships would arrive, ready to carry on the trade. The Sapitapa, interested in personal gain, saw the wisdom of a commercial compact rather than war, and quickly told Eaton that he would speak with the Bey.

While Eaton waited, he received an invitation to dine with the Bey's physician. Over a sumptuous meal, Eaton finally received confirmation of his suspicions about Famin. According to the physician, after Eaton had arrived in Tunis, Famin had told the Sapitapa to make the demand for jewels. When the Sapitapa had hesitated, saying that in no communication was a demand for jewels stated, Famin told the minister that he would find documentation to support the demand. Eaton listened attentively, his blood boiling. Famin had been a thorn in his side, and now he had proof that the Frenchman had been polite on the surface while seeking Eaton's downfall. Eaton vowed to defeat him.

But as the New Year unfolded, no store ship arrived and Eaton watched as the corsairs were readied for a cruise, no doubt against Americans. Meanwhile, Famin continued to prod the Bey toward a war with the United States. Instead, the Bey held off, granting Eaton a sixty-day forbearance. Famin continued to stir the pot. In February, Famin reported

to the Bey that American merchant ships had arrived in
Leghorn. Eaton tried to calm the Bey, but he realized that
time had almost run out for peace. If a store ship or dispatches did not arrive soon, the corsairs would be let loose
on American shipping, and the Tunisians would take what
they had been promised. Each day, Eaton prayed that a message would arrive, but the waters off the Goulette remained
empty of American shipping.

Finally, on March 24, 1800, the brig *Sophia,* on which Dr.
Shaw had sailed for Philadelphia, returned to Tunis. Eaton
received dispatches from Pickering, a letter to the Bey from
President John Adams, and, at last, a copy of the ratified
treaty. As Eaton scanned the dispatches, he was relieved to
learn that the store ship *Hero* was on its way to Tunis, and
read with great interest Pickering's response to his repeated
requests for armed American warships to make an appearance off the Barbary Coast:

> The importance of sending a naval force into the Mediterranean,
> to shew to the Barbary powers our capacity to defend our com-
> merce, and to annoy them, has repeatedly been urged; and prob-
> ably the period is near at hand when this measure will be
> practicable.

However, noted Pickering, the Danes and Swedes had
strong naval forces and had often fought with Barbary pirates, and each time they had lapsed back to peace based on
an annual tribute. Pickering asked Eaton if it was simply a
matter of spirit? Eaton continued to read Pickering's letter:

> . . . should our differences with France be settled by our Envoys
> now in Paris, and either of the Regencies break their peace with
> us, our whole naval force may be sent against them: and consist-
> ing of Frigates, smaller ships, brigs, and Schooners, no fleet
> would be equally adapted for service on the coast of Barbary:
> and by their numbers and strength, according to the enclosed list,
> you will see they are sufficient to destroy the Corsairs of any one
> or of all the three regencies together.

Quickly finishing the letter, Eaton made his way to the Kasba, where he was admitted to the apartment of the Sapitapa. Eaton told the minister that he had received news from his government and wished to communicate it to the Bey.

"Do you take us for dupes?" the Sapitapa asked Eaton. "You at one time showed us letters from your minister at Portugal, at another from your consul-general at Algiers, at another from your consul at Leghorn. At one period your presents were under convoy of two frigates; at another in quarantine at Lisbon; and then we are placed at our windows with spy-glasses, looking for the arrival of vessels which sail in air. We are no longer to be amused. It is not necessary that you take the trouble of a formal communication. I now candidly inform you, that the corsairs now bound on a cruise, have orders to bring in Americans; and for this purpose, they are ordered to cruise off the coast of Spain and Portugal."

Eaton explained that he had already alerted American merchantmen to be on their guard. At this, the Sapitapa became attentive and Eaton continued, explaining that prior to this day the communications he had submitted to the Bey were unofficial. Eaton took out the president's letter and handed it to the Sapitapa, telling him that this was a formal communication to the Bey from President Adams, written in his own hand, as well as a copy of the ratified treaty. Finally, he told the Sapitapa that a store ship was on its way, laden with stores. He also told the minister that he had been authorized to meet the Bey's demands for jewels.

The Sapitapa reviewed the documents presented by Eaton. "This looks a little more like the truth," he said, "but will not arrest the cruise. If we make captures of Americans we will send the Christians to your house, your vessels to Porto Farina, and their cargoes we will safely store. They shall be held in sequestration a given number of days, in expectation of the arrival of your presents so much talked about, on failure of which they shall be good prize."

Eaton remarked as both a diplomat and soldier, indicating that taking Americans would defeat the objective of the cruise, since American sailors would fight if they were attacked, and the consequences would be bloodshed and war. The Sapitapa listened as Eaton asked, again, to present the formal communications from his government to the Bey.

The Sapitapa said he would meet with the Bey tomorrow.

Two days later, Eaton returned to the Kasba, took off his shoes, and entered the audience chamber, where he presented Adams's letter to the Bey. The Bey told Eaton he was flattered by the letter, hoped for the safe arrival of the ship, but asked why the president had mentioned nothing about the jewels.

Eaton quickly responded that he had been authorized to purchase the present in England, but that limits had been placed on the sum he could spend.

"To me," replied the Bey, "the sum limited is of no import. I shall be satisfied, provided the articles come according to the note." Eaton breathed a sigh of relief. As he left the audience chambers and blinked in the bright sunlight, he realized that he had done it. War had been averted, though it irritated him that the United States had had to resort to payments to achieve its ends. Eaton was a soldier at heart. Knowing the disposition of the Tunisians, he would have preferred war, but that would have to wait until either Washington, the new capital of the United States, had the stomach for engaging in a far-off conflict, or the Barbary declared war on the United States.

On April 12, 1800, the store ship *Hero* arrived off the Goulette.

III

DARK CLOUDS

While the arrival of the *Hero* helped smooth over the ruffled feathers of the Bey, news of Eaton's promise to provide the Bey with jewels caused problems to the east. It was May 25, 1800, and James Cathcart had just returned from an audience with the Bashaw of Tripoli in which the Bashaw told Cathcart he had received news about the presents—diamond-studded rifles, pistols, daggers, watches, and other bejeweled objects—Eaton had promised the Bey. He asked Cathcart why no such present had been offered to him.

The Bashaw had demanded that Cathcart provide him with presents of similar value and told him that if he did not receive them, he would let loose his corsairs on American shipping. Cathcart had asked the Bashaw to write a letter directly to the president stating his demand, which Cathcart would send along with his dispatches. A letter to the president would buy the United States some time, thought Cathcart, but even if Adams acceded to the demand, Cathcart knew it would only satisfy the tyrant for a year, at most. Algiers, Tunis, Tripoli, and to some extent Morocco operated in league with one another, sharing intelligence to ensure that what one received as tribute, the others would receive as well. Cathcart sat down and thought over the note he would write to Pickering. He would again press for the government to send warships to show the tyrants that America was not weak, but if the past was any guide, this request would again be ignored.

* * *

Almost a month later, on June 23, Eaton read Cathcart's message along with the Bashaw's letter to the president. Eaton agreed entirely with Cathcart's call for armed frigates, and setting pen to paper, added his own note to the package addressed to Pickering:

> If further testimony be necessary to inforce a conviction of the correctness of the conclusion, so often reiterated, that no profusion of generosity can satisfy these begging thieves we shall undoubtedly have that testimony—The Bey of Tunis holds to his claim for a cruiser—I refused to communicate his message—He gave me to understand that I would be ordered out of his kingdom—I intimated to him in return my sense of the Honor he would do me by such a measure—I will not yield to the claim. Let him send me away—He dare not make war upon us if the U. States use their proper means to deter him. Without the use of these means we are considered tributaries—and shall be treated as such.

Eaton continued writing, his pen scratching furiously against the parchment:

> Nobody here, acquainted with our concessions, could be persuaded that we are the same Americans who, twenty years ago, braved the resentment of Great Britain, if that fact were not recorded. There is, indeed, no nation so much humiliated in matters of tribute—And it is a burlesque upon every thing manly or political to see nations pouring into the ports of these kingdoms, which have not of their own produce a single article of naval material, stores and builders to construct navies to be employed as pirates against themselves—In this list of inconsentents the U. States at present have the honor to stand at the head—Our whole system of Negociation must be changed—There is no devination in this prediction: But it will be found as true as divinity—
> Pardon, I pray you, Sir, this rhapsody—No American can be cool and suffer as I do—And say to the Govt of the U. States they must either send a show of force to the Tunis—or a Slave!

Eaton went on to conclude that if the Bashaw of Tripoli persisted in his demand for a present similar to that de-

manded by the Bey of Tunis, that America should use this
opportunity to send a fleet of warships to show the Bashaw
that the United States would not yield. Eaton wrote, trying to
convince Pickering, and the government, that it was not in
America's interest to submit to this request. He also noted
that of the four Barbary States, Tripoli was the smallest and
weakest of them all. What better tyrant's demand to refuse
than that of Tripoli?

Finished with his dispatches, Eaton stood up from his
writing desk and paced the room. He was angry over the reports he had lately heard concerning the scoundrel Famin.
The former American consul had been a thorn in Eaton's
side ever since he arrived. The man had actively tried to
thwart peace between Tunis and the United States and had
spread rumors and falsehoods at every opportunity in an attempt to damage America's relations with Tunis. Since the
arrival of the *Hero* in April, relations between Tunis and the
United States had been good. The Bey still demanded jewels,
but the corsairs had not been sent to bring in American ships.
So now Famin was spreading reports that America was weak
and dependent upon France for her independence.

Eaton decided to take a walk to cool his anger. Certainly
Famin's statements would ring true to the Bey. The *Hero* was
a decrepit hulk, which hardly improved the image of the
United States in the Bey's eyes, and America could not send
a squadron to the Mediterranean as long as French privateers
in the Mediterranean threatened American shipping. Eaton
cursed the man, and then, coincidently, as he was passing the
Marine Gate, he spied the scoundrel in the flesh. The impu-
dent man was walking toward Eaton. Eaton's temper rose to
the boil. Diplomacy had not worked. Perhaps it was time to
teach Famin a lesson.

Eaton spied an Arab urging his donkey on with a horsewhip. Eaton seized the horsewhip from the surprised man
and bellowed out Famin's name. The Frenchman looked up,
and seeing Eaton brandishing the whip, cowered as Eaton
strode toward him, raised the whip, and slashed down with
all of his fury. As Eaton horsewhipped the unfortunate man,

a crowd gathered to watch Eaton strike Famin repeatedly. When Eaton had finished, he handed the whip back to the dumbfounded owner and stalked off, well pleased with the chance encounter and the opportunity to teach the French pirate a lesson he would never forget.

The next day, Eaton received a summons to the Kasba, and promptly made his way to the audience chamber, where he saw Famin seated before the Bey. After Eaton took his seat, the Bey gave Eaton a stern warning.

"I will send you out of the country," the Bey said.

"You will do me an honor, which I will take care to appreciate," replied Eaton.

"How dare you lift your hand against a subject of mine in my kingdom?" responded the Bey.

"If your renegade had been in the kingdom of heaven, and had given me the same provocation, I would have given him the same discipline," said Eaton. "But the Bey of Tunis has too much penetration to believe that abject wretch faithful even to his patron. If he were such, if he were a true Frenchman, I would respect him as such; if an American, I would protect him as such; if a good Mussulman, I would honor him as such; or, if a Christian, he should be duly respected. He is neither one nor the other. I have documents to convince you that he would sell your head for caroubes, and barter away the reputation of your court for piastres. See here his statement to an American, who, by this means, has been entrapped into his hands. Hear him call your prime minister and his mercantile agents a set of thieves and robbers."

"How!" said the Bey.

"Yes, thieves and robbers!" replied Eaton.

"Mercy! Forbearance!" Famin cried.

"Yes, thieves and robbers!" shouted Eaton. "This is the man of your confidence. This is the man of mediation between your Excellency and my master, the president; and these are the measures he uses to maintain the good understanding subsisting between us. Had he been faithful, either in his representations of your Excellency's character to the president, or in that of my nation to you, you would long since have received, whatever they might have been, the presents stipulated as tokens of friendship. It is his treachery, his falsehood, his sleek and plausible misrepresentations, which have generated the misintelligence between us. Do not suppose I am ignorant of his intrigues. Full well I know that he labored three days, incessantly, after my arrival in Biserta, to prevail on your Excellency to refuse me an audience. Full well I know that, during our negotiation, he was playing a double game with us. And full well I know that he has uniformly insinuated that my government were flattering you with elusive expectations and insincere promises, and that I myself am sent here to be the instrument of this hypocrisy."

"But how do you know these things?" asked the Bey. "Whatever passed between him and me was tête-à-tête."

"Yes," replied Eaton. "But the fellow had not prudence enough to keep your confidence. Elated with the prospect of success, he blabbed everything to the woman he keeps; she to her neighbors; so that it has been the topic of conversation in half the Christian taverns in Tunis, that his Excellency the Bey was going to send away the American consul to accommodate an apostate Frenchman, as if the Bey of Tunis had not independence of mind, nor discernment to discriminate between the event of insulting a nation and disobliging a slave. Permit me to suggest to your Excellency, your reputation has been brought into disrespect in the event."

Famin, concerned by the turn of the conversation, addressed the Bey in Arabic.

"Speak in French," the Bey demanded.

Famin did so, denying the charges. But given the facts against him, his denial fell flat. The Bey, having heard enough, signaled that the audience was over. As Eaton paid his respects, the Bey took Eaton's hand in his and announced to the court: "The American consul has been heated, but truly he has had reason. I have always found him a very plain, candid man, and his concern for his fellow citizens is not a crime."

* * *

The next day, as Eaton wrote in his journal, his thoughts were interrupted by a knock at the door. Danielson ushered in the Danish consul, Mr. Hammekin, who had the worried appearance of a man under a great deal of stress. Eaton begged him to be seated and learned that the Tunisians had seized two Danish ships, one at the Goulette, the other in Bizerte. Mr. Hammekin told Eaton he fully expected the Bey to declare war and asked Eaton if he would take charge of Danish affairs if he had to leave the kingdom. Eaton understood why the ships had been taken; denied American ships, the Tunisian corsairs had set their sights on Danish shipping. The Bey had harbored a grudge ever since Denmark had sent him naval stores to satisfy her treaty obligations with Tunis. The Bey had rejected the stores, which he had considered inferior.

Eaton gave his assent, and several days later, on June 28, Tunisian troops chopped down the Danish flagstaff to announce that Tunis had declared war on the kingdom of Denmark. He learned that Mr. Hammekin had been confined to his house and that more than seventy Danes had been sold into slavery.

Eaton picked up his hat and made his way immediately to the Kasba, where he was admitted to the audience chamber.

The Sapitapa welcomed Eaton and listened attentively as Eaton explained that he had been asked to take over Danish affairs for Mr. Hammekin. The Sapitapa explained why Tunis had declared war: "The Bey had demanded presents, and the king of Denmark had violated his good faith by treating that demand contemptuously," remarked the Sapitapa.

The Sapitapa also told Eaton that the war had been intended to be against the Americans, but the president's letters, and the excellent quality of the stores, had caused them to suspend the war.

Eaton remarked that he could have saved the Bey and himself much trouble if they had listened to his promises all along and ignored the counsel of meddling fellows who would betray the Bey and Eaton if the occasion suited them.

"That is past," said the minister, "and you have had your

own way of revenge. We are convinced you have dealt candidly with us, though we sometimes thought you a little hard-bitted. But you are a sort of Englishmen, you Americans, are you not?"

"We are not Italians," replied Eaton, as they had a reputation for cowardice among the Barbary pirates.

"Have you no pope in America?" asked the Sapitapa.

"Yes," replied Eaton. "Once a year our boys and girls of the streets, accompanied by our sailors and fiddlers, make a pope and a devil of old cast clothes, mount them both on a borrico [jackass], and, after driving them about till they are wearied, tar and feather and burn them together, by way of amusement."

The minister laughed. "I believe you are just such another hard-headed race as the English; but, thank God, we are friends."

Indeed, Eaton reflected, he was glad. Several weeks had passed since he had met with the minister. It was now July 16, and he had learned that the war had gone badly for the Danes. Eight vessels had been captured, and their crews, totaling almost one hundred men, had been sold into slavery. The value of the ships, cargoes, and slaves was estimated at 411,000 Spanish dollars. Therefore, Eaton was not at all surprised when later that day he heard a knock at the door announcing the arrival of the masters of six of the vessels. After they had taken seats and refreshments had been served, Eaton listened to their case. They told Eaton that the Tunisians were going to sell the ships, and requested that Eaton bid on them. They promised Eaton that they would open a line of credit in Leghorn, with which they would repay the consul. Eaton immediately accepted their proposal and set off to view the ships.

They were a forlorn lot, bobbing at anchor, riding high in the water, their cargoes already offloaded and dispersed. Eaton made a cursory inspection and then made his way to the Kasba, where he met with the Sapitapa and told him he would like to buy the Danish ships and named his price.

44   David Smethurst

The Sapitapa acknowledged Eaton's bid and told him that he would consider the offer. Eaton asked why he could not merely accept the offer, which was fair, but the Sapitapa remained firm, and told him he would need to speak with the Bey.

The following day, Eaton was again interrupted by the Danish masters, who arrived this time to report that they had decided to forgo the project, and asked Eaton to cancel his bid. Eaton demanded to know why they had changed their minds, but the masters would not spell out the details, alluding only to the fear that the project was too risky to pursue at this time. After the Danes had departed, Eaton realized that he had stuck his neck out while the Danes had withdrawn into their shell, leaving him, if his offer was accepted, with an obligation of 411,000 Spanish dollars.

Eaton did not worry for long. Later that afternoon, Danielson delivered a message from the Sapitapa. Eaton tore it open and scanned the contents. The scoundrel Famin had outbid him. A smile spread across Eaton's face. He wished Famin luck in coming up with the money, for he knew that most likely the Sapitapa had put the pirate up to it, in an effort to extract a higher bid from Eaton.

Eaton sat down and quickly penned a note in response. He wrote to the Sapitapa that he considered the business now at an end since his bid was fixed. The following day, he left for Bizerte, where the Bey had provided him with a weekend home by the sea. Eaton arrived and had only just begun to relax when he received another dispatch from the government in which the Sapitapa expressed his astonishment at his departure since they had decided to close with Eaton's offer.

Eaton laughed. He had learned the ways of the Tunisians in the year and a half since he had arrived, and quickly made his way back to Tunis where, before the Sapitapa could extract additional money from him, he closed the deal, offering credit to secure the ships. Eaton then turned the vessels over to the Danes, asking only that they assume his credit obligation. By the end of August, after peace had been signed between Tunis and Denmark, the vessels were returned to their masters and Eaton received the thanks of a grateful monarch.

Meanwhile, Eaton learned that his friend and benefactor, Timothy Pickering, had been fired by President Adams on May 12, and replaced by Charles Lee. Eaton hoped Lee could do what Pickering could not: convince Adams to send a warship to the Barbary Coast, to show the despots that the United States had the means to fight them, if it proved necessary.

Through his telescope, Captain William Bainbridge stood on the deck of the *George Washington* and scanned the capital city of the most powerful Barbary State. After a passage of forty days from Philadelphia they had arrived at this strange port on the North Africa coast. The date was September 17, 1800.

Bainbridge stood six feet tall, a shock of jet-black hair atop his head, his face bracketed by long sideburns. He had been at sea since he was fifteen, beginning as a seaman in the merchant marine and rising to the rank of captain in the navy. He was twenty-six years old, a native of Princeton, New Jersey, and mindful of the historic importance of his mission. The *George Washington* was actually a converted merchantman, and carried a crew of only one hundred and thirty to make room for six months of provisions as well as the tribute to be paid to Algiers: specie and naval stores such as plank, cables, and cannon. Yet she was also the first American warship to enter the Mediterranean. Bainbridge's mission was to deliver the tribute and show the Barbary pirates that, while America had purchased peace, the young nation also had the means to conduct war.

Eight bells in the afternoon watch indicated the hour of four o'clock. As the last of the bells struck, the pleasant breeze propelled the frigate into the anchorage as a small boat arrived carrying the consul, Richard O'Brien, and another man who, by the looks of him, was an Algerian. Moments later, the small boat touched and the two men climbed aboard. The Algerian was the captain of the port, who piloted the frigate to an anchorage beneath the fort and shore batteries. Bainbridge eyed the snouts of cannons protruding from the thick, stone walls, but put them out of his mind. There was no cause for alarm. The United States and Algiers were, after all, at peace.

Over the course of the next two days, his men began unloading the cargo: coffee, tea, sugar, herring, gunpowder, and other items deemed worthy of tribute. After the delivery was complete, Bainbridge and O'Brien made their way to the Dey's palace, to pay their respect to Bobba Mustapha. As they entered the ornate chambers, they saw a large, shaggy man sitting on a low bench covered with cushions. The Dey held out his hand and an attendant hissed: "Kiss the Dey's hand." The formal greeting over, O'Brien and Bainbridge stood before him, and the Dey made a final request to the Americans: He wished for Bainbridge to transport his ambassador to Constantinople. O'Brien, who was used to the demands of the pirates, told the Dey that the captain's orders were specific: He could not transport the ambassador, nor could he defend the ambassador or his property from Portuguese or Neapolitan vessels since they were only authorized to fight French vessels.

The Dey nodded, and dismissed them, but the matter did not end. Several days later, the Dey summoned O'Brien to his chambers and restated his demands. The Dey told him that there was no alternative, that the U.S. frigate would do him the favor of carrying his ambassador and presents to Constantinople. "You pay me tribute, by that you become my slaves," the Dey told them. Furthermore, he told them that if they did not comply, he would no longer hold himself to his treaty with the United States.

O'Brien argued that Bainbridge had no orders that would allow him to convey the ambassador and his gifts to Constantinople. At this, the Dey flew into a rage and declared that this was merely an excuse. Then he repeated himself: The favor was required. If O'Brien did not acquiesce, he knew what to do. The Dey told O'Brien that he would send his flag to be hoisted on the masthead, and that the matter was settled. O'Brien did not argue. The Americans had no choice: The *George Washington* was anchored beneath the guns of the fortress. If she tried to leave without permission, she would be blasted to pieces. And even if she managed to leave, America would once again be at war with Algiers.

With a heavy heart, O'Brien took a jolly boat to the frigate, accompanied by the general of the marine. The Stars and Stripes fluttered at the masthead of the frigate, which rocked gently at anchor beneath the fortress guns. O'Brien clambered aboard ship and once inside Bainbridge's cabin, told him the awful news. Bainbridge was an officer, and was used to following orders, no matter how difficult. As four bells struck in the afternoon watch, he walked on deck and ordered all hands piped to quarters. Then, as the crew watched, aghast, the American flag was struck down and the Algerian pendant was sent up the main topgallant masthead. Bainbridge stood rigid, trying not to show his feelings as seven guns were fired in salute, and answered by the castle. He would take the ambassador and his presents to Constantinople under orders from O'Brien, but he eagerly looked forward to the day when this injustice could be reconciled.

James Carpenter wiped the lens of his glass with a soft cloth and peered intently at the sail that appeared to be on a course to intercept their path. As the deck of the *Catherine* pitched in the swell seven leagues south of Majorca, Carpenter gazed intently at the ship. As far as he knew, American ships had had no enemies in the Mediterranean; the Quasi-War was over and the Barbary Coast was, for the most part, quiet. Carpenter, however, was concerned. The brig rolled heavily in the moderate seas, her hold laden with sugar, coffee, pimento, beef, logwood, and whalebone. They had left New York on July 26, and now, almost two months later, they were nearing their destination of Leghorn. Carpenter again peered through his glass and saw that the vessel was a polacre, which meant she was more than likely a Barbary vessel. They would know soon enough if she was merely curious or hostile.

An hour later, they were brought to by the eighteen-gun polacre *Tripolino*. The captain of the vessel ordered Carpenter aboard. Stuffing his papers into a pocket, Carpenter clambered down into a waiting rowboat and made his way between the two vessels. Moments later, he entered the captain's cabin and handed his papers to the commander. The captain looked them over, then placed them to one side. The captain told Carpenter that he, Raiz, Amor, and Shelli, would take the *Catherine* and her cargo as prize for the Bashaw of Tripoli.

On October 15, Cathcart stood on the rooftop deck of the American consular house and saw a brig, American by the looks of her, being escorted into the harbor. He quickly donned his hat and made his way down the winding streets to the beach, where he learned that the brig was indeed American, and had been captured by the *Tripolino*.

Cathcart was enraged, and spent the rest of the day seeing to the welfare of the crew, offering James Carpenter lodging at the consular house. On the following day, he and Carpenter paid a visit to the Bashaw.

After they had removed their shoes and taken seats upon the proffered cushions, Cathcart spoke.

He demanded satisfaction for the insult to the American flag suffered by the *Catherine,* stating that her papers were in good order and demanding restitution of the property seized from her.

The Bashaw replied that he had not ordered Raiz to capture the American brig and had given orders to the minister of the marine to dismiss him from the service and return all articles to the brig.

The Bashaw continued: "Consul, there is no nation I wish more to be at peace with than yours, but all nations pay me and so must the Americans."

Cathcart responded by stating that the United States had already paid everything owed Tripoli, and was not in arrears.

The Bashaw replied that for the peace, the United States

had paid him, it was true, but to maintain the peace she had given him nothing.

Cathcart observed that the terms of the treaty indicated that the United States would pay him in stores and cash.

The Bashaw responded by stating that the United States had given more to Algiers and Tunis and that a certain Portuguese captain who had passed Algiers in September had told him he had seen an American frigate in the bay, bringing more presents to the Dey. The Bashaw asked Cathcart why the United States was neglecting him.

Cathcart responded that the American frigate had stopped in at Algiers as part of a three-ship squadron sent to protect American shipping and that as far as he knew she carried no gifts for the Dey.

The Bashaw, however, was unmoved. "Well then, let your government give me a sum of money and I will be content, but paid I will be one way or the other." The Bashaw continued: "I now desire you to inform your government that I will wait six months for an answer to my letter to the president, that if it does not arrive in that period and if it is not satisfactory if it does arrive that I will declare war in form against the United States." Cathcart nodded in understanding. The Bashaw had effectively annulled the treaty and was relying on force to negotiate a new one. If the Bashaw's words were true, if America did nothing, Tripoli and the United States would be at war by early spring 1801.

Meanwhile, in Tunis, Eaton could sense the Bey's growing anger over not receiving either the presents he had demanded or additional naval stores as stipulated in the peace treaty. Eaton knew the Bey would not wait much longer before sending out his corsairs to claim on the high seas what had been stipulated in the treaty. Eaton made repeated trips to Porto Farina and watched as corsairs were outfitted for sea. He feared that if the store ship and promised presents didn't arrive soon, the corsairs would be used to hunt for Americans, who were, as far as Eaton knew, the only delinquent tributary nation. Not only that, but according to Thomas Appleton, U.S. consul at Leghorn, American ships carried almost as much commerce in the Mediterranean as all other nations combined. The United States was an easy target, and the delay in sending presents and stores made Eaton uncomfortable.

On October 31, Eaton was called to the Kasba, where he received a dressing-down by the Bey.

"What am I to deduce from all your assurances of punctuality on the part of your government?" demanded the Bey.

"Your Excellency will have the goodness to believe that when the information of our definite arrangements was received in the United States, the stores which we have stipulated as the condition of peace with you were growing on our mountains, at the sources of our rivers—"

The Bey cut Eaton off. "Am I to suppose then that your guns and your powder, comprised in that stipulation, were growing on your mountains? You find no difficulty in discharging your obligations with Algiers. Do you suppose me less able than Algiers to compel the punctual observance of treaties?"

"By no means," responded Eaton. "If we have been more attentive to Algiers than to you it is not because we consider you less respectable but more just than Algiers."

"We must make an end to compliment," said the Bey. "It would give me pain to affront you, but facts justify the conclusion that if you suppose me just; you study to amuse my justice. Denmark may furnish you a caution against such a reliance."

"I supposed," responded Eaton, "your Excellency can have no doubt that the residue of our peace presents have long since been at sea, but the winds have been many days against us—"

The Bey interjected. "They have been against us three years."

"Your Excellency will recollect they were very favorable last spring," replied Eaton.

"Not so favorable as I had been flattered to believe they would have been," said the Bey.

"What shall be done?" Eaton asked. "Shall we make war upon the elements?"

"You choose your measures," replied the Bey, "and you need not be surprised if I reserve to myself the same privilege."

"Permit me to demand an explanation for this entendre," Eaton replied.

"Events will explain it," replied the Bey.

Eaton asked the Bey if his comments were meant to imply a menace to American shipping. If so, continued Eaton, he would need to let his government know so that they could use this information when providing passports to Tunisian corsairs.

"In this you will use your own discretion," replied the Bey. "If you give them it is an evidence that you are at pcace with me. If you refuse them I have nothing serious to apprehend from it."

Eaton nodded and the audience concluded. As he walked out, he wondered if he needed to send out a circular warning American ships or one indicating that all was well. As his carriage clattered through the souks toward his home, he hoped American warships would arrive offshore and back his diplomatic efforts. If they did not arrive, Eaton believed he would soon be sending notes to the secretary of state indicating the number of new American slaves in Tunis.

On November 10, Eaton received dispatches from O'Brien and learned that the government had sent a warship to the Mediterranean but had made America the laughing-stock of the Barbary Coast in the process. Eaton read with growing anger how Bainbridge had allowed the Dey of Algiers to commandeer the *George Washington*. This was even worse than sending no ship at all. Eaton finished reading O'Brien's letter and then took out a clean piece of paper and wrote a letter to Charles Lee. Eaton wrote not as a diplomat, but as a soldier and an American.

Genius of My Country! How art thou prostrate! Hast thou not yet one son whose soul revolts, whose nerves convulse, blood

vessels burst, and heart indignant swells at thoughts of such de-
basement!

Shade of Washington! Behold thy orphan'd sword hang on a
slave—A voluntary slave, and serve a pirate!

I never thought to find a corner of this slanderous world where
baseness and American were wedded—But here we are the by-
word of derision; quoted as precedents of baseness—even by a
Dane!

Shall Tunis also lift his thievish arm, smite our scared cheek,
then bid us kiss the rod! This is the price of peace! But if we will
have peace at such a price, recall me, and send a slave, accus-
tomed to abasement, to represent the nation—And furnish ships
of war, and funds and slaves to his support, and Our immortal
shame—

History shall tell that the United States first volunteer'd a ship
of war, equipt, a carrier for a pirate—It is written—Nothing but
blood can blot the impression out—Frankly I own, I would have
lost the peace, and been empaled myself rather than yielded this
concession—Will nothing rouse my country!

To make matters worse, several days later, Eaton learned
that the *Catherine* had been taken and released. He had also
learned that the condition of continued peace between
Tripoli and the United States was an additional annual payment. Meanwhile, news of the *George Washington* had reached
the Bey, who had told Eaton on the previous day that he would
wait one more month for the arrival of the store ship, the *Anna
Maria,* which O'Brien wrote had sailed on August 30.

Meanwhile, the corsairs were being fitted out, and the target, Eaton knew, was American shipping. And why not?
America's commerce was the richest in all the Mediterranean, and, as the *George Washington* had shown, unguarded. If the *Anna Maria* did not arrive soon, the corsairs
would snatch up American ships, and American sailors would
be sold into slavery.

But the *Anna Maria* did arrive, and on November 27,
Eaton received a note from Captain George Coffin that the
ship was in the road at Porto Farina. Eaton requested permission to visit the ship and on November 30 reached the *Anna*

Maria, where he took possession of the bill of lading and in-voice. The following day, he traveled to the Kasba, where he presented the documents to the Bey. The ministers reviewed the documents, and complained about the length of the planks. But Eaton knew that their real complaint was that Eaton had learned of the arrival of the vessel. Captain Coffin had arrived on November 16 but had not been allowed to send a message to Eaton. Instead, the captain had smuggled a letter off the ship. Eaton received it just in time. Tunis had been spoiling for this war, and Eaton's timely arrival at the Kasba had ruined the Bey's plans.

But the Bey would not roll over. He had learned how the Dey of Algiers had commandeered the *George Washington,* and had decided he would do the same with the *Anna Maria.* When Eaton was called to the palace again on December 20, the Sapitapa demanded that the *Anna Maria* carry a cargo of Tunisian goods to Marseilles without charging freight.

Eaton replied smoothly that she was available for charter.

The Sapitapa countered by saying that the *George Washington* had performed this service for Algiers, and the *Anna Maria* would do so for the Bey, by force if necessary.

Eaton pointed out that the treaty between Tunis and the United States forbade the impressments of either country's ships.

The Sapitapa grew angry but in the end agreed to pay $4,000 for freight, which Eaton accepted. It was much less than she should have received, but it averted war. As the year 1800 came to an end, Eaton wondered if the consuls would be able to maintain the peace for another year. He thought it unlikely, and found himself wishing for war.

Meanwhile, in Tripoli, Cathcart sat down heavily at his desk, dipped the nib of his pen in the inkpot, and wrote the date, February 21, 1801. He continued writing, addressing the circular to all U.S. agents and consuls in Europe.

Gentlemen. I had the honor to inform you in my Circular Letters of November 1800 and January 1801 of the State of our affairs with this Regency, I have now to add that all hopes of accommodation has subsided, I therefore request you to detain all Merchant Vessels Navegating under the Flag of the U. States in Port and by no means to permit any of them to Sail unless under Convoy, as I am convinced that the Bashaw of Tripoli will commence Hostilitys against the U. States of America in less than Sixty Days from the date hereof. . . .

IV

TRIPOLI DECLARES WAR

At noon on March 4, 1801, Jefferson stepped out of his lodgings at Conrad & McMunn's boardinghouse, at the corner of New Jersey and C Street, and began walking toward the Capitol, a walk, he knew, that would change him forever, completing the voyage he had embarked on when he authored the Declaration of Independence many long years ago. Jefferson, a month shy of his fifty-eighth birthday, walked the two blocks, accompanied by Benjamin Stoddert, secretary of the navy; Samuel Dexter, secretary of the treasury; and a group of Republican members of Congress and lodgers from his boardinghouse. A company of Maryland artillery, parading with their cannons in tow, accompanied them.

As they made their way toward the Capitol, Jefferson remarked on the progress the builders had made; the north wing was complete, now occupied by the Senate, the courts, and a library. The south wing was incomplete, and the center was unfinished. As Jefferson and his entourage climbed the steps to the north wing, heading for the Senate chambers, the militia fired their cannons, announcing the arrival of America's third president.

Inside the Senate chamber, the members of both the Senate and House were waiting for him. As Jefferson entered, the members, including Aaron Burr, rose, and Burr motioned for Jefferson to take his seat. Burr sat on his right hand and John Marshall sat to his left. As the members of Congress settled into their seats, the room was quiet for a moment. Then Jefferson stood, manuscript in hand, and read his inaugural address in almost a whisper, the first ever to be delivered in the nation's new Capitol.

After concluding his speech, Jefferson walked back to his boardinghouse with his entourage, taking supper at the long table in his regular place at the bottom of the table, far from the roaring fire. He was still unaccustomed to his new title, president of the United States, as well as the prerogatives of power.

Jefferson stayed at the boardinghouse until March 19, when he moved into the unfinished White House: the slate roof leaked, the East Room's walls needed plaster, there was no main staircase, and the grounds were bare. Still, Jefferson set up office in what is today the Cabinet Room, decorating it with potted plants and keeping his favorite gardening tools in the drawers of his desk.

Jefferson did not affect the image of an eager warrior. Guests who came to the White House to visit found him wearing an old brown coat, a red waistcoat, old corduroy britches, woolen hose, and slippers without heels. Yet late at night, which he found the best time to work, he sat at his desk, his pet mockingbird perched on his shoulder, and rapidly set in motion the plans and ideas he had formulated over the course of the past fifteen years.

The Barbary pirates were a thorn in America's side that would not go away. A month and a half after taking office, Jefferson was deeply upset upon learning of the requisition of the *George Washington* by the Dey of Algiers. Captain Bainbridge had reached Philadelphia on April 19, and Jefferson had received him a short time later. The president listened to Bainbridge's account of the Dey's insult to American sovereignty. Jefferson understood that, by sailing to Constantinople, Bainbridge had averted war, but he also knew that this sort of affront to American independence could never be tolerated again.

On May 15, almost two months after his inauguration, Jefferson assembled his cabinet and posed two questions that were the culmination of years of studying the problem of the

Barbary pirates. Jefferson looked around the room at the faces of the assembled men—Secretary of State James Madison, Secretary of the Navy General Samuel Smith, head of the War Department Henry Dearborn, Secretary of the Treasury Albert Gallatin, Attorney General Levi Lincoln, and his personal secretary, a young man who lived near his home in Virginia, Lieutenant Meriwether Lewis.

He looked into the eyes of each of these men and asked them two questions: "Shall the squadron now at Norfolk be ordered to cruise in the Mediterranean?" and "What shall be the objective of the cruise?" Jefferson's questions telegraphed his answers. Each of the men, in turn, nodded assent. The president was pleased. It had taken sixteen years, but he was finally able to thwart the corsairs, with whom he had become acquainted in 1785. Jefferson was sending America's navy on its first mission: to defeat the Barbary pirates who had preyed on American shipping ever since the nation had been born. Jefferson knew that it was well and good to declare independence, but understood that the Barbary pirates had been testing that independence for fifteen years, and now, America had the tools, and the will, with which to respond.

The U.S.S. *President* rode at anchor off Hampton Roads, Virginia. The freshening westward breeze ruffled the water and tugged at her towering white sails, unfurled for her imminent departure. She was a trim, forty-four-gun frigate, one of America's finest, thought Captain William Bainbridge, who surveyed her from the quarterdeck of the U.S.S. *Essex,* which rocked gently against its anchor, fast in the muddy depths of the blue-green waters at the confluence of the Chesapeake Bay and the James River.

Bainbridge peered out through the dim morning light and closely examined the *President,* the squadron's flagship and one of six frigates built to defend America's fast-growing maritime trade. She was a three-masted frigate, whose main mast towered one hundred feet above the deck and was held up by an intricate web of cords and rope. Climbing from the port and starboard side were the shrouds, which were connected by horizontal ratlines that made a ladder for seamen to climb. Shrouds climbed to each fighting top, where more shrouds were anchored and extended to the lookouts. To keep the masts from pitching forward, they were anchored to both the bow and the stern; stays prevented them from pitching forward, and backstays prevented them from falling aft. Attached to the masts were long, horizontal crossbeams called yards. Sails hung from the yards, and each of the multitudes of billowing canvas sheets had a distinct name and a unique role.

The *President* was the first of the squadron. The early-morning mist softened the lines of the one-hundred-and-seventy-five-foot frigate; a wall of live oak pierced on either side by two rows of gun ports, closed now, the guns stowed for their departure. Although rated a forty-four-gun frigate, the flagship contained more than that, making her a heavily armed, dangerous adversary. Thirty twenty-four-pounders squatted charged and ready on her lower gun deck, fifteen to a side; twenty long twelve-pounders lay behind the gunwales of her upper deck. On her forecastle, she carried two long twenty-four-pounders; on her bow and stern she carried several carronades, short, stocky cannons that were devastating at close quarters. She would undoubtedly be a fast sailor, thought Bainbridge. To handle the ship and man the guns required three hundred and fifty souls: midshipmen, lieutenants, seamen, gunners, surgeons, carpenters, boatswain, and a complement of forty marines.

To Bainbridge's eyes, the *President* was a beautiful vessel with sleek, taut lines. She was newly launched, and had entered the country's fledgling navy several months earlier with only a shakedown cruise to her credit. On her quarterdeck, Bainbridge saw the commodore, Richard Dale, newly appointed commander of the squadron, dressed in the dark blue uniform of the U.S. Navy. Dale was forty-four years old, an intrepid, staunch veteran of the Revolutionary War, where he had been John Paul Jones's first lieutenant. He was a good choice, and a good leader.

Bainbridge swung his telescope across the gray-blue water, and focused on the other vessels that made up Dale's squadron: the thirty-six-gun *Philadelphia,* commanded by Captain Samuel Barron, and the twelve-gun sloop-of-war *Enterprise,* commanded by Lieutenant Andrew Sterett.

Aboard the U.S.S. *Essex,* four bells announced the hour of six o'clock in the morning on June 2, 1801. Across the water, Bainbridge heard the ringing of bells and the piping of whistles aboard the squadron's vessels. Aboard the *President,* men scurried to and fro as a signal flag was hauled up, flapping in the freshening breeze. Their hour had finally arrived; Dale was signaling the squadron to make sail and head for sea.

Bainbridge felt a surge of pride and purpose, aware of the historic moment. Recently returned from the Mediterranean, where his ship had been commandeered by Dey Bobba Mustapha and sent to Constantinople to carry the Dey's tribute to Selim III, the sultan of Turkey, he well remembered the Dey's words as he stood before him in his chambers: "You pay me tribute, by that you become my slaves." Now, almost nine months later, Commodore Dale had signaled that the squadron would sail to the Barbary Coast to show the pirate states that the United States now possessed a navy to protect American shipping—and the will to use it.

As the *President*'s bow cut through the blue waters of Hampton Roads, throwing a fine, white spray of foaming water to each side, she headed out into Chesapeake Bay and thence on into the North Atlantic. As the ship gained speed, Commodore Dale cast a glance at the green hills that slid by on either side. To the starboard, the Elizabeth River wound its way to the naval yard at Portsmouth. To the portside lay Virginia, and the towns of Newport News and Hampton. Seeing that the ship was in capable hands, he nodded to his first officer, and went below to his great cabin in the stern of the ship. Through the sweeping, wide windows that spanned the stern of the vessel, he saw the foaming wake of his ship and the prows of the *Essex, Philadelphia,* and *Enterprise* as they followed him out to sea.

Dale sat down at his desk, reached for a sheaf of papers, and found the one he was looking for, his orders, dated May 20, 1801, from Samuel Smith, the acting secretary of the navy. Dale scanned the orders again to better understand the mission ahead and the intentions of Thomas Jefferson, who had been inaugurated not three months ago as America's third president.

He scanned the elegantly written orders, his eyes resting on the two paragraphs that interested him most:

> Recent accounts received from the Consul of the United States, employed near the Regencies of Algiers, Tunis & Tripoli, give cause to fear, that they will attack our commerce, if unprotected, within the Mediterranean; but particularly such apprehension is justified by absolute threats on the part of the Bey of Tripoli.

Dale skimmed over the closely packed text, finding the second paragraph of interest:

> Should the Bey of Tripoli have declared War (as he has threatened) against the United States—you will then proceed direct to that Port, where you will lay your ships in such a position as effectually to prevent any of their Vessels from going in or out. The *Essex & Enterprize* by cruising well on toward Tunis, will have it in their power to intercept any vessels which they may have captured, —By disguising your ships, it will be some weeks before they will know that the Squadron is cruising in the Mediterranean—and give you a fair chance of punishing them.

The commodore leaned back in his chair and rubbed a hand over his face, weathered from many years of hard action and life at sea. He knew war, had tasted it, smelled it, and lived it for much of his life. And now he was leading a squadron of powerfully built American warships to the Mediterranean. He pondered again the gravest question to

which, he knew, he would only find the answer once the
squadron reached the far shores of the Atlantic: Was America at war?

One bell in the last dog watch announced the hour of six-
thirty in the evening. It was June 27, a Saturday, recollected
Bainbridge, who strode the quarterdeck of the *Essex*. The
weather was pleasant, unlike much of their passage across
the Atlantic, which had been wet and miserable, especially
for those aboard the *President,* which, heavily laden with
stores to last them for a year's cruise, wallowed in the heavy
swells, splitting several seams. The carpenters had caulked
and filled, but the *President* had shown that although heavily
armed and the fastest of the new frigates, the *Enterprise* was
the fleetest vessel of the squadron.

Bainbridge peered through his telescope and scanned the
seas ahead searching for pirates. Was America at war with
Tripoli? Had the Tripolitan fleet sailed? Were they prowling
the North Atlantic in search of American ships to take their
cargos and enslave their crews? It was possible, given the
state of the Bashaw's temperament and love for plunder.
Tripoli had broken the treaty in the past. On July 25, 1800, a
little less than a year ago, the Tripolitan polacre *Tripolino*
had captured the brig *Catherine,* which was bound from
New York to Leghorn with a cargo of coffee, sugar, beef, and
goods valued at $50,000. In spite of the treaty between
Tripoli and the United States, the Tripolitans had boarded the
ship and brought it back to Tripoli. Although it was eventually released, it was understood by all captains aboard U.S.
vessels that Tripoli was unhappy with the terms of the treaty
it had signed with the United States, since its neighbor, Algiers, had received a much larger tribute. And Bainbridge
knew that Yusuf Karamanli was the sort of man who would
try to renegotiate a treaty by the application of force.

So he scanned the seas carefully, also on the lookout for
the *Enterprise,* which Dale had dispatched ahead of them.
Finding no sail on the horizon, he focused instead on the

heavy clouds, a telltale sign of landfall. A signal flag rose
aboard the flagship. Bainbridge's signal officer informed him
that Dale wanted to speak to the *Essex*. Very well, thought
Bainbridge, who ordered the master to bear down on the
President.

As they approached the flagship, which labored less now
that the seas were fair and the crew had learned how to handle the frigate, a signal flag flew up the mainmast; Dale ordered the *Essex* to sail ahead and keep a good lookout.
Bainbridge acknowledged the signal and ordered sails unfurled. Soon, they left the *President* far behind, a nick of
white sail against a backdrop of blue and gray.

As darkness descended upon the *Essex,* the binnacles and
lanterns glowed, swaying to the vessel's easy motion. As the
night wore on, marked by the sounding of the ship's bells and
the changing of watches, Bainbridge kept pacing the quarterdeck, certain that land was near. Finally, at 10 a.m., the lookout cried out and pointed to the northeast. There, at a
distance he reckoned to be ten leagues, lay the two hills that
formed Monte Chico, and the southernmost of those hills
sloped toward Cape Saint Vincent. They had crossed the Atlantic, and were only a few days' sail from Gibraltar, the
gateway to the Mediterranean. Soon enough, thought Bainbridge, they would know if they were at war.

On June 20, Eaton was summoned to the palace. He had
been confined to his bed, suffering from a bilious fever, but
knew that a summons from the Bey must be answered, so he
dressed and made his way to the Kasba, where he was ushered into the audience chamber. The minister came quickly
to the point: A fire two days earlier had consumed fifty thousand stands of arms, and he demanded that Eaton write to his
government and request ten thousand stands of arms.

"I have proportioned my loss among my friends, and this
falls to you to furnish," explained the minister. "Tell your
government to send them without delay."

Eaton told the minister it would be quite impossible to
state this demand to his government. "We have no magazines

of small arms; the organization of our national strength is different from that of any other nation on earth. Each citizen carries his own arms, always ready for battle. When threatened from invasion, or actually invaded, detachments form the whole national body and are sent, by rotation, to serve in the field; so that we have no need of standing armies, nor depositories of arms. It would be an affront to my government, and an imposition on the Bey, to state to them this demand, or to flatter him a prospect of receiving it."

"Send for them to France or England," said his minister.

"You are in a much more eligible position to make this commission to Europe than we are," replied Eaton.

"If the Bey had any intention of purchasing the arms from Europe he could do it without your agency," said the minister. "He did not send for you to ask your advice, but to order you to communicate his demands to your government."

"I came here to assure you that I will make no such communication to my government," replied Eaton.

"The Bey will write himself," said the minister.

"If so, it will become my duty to forward his letter; but, at the same time, it is equally obligatory on me to let the Bey be aforehand apprised that he never will receive a single musket from the United States." Eaton argued that the United States had delivered all it had promised in the treaty, apart from the jewels, which the Bey still demanded, and told the minister and the Bey that the discharge of treaty obligations would put an end to any additional contributions.

"Your contributions, as you think proper to call them, will never have an end," replied the minister. "If this be the language you think of holding at this court, you may prepare yourself to leave the country, and that very soon."

"If change of style on my part be the condition of residence here, I will leave the Bey's kingdom tomorrow morning," replied Eaton.

"We will give you a month," said the minister.

"I ask but six hours," Eaton replied.

"But you will write?" implored the minister.

"No," replied Eaton.

"But it is your duty to write," said the minister, in an exasperated tone.

"For deficiency in duty this is not the place where I am to be questioned," said Eaton.

"I tell you again, your peace depends on your compliance with this demand of my master."

"If so, on me be the responsibility of breaking the peace. I wish you a good morning," said Eaton and made his way toward the exit. As he left, he heard the minister remark: "By God, that man is mad! But we shall bring him to terms; never fear."

On July 1, Commodore Dale stood on the quarterdeck of the *President,* following the *Essex* into the harbor at Gibraltar. As they passed into Gibraltar Bay, bounded by Cabreta Point to port and Europa Point to starboard, the great rock of Gibraltar, some three miles long and a mile wide, rose fourteen hundred feet above the glistening blue waters of the bay, framed against a brilliant blue sky. The *Philadelphia* followed the flagship in. As Dale peered through his telescope, he noticed that there were no British warships in the harbor. He did, however, spy the *Enterprise,* and then, to his surprise, he saw two Tripolitan warships. Did this mean America was still at peace?

As they approached the anchorage, Dale studied the two Tripolitan vessels. The first he recognized as the *Betsey,* an American-built brig that had been captured by Tripolitan pirates in 1796 and converted into a schooner. She was also the flagship of the Tripolitan navy, commanded by High Admiral Murad Reis and now known as the *Meshouda.* She no longer looked like a sober New England brig; the coppered and deep-waisted vessel gave the impression of being a pirate ship. Her hull was painted yellow with a white streak. The stern was painted green, with flowers decorating her stern windows. Her gun muzzles were painted red, and a woman's head decorated the transom. She was also heavily armed with twenty-eight guns: eighteen nine-pounders on her main deck, six four-pounders on her quarterdeck, two bow chasers, and two stern chasers. Beside her was a sixteen-gun Swedish-built brig also flying the Tripolitan ensign. Together, they were a powerful force, enough to overtake and outgun any American merchantman.

From the crowded quay, Dale saw a jolly boat depart for the *President*. In all likelihood it was John Gavino, U.S. consul to Gibraltar. Dale ordered the *President* to anchor close to the *Enterprise* and Tripolitan vessels. As they hove to, Dale hailed Murad Reis, who stood on the quarterdeck of the *Meshouda,* and asked if Tripoli was at war with the United States.

Reis replied that Tripoli and the United States were at peace. Dale knew that if they were at war, Reis would probably not tell the truth. He was a renegade and a traitor. The real name of the blond-haired, sandy-bearded man Dale spoke to was Peter Lisle, a Scotsman who had been a deckhand aboard the *Betsey.* Dale knew that after her capture, Lisle had converted to Islam and had married the Bashaw's daughter. Dale also knew that he hated Americans, and was a fine seaman. His Muslim name also had significance: It was the name of a Barbary corsair who had raided Iceland and Ireland in 1631.

Dale shouted back across the narrow gap of blue water that separated the two ships and asked if James Leander Cathcart, U.S. consul to Tripoli, was in good health. Reis replied that Cathcart had left for Tunis and "was no friend of the Americans." As the *President* passed by, Dale could not help but notice that the *Meshouda* was well armed and well stocked, and carried a large crew. That, and Reis's response to his inquiry about Cathcart, did not bode well for peace.

As the *President*'s anchor chain rattled through the hawseholes and the anchor plunged into the soft mud of the bay, Dale heard the welcoming sound of cannon fire, as gun after gun from the garrison fired in salute of the first American war fleet to arrive in Gibraltar. Dale returned the salute, gun for gun, and ordered a midshipman to signal all captains to repair aboard the flagship.

They arrived soon enough, the handsome, curly-haired

Andrew Sterett, whose high spirits seemed to emanate from his person; Bainbridge, who took a seat next to Gavino; and Samuel Barron, whose father, James, had been commander of the Commonwealth of Virginia navy during the Revolutionary War.

When they had all taken a seat, Dale began the meeting by asking Gavino whether the United States was indeed at peace with Tripoli, as Reis had indicated. Gavino announced that two days ago, the Tripolitan ships had arrived in Gibraltar after cruising for thirty-five days. Gavino told the assembled captains that when the harbor master had asked him if Tripoli was at war with the United States he had indicated that they were not. However, when asked if Reis had taken any prizes, he also indicated that he had not. The answer to the latter question, Gavino believed, indicated that there was a possibility that war had been declared.

Dale agreed, especially since Reis had indicated that Cathcart had left Tripoli. Dale knew that he would only have done so if the Bashaw had declared war. But what Dale needed was conclusive proof. He instructed Gavino to call on Reis the following morning and invite him to dine either aboard the *President* or at Gavino's house ashore. If he accepted, that would mean that the two countries were at peace. If he declined, it meant they were at war.

Gavino nodded his assent to Dale's plans, and then produced a package of letters from Richard O'Brien, U.S. consul general, Algiers, and asked Dale if he might read aloud a passage from the letter, dated May 12, 1801. Dale nodded. Perhaps O'Brien's letters would provide some intelligence. His words were frank and to the point:

In February The Bashaw of Tripoli declared he no longer held to his friendship with the United States has demanded vast Sums and disregarded The deys letters and Gaurenteee. And every reasonable offer which Consul Cathcart Could make, & has sent his Corsairs to Sea to Capture Americans—

At Algiers we are two & a half Years in arrears in the Annuities we are threatened with war if The Stores does not arrives

Shortly—The Consuls in Barbary has neither Money or Credit.
And the Government of the U. States pays no attention to our
Communications it is 10 Months that I have not had any letter
from the department of State

War Sir will shortly be the result of detention and neglect.

Gavino put the letter down, waiting for Dale to speak.
Dale, his face showing the gravity of the situation, indicated
to the assembled captains that O'Brien's letter left little
doubt that they were at war, and the presence of two corsairs
at anchor here, commanded by the high admiral, gave added
appearance that war had been declared. Yet until this could
be confirmed, Dale instructed his captains to keep a sharp
watch over the Tripolitan corsairs. While they could not be
attacked in a neutral harbor, Dale was adamant that neither
of the pirate ships should be allowed to leave.

The following morning, Gavino rowed over to the *Meshouda* and presented Murad Reis with an invitation to dine
either aboard the *President* or at the house of the U.S. consul
on shore. Murad Reis stood high above Gavino, on the quarterdeck of the *Meshouda,* and politely declined both invita-
tions. Instead, he suggested meeting on neutral ground, and
named a tavern onshore.

Gavino took Reis's response back to Dale, who was seated
at his desk in the midst of writing a letter to the secretary of
the navy. Dale realized that the probability that peace still ex-
isted between Tripoli and the United States was steadily de-
creasing with each passing moment. He thanked Gavino and
then invited him on an excursion to shore. They had been invited to dine with General O'Hara, governor of Gibraltar.
Perhaps the British would possess the conclusive answer
Dale sought.

Neither O'Hara nor any other British official in attendance
could provide Dale with a concrete assertion that the United
States was at war with Tripoli. However, Dale and Gavino
did learn that four other Tripolitan cruisers were cruising the
Mediterranean, which accounted, in part, for why the American vessel *Grand Turk,* loaded with presents for the Bey of

Tunis, had been waiting in the harbor seven weeks for an escort. The captain had been fearful, for good reason it now appeared, of being captured. Dale sent a note to the captain
instructing him to ready his ship for sea; he would escort him
to Tunis, and would be leaving as soon as he had completed
watering and replenishing his stores.

After dinner, Dale returned to the *President,* his crew
pulling hard on their oars, propelling the launch across the
wind-ruffled waters. Dale pondered the situation and his bad
luck. If only the squadron had not been delayed in its passage
across the western ocean by ten days of storms and gales, he
would have met Reis at sea, and taken him. Instead, here he
was, right under his nose. But Gibraltar was a neutral harbor,
and Dale could not act out of fear of offending his British
hosts.

Dale decided, as the oarsmen pulled and propelled the
small craft across the bay, that he would leave Captain
Samuel Barron in the *Philadelphia* to watch over Murad
Reis. Although both of the pirate ships were well manned,
with two hundred and sixty men aboard the *Meshouda* and
one hundred and sixty more aboard the brig, the *Philadelphia* was more than a match for the two of them. As the
launch bumped against the towering hull of the flagship,
Dale heard the familiar piping of the boatswain's call indicating his arrival. He climbed the ladder, firm in his purpose
to leave for Algiers as soon as his ships could be readied for
sea.

The following day, July 3, Dale spent much of the afternoon writing orders to his captains for their imminent departure, and letters to the secretary of the navy, announcing their
safe arrival in the Mediterranean. Gavino would send his dispatches to Washington aboard the first sail headed west. Currently, however, the British and French fleets were at sea,
readying for action near Cadiz. Indeed, the squadron had
seen seven English ships of the line commanded by Sir
James Saumerez blockading Cadiz, and three French ships
of the line near Gibraltar, headed for Cadiz to break the
blockade. He would instruct Gavino to wait a few days be-

fore sending the messages, until after the action had concluded.

The morning of the fourth dawned bright and clear, with a southerly breeze blowing from North Africa, only a short distance across the straits. Aboard the *Essex,* Captain Bainbridge watched as a signal flag flew up the mainmast of the *President,* and the clang of three bells in the morning watch indicated the hour of five o'clock. The signal instructed the *Essex, Philadelphia,* and *Enterprise* to unmoor. They were heading out to sea.

Seated in his cabin, Dale continued writing out orders as the sound of running feet pounded on the deck above him. He could hear the stamp and go of the men at the capstan bars, slowly winching the heavy anchor, stuck deep in the harbor mud, back into the frigate. He heard the shouts of lieutenants and the cries of midshipmen, urging their watches to their duty. The *President* was a well-run ship, and the passage from Hampton Roads to Gibraltar had meshed the crew into a tightly knit, efficient community of sailors. But how would they fight? Dale knew that the Barbary pirates' strength was not gunnery. They preferred to rush in and board their prey, overmatching merchant ships with a much larger force of men and arms. He also knew that only in the heat of battle would he know how well his men would fare. He had trained them in gunnery and small arms, and a professional officer commanded the marine contingent aboard each of the vessels, but only battle would tell him whether the U.S. Navy was ready. Dale hoped that battle would come soon.

As Dale put down his pen, he realized the irony of their departure date: July 4, the fifteenth birthday of the new nation. And here, for the first time, was an American war fleet in the harbor at Gibraltar ready to fight to maintain America's liberty if the occasion arose. And if it did, it would be the young country's first war as an independent nation.

The squadron sailed out of Gibraltar Bay, heading for Algiers, some four hundred and sixteen nautical miles to the east. They stayed close to Europa Point, which lay just off the port side. Surveying the open sea to starboard, Dale saw the faint brown smudge on the horizon where Morocco and the town of Ceuta lay, some twelve miles distant. They sailed under a favorable southerly breeze amid clear weather and sparkling blue skies. Summer had arrived and the weather was hot. The dry wind blowing from North Africa brought little rain or moisture. Dale rose from his seat and walked toward the door, which a sentry opened for him. He passed through and climbed to the quarterdeck, where he gazed to the stern, watching as the ships of the squadron, along with two merchantmen, the *Hope* and *Grand Turk,* followed in his lee. Well satisfied with their stations, Dale returned below to finish the orders he would deliver to his captains on the morrow.

Sunday, July 5, dawned bright and clear, with a light wind out of the east. At half past noon, Dale shouted for his orderly and asked him to send word for Captains Barron, Sterett, and Bainbridge. A short time later, Captain Bainbridge was ushered into Dale's cabin. As the marine sentry stood to let him pass, Bainbridge took off his hat and stooped to allow his six-foot frame to clear the door. Stepping into the great cabin, with its sweeping view of the blue Mediterranean and the ships of the squadron through its stern gallery, Bainbridge stood at attention. Dale bade him take a seat and handed him written orders.

He told Bainbridge of his intention to leave the *Philadelphia* off Gibraltar to watch over Murad Reis and prevent him from escaping, while the rest of the squadron proceeded to Tunis. He instructed Bainbridge to convoy the *Grand Turk,* as well as the American brig *Hope,* to Algiers. Dale was careful to state that Bainbridge should do nothing to upset either the Bey of Tunis or the Dey of Algiers. Knowing full well the humiliation Bainbridge had suffered under the latter as captain of the *George Washington,* Dale made Bainbridge aware that if war had indeed been declared by the Bashaw of Tripoli, the United States would be better off fighting a war against only one of the Barbary States rather than two of them. After safely seeing the *Grand Turk* and *Hope* to Algiers, Bainbridge was to touch in at Tunis, where William Eaton was in residence. If Bainbridge had not learned by then whether America and Tripoli were at war, Eaton would know. If they were at war, Dale told Bainbridge, he was to cruise to Tripoli and blockade the harbor.

The orders were simple and to the point. Bainbridge acknowledged them, and took his leave. After he had departed, another knock at the door announced Captain Barron. Dale motioned for him to sit and as he did so, passed him his set of orders, which Barron put into his pocket. Dale began by telling Barron that all information he had received indicated that Tripoli was at war with the United States. Since he had not received word from Consul Cathcart to confirm that, he was operating under the assumption that war had been declared. The one salient fact, Dale pointed out, was the presence of High Admiral Murad Reis in port in command of two corsairs that had just returned from a long cruise. It was unlikely, Dale observed, that Bashaw Yusuf Karamanli would send his ships to sea if Tripoli was not at war. He also noted his belief that Reis was lying and had every intention of capturing American ships once the squadron had departed.

To stop him, Dale told Barron to take the *Philadelphia* and lay off Gibraltar, keeping a close watch on the pirates, and to take them when they left. Dale told him to keep far enough away from the harbor so that no one could call his action a blockade, but close enough so as not to allow Reis to slip away into the western ocean. Dale also told Barron that Gavino would assist him, sending out a boat to let Barron know if Reis had sailed. Finally, he instructed Barron to hoist English colors so as to keep the presence of the American warship secret. If Reis sailed west, through the strait and into the western ocean, Barron was to give chase. If Reis managed to slip away, Dale instructed Barron to head for Algiers, where he would join up with Dale and the rest of the fleet. If he was not there, he was to touch in at Tunis and then proceed to Tripoli.

Barron thanked Dale for the honor of watching over Reis. He would take him if he came out, of that he assured the commodore. With a salute, he tucked his hat into the crook of his arm and a marine sentry opened the door, allowing him to depart. Dale watched him go. Barron was a good man and a good captain. He trusted him to capture Reis if the opportunity presented itself. But Dale also knew that Murad Reis had lived by his wits and seamanship for many years and would not be captured easily. Still, if he could be taken, the war, if indeed they were at war already, would be over in one fell swoop.

After Barron had taken his leave, the marine sentry knocked again and Dale looked up from his desk to see Lieutenant Sterett, commander of the *Enterprise,* the fastest sailor of the squadron. Dale knew that the *President,* though fast for a frigate, was much slower than the speedy *Enterprise,* so he told Sterett that if they were to lose sight of each other, to sail for Algiers, and remain there until he arrived. Mindful of Bainbridge's experience there—when he had naively anchored beneath the guns of the fortress and his ship was requisitioned and forced to take specie and presents to Constantinople—Dale told Sterett to anchor out of range of the guns.

Dale examined the younger officer closely, marveling at the youthful vigor but also the strong sense of discipline and decisiveness about the man. He told him to hoist a red flag at the foremast, which would be a signal for Richard O'Brien, U.S. consul, to come out to the vessel. Lastly, he reminded Sterett that they were possibly at war with Tripoli and other Barbary States, and that he should be ever watchful for enemy cruisers. To lull the pirates into a false sense of security, he instructed Sterett to hoist the English colors at sea, and only to hoist the American colors if attacked. Dale reminded the young lieutenant that disguise and secrecy were as important as projecting power at this point, so early in their cruise. Sterett nodded his understanding, stood and saluted the commodore, and took his leave.

Finished with writing orders, Dale stood and stretched, then took up his hat and made his way to the quarterdeck. The sea was ruffled with flecks of white foam, produced by the steady headwind, which the squadron labored against, tacking to make any progress at all. If the wind did not change direction, Dale knew it would be a slow, tedious passage to Algiers. Pacing the quarterdeck beside the windward taffrail, Dale watched as the lieutenant in command of the watch ordered the log to be thrown. A midshipman held on to a reel of rope that was fastened to a small, weighted wooden panel. As the lieutenant gave the signal, the midshipman threw the log over the rail into the sea and another midshipman turned the glass, which measured half a minute. As the panel struck the water, the rope, which was knotted at equal lengths, began to quickly unwind. "Mark," cried the lieutenant, and the midshipman grabbed the rope, noting the number of knots that had gone overboard in thirty seconds and thereby determining the ship's speed, measured in knots. Taking into account the zigzag progress of the squadron, the speed was not nearly fast enough, thought Dale.

Indeed, subsequent days of calm followed and it was not until July 9 that they arrived in Algiers. Careful to avoid placing the *President* beneath the fortress guns, Dale anchored well out of reach, in thirty fathoms of water. As the anchor chains clattered through the hawseholes and the anchor splashed into the blue-green water of the Mediterranean, a lieutenant announced that a small cutter was making its way toward the *President.* Dale peered through his telescope and saw the hunched form of Richard O'Brien, U.S. consul to Algiers. In a few moments, he would know whether or not America was at war.

Mr. O'Brien appeared on deck moments later, assisted by the firm hands of two marines. Dale could see that O'Brien was not at all in good health; his years of captivity had taken their toll. Dale took O'Brien to his cabin and asked him if they were at war. O'Brien nodded. Yes, the United States and Tripoli were at war, which the Bashaw had declared on the fourteenth of May.

O'Brien recounted Cathcart's story, which the former consul had detailed in a letter. On May 14, Cathcart had bade Hadgi Mahamude la Sore, emissary to Bashaw Yusuf Kara-

manli of Tripoli, enter his office. As la Sore entered, Cathcart
noted the hour, one p.m., then turned his attention to the
emissary, who announced the news that Cathcart had tried
for years to prevent: The Bashaw was sending soldiers to the
U.S. consulate to take down the flagpole. Cathcart, who had
been a slave of the Algerians for more than a decade, had
known what that meant: It was the customary way the Barbary pirates declared war.

La Sore's message delivered, Cathcart then watched as he
left the room. Cathcart watched from the window as the
Bashaw's soldiers marched to the flagpole. He had seen an
officer instruct his men to haul on the halyards in an attempt
to snap the pole in half. They struggled and pulled, but the
flagpole did not come down, so the officer ordered his men
to chop down the flagpole. The flagpole, cut at a height of six
feet above the ground, crashed down at half past two in the
afternoon, its slender length lying on the consulate's terrace.
Cathcart saw that one of the Tripolitan officers had bundled
up the Stars and Stripes and taken the flag away. Hours later,
he saw the American flag hoisted aboard a Tripolitan cruiser,
in the customary place where the flags of nations at war with
the Bashaw were flown.

Dale listened attentively until O'Brien had finished his account, then, remembering his duty, provided O'Brien with
dispatches from Washington and told him that the frigate
George Washington, which was scheduled to sail from Washington to Algiers in July, contained the tribute required to
fulfill the treaty obligation. Much as he disliked doing so, he
had handed to O'Brien the letters containing invoices of the
stores aboard the frigate. O'Brien scanned the list: timber,
naval and military stores, cables and gun carriages, and
masts. O'Brien nodded; the Dey would be pleased. O'Brien
also noted that with only four ships in the Mediterranean, the
United States could only fight one pirate state at a time. So
this cargo, and the cargo aboard the *Peace & Plenty,* which
was bound for Tunis, would keep the two other restive pirate
states happy until Tripoli could be defeated.

* * *

James Leander Cathcart sat down at his writing desk and began to write to Eaton. Cathcart had managed to escape Tripoli and was now in Leghorn, a consul in exile. And he had important news for his fellow consul.

In the latest post from London, Cathcart had learned that the American squadron was on its way. The happiness of the news made his pen scratch faster and faster against the paper as he wrote: "The same letters informs us that (if rumor is to be credited) the government of the United States have resolved to pay no more subsidy's (they are ashamed of the name of paying Tribute, thank God) to the Barbary States."

Next, Cathcart laid out his plan to defeat the Barbary, a plan in which he needed the assistance of Eaton, and which he knew Eaton would enjoy:

In my last letters I informed you that I do not merely contemplate to conclude an honorable & advantageous peace at Tripoli no Sir more must be done, we must establish a national character in Barbary by effecting a revolution in favor of Hamet the Bashaws Brother who is at Tunis, for so long as Joseph Bashaw lives, our commerce will not be secure, allowing that we conclude a peace upon our own terms.

Cathcart knew Yusuf Karamanli well. If peace were concluded on America's terms, the first time U.S. frigates were off on other duty the Bashaw would try and capture American merchantmen. Karamanli would never accept any peace on America's terms. Therefore, Cathcart believed, the United States must be rid of him. He finished the letter by asking a favor of Eaton: "I therefore request you to give me what Information you are master of upon the above head, and how far you can engage said Hamet in an expedition of that nature."

When he was finished, Cathcart carefully blotted the paper dry and put it in an envelope. He was already impatient for a response. Would Hamet agree to the plan? Could he be trusted? Would he make a suitable Bashaw? Cathcart wanted answers, but his mind would not rest as he thought through how best to effect a change in leadership in Tripoli.

On July 17, the *President* and the *Enterprise* rounded Point Farina, a hooked point of land that shoaled well out into the sea, and entered the Gulf of Tunis. The *President* cut through the waters, heading for the anchorage. A short time later, the *President*'s anchor slashed the surface of the bay off the Goulette.

Dale sent a letter to Eaton, asking him to come aboard. He did not intend to step ashore himself. He remembered too well Bainbridge's troubles with the Dey of Algiers. Furthermore, he was pressed for time. He wished to provision and water his ships and then proceed to Tripoli, where he intended to capture Tripolitan vessels and bottle up the harbor. War had been declared, and it was time to fight it.

There was also another purpose to his visit here. Dale intended to show the Bey of Tunis America's new might. Dale was keenly aware that the Tunisians would be watching and wondering what America's response would be to Yusuf's declaration of war. Commodore Dale stared back at his reflection in the looking glass. He wore his full dress uniform: a long, blue coat faced by a row of buttons containing an anchor and an American eagle surrounded by fifteen stars. The standing collar was stiff against his neck, and trimmed with gold lace. Gold epaulettes adorned each shoulder. Satisfied with his appearance, he left his cabin and strode along the gangway and climbed up to the quarterdeck. Let the Tunisians see him; this was the American response. Dale watched as small boats plied to and fro between the warship and shore, bringing empty water casks to be filled and fresh provisions that would allow the *President* to remain off Tripoli for as long as possible.

Dale waited several hours for his letter to be carried to shore and then spied a boat carrying a solitary figure. Dale watched as the boat approached the frigate and confirmed his suspicions; it was Eaton. As the bluff, hearty Eaton climbed the ladder to the deck, Dale saw that the consul looked weak. Taking him below to his cabin, he asked about his health. Eaton told him that he had suffered a bilious fever that had confined him to bed in late June. In addition, the strain of living in Tunis was immense. Dale and Eaton conversed late into the evening, Eaton filling Dale in on the present situation in the Mediterranean and Tunis, Dale telling Eaton about the blockade of Murad Reis in Gibraltar, American forces now in the Mediterranean, and his plan to leave for Tripoli on the morrow. Before leaving, Eaton made sure that Dale understood one characteristic of the Barbary pirates: They respected force, and only force. He urged Dale, as he had argued the secretary of state, that in order to have free commerce in the Mediterranean, the United States would have to defend it. There was no alternative.

On July 24, the *President* and the *Enterprise* arrived off Tripoli to begin their blockade of the port. Dale had sent the *Essex* to Barcelona to collect American merchantmen and convoy them safely out of the Mediterranean and into the Atlantic.

Dale braced himself against the taffrail as the frigate rolled in the light Mediterranean swell, peering through his telescope at the enemy capital. Set in a wide bay, Tripoli was a walled city of buff and white houses set against a background of olive trees and palms. It was early morning and the warm breeze that blew from shore brought with it the faint scent of jasmine, oleander, and flowering hibiscus. Secluded behind a rocky reef, Tripoli was built for pirates. It would be hard to thread a large frigate into the harbor, past the jagged procession of rocks running in a line across the harbor entrance. Small, shallow draft vessels, such as those that the pirates preferred, could easily escape any of Dale's warships and hide in the harbor.

The obstacles, Dale knew based on local charts, marked the outer limit of the Kaliusa reef, which formed a natural breakwater. The rocks extended from the western edge of the bay, on which rose the hulking shape of the Mandrach, a fortress that anchored the right flank of the bay. Farther along the shore to the west was the round form of the French fort, which guarded Tripoli against both a sea invasion and attack from the desert. Just beyond these two forts was the town itself, guarded by the massive walls of the Bashaw's castle. Dale peered at the town, taking in the disorderly walls, the rows of houses, and the domed roofs of a multitude of mosques interspersed with fruit trees and date palms swaying softly in the morning breeze. He swung his telescope to the left, and saw a sandy beach lined with palms, and behind them fields of tobacco, millet, and barley. On the far left side of the bay, near where the reef shoaled and deep-draft ships could not pass, were two other forts, the American fort and the English fort. Dale gazed further at the scene before him, then snapped shut the telescope. Tripoli was indeed well defended, and would be difficult to attack from the sea. With the force that he possessed, a blockade was his only option.

Dale knew, however, that in spite of what he had heard from Cathcart, O'Brien, and Eaton, duty required that he send a letter to Yusuf Karamanli, to confirm that the two countries were at war and, furthermore, to determine if a peace could be effected. So, on July 25, he sat at his desk and penned a letter, instructing the Bashaw that if he wished to make peace, he had only to send a boat out to the *President* indicating that the war was over.

Two days passed as he waited for the Bashaw's reply. Finally, on July 27, a lookout spied a boat, pulling hard from shore, headed for the flagship. As it touched, a Tripolitan officer stood up, steadied himself against the side of the ship, and handed a letter to one of Dale's officers who had clambered down the ladder. As the boat departed, Dale took the letter and scanned its contents. He frowned as he read the note, in which the Bashaw stated his reasons for going to war and effectively closed the door on peace. Dale put the letter in his pocket and took a stroll on the quarterdeck, the fresh breeze ruffling the waters of the Mediterranean, which foamed alongside the frigate as it tacked, to and fro, across the mouth of the bay, keeping an ever-watchful eye for any sign that the corsairs were readying for sea.

Aboard the *Enterprise,* Sterett used his time well, studying the fleet arrayed against him. In addition to the two enemy cruisers that Barron had bottled up at Gibraltar, High Admiral Murad Reis possessed ten additional ships, which were at anchor in the harbor. Through his glass Sterett saw two gunboats, hauled up on shore; two spalonards, open boats that contained twenty oars and four mounted swivel guns; a quarter galley mounting four guns; an eighteen-gun Neapolitan polacre; two three-masted eighteen-gun polacres; a ten-gun polacre that appeared to have been converted into a transport; and an old thirty-two-gun vessel that appeared to be undergoing repairs.

If the Tripolitans chose to attack, the *Enterprise* and *President* could handle this force. But they could not attack Tripoli with only two vessels. They did not know the harbor, which had every indication of being treacherous. Furthermore, more than a hundred cannons could be thrust from the embrasures of the town's numerous batteries to defend the harbor. They were at a standoff. All they could do, surmised Sterett, was to make a show of force, and wait for the Bashaw to come out and fight. On the other hand, the Bashaw must know that they could not sail indefinitely. Already, the purser reported that they only had a few remaining barrels of fresh water. They would have to leave soon. Yet they had accomplished something. They had turned away some vessels carrying goods and food to the Bashaw, so Tripoli, too, would suffer. Yet clearly the Bashaw had the upper hand. The *Enterprise* would run out of water far sooner than Tripoli ran out of food.

As if reading his mind, Dale sent a signal to the *Enterprise,* instructing Sterett to come aboard. Sterett's fears were confirmed as he took a packet of letters and correspondence from Dale, along with his orders. Dale asked him to head for Malta, some one hundred and ninety-two nautical miles to the northwest. There he would deliver the mail to any packet boat on its way west to Gibraltar, and take on as much water as he could carry back.

Sterett sailed on the following morning. The winds were favorable and the nimble *Enterprise* cut easily through the sea, leaving only a foaming wake to mark its rapid progress. Sterett packed on as many sails as the sloop of war could manage, hoping to return to the blockade in a few days.

V

A WILY ENEMY

The morning of August 1 dawned bright and clear. The *Enterprise* was momentarily quiet, apart from the creak of cords and the splash and gurgle of water as she cut through the rolling swell. Sterett stood on the windward side of the quarterdeck, which was newly wet after being scrubbed and cleaned by his crew. Hammocks now hung in the rigging, their usual place after a night's use, where they were out of the way should the crew need to clear the decks and fight, and a rolled-up hammock could stop a splinter or musket ball. What other noise there was came from the hubbub below, where the crew was eating breakfast.

Sterett glanced up at the sky and remarked that it was somehow lighter in color and more stark and clear than the sky of his native land. Perhaps it was due to the lack of moisture in the air, dried from its passage over the Sahara. Sterett was brought back from his reminiscence by the hail of a lookout in the main top. There was a sail on the horizon. Sterett propped his telescope against the binnacle and peered through the eyepiece, sighting a vessel ahead of them, a lateen-rigged two-masted vessel, a xebec by the looks of her, mounting fourteen guns, two more than the *Enterprise.* Sterett examined the vessel in detail, noting the size of the gun muzzles, which indicated that they were probably six-pounders, just like his own. He took his eye off the telescope for a moment and looked up at the mainmast, seeing that their ruse was in place. The *Enterprise,* following Dale's instructions, was flying English colors. The ship ahead, who-ever she was, would think her British, and this would allow

Sterett to speak to the captain of the vessel and find out whether he was friend or foe. Sterett hoped she was foe. They were at war with a despotic pirate state, and had been at sea now for two months, yet they had not seen any action. Sterett wanted to prove that his ship and his men, whom he had drilled and trained during those long months from Hampton Roads to Tripoli, were ready.

Sterett instructed his executive officer to beat to quarters. The drummer beat the drums as the ship was cleared for action. Preparing for battle was a carefully choreographed series of tasks performed by each of the eighty-nine crew-members. Below him, on the gun deck, the gunner took out the key to the magazine and opened it, instructing the powder boys to bring shot and powder to the guns. Meanwhile, the captain of each of the guns repaired to the great cabin to receive his saltbox, which contained two cartridges, a powder horn, and a pistol with a dozen cartridges. The pistols were to repel boarders. The officers of each division shouted commands, ordering the guns cast off, and tampions out. As an officer walked alongside each of the twelve hulking weapons, he nodded as he was shown that the rammers, sponges, and worms were in their proper places, and that match tubs with water and another bucket full of water stood ready to dowse fires on the gun deck.

The gun captains now ordered their crews to load the guns. The powder boys distributed flannel bags containing powder to each of the spongers, who took the bags and rammed them down the muzzles. Using a priming iron thrust through the priming hole, the captain of the gun felt for the flannel bag. The cry of "home" in rapid succession echoed through the gun deck. Next, the sponger rammed a six-pound shot into the muzzle, followed by a wad, to keep the ball in place. Finished loading, each gun crew now hauled on the tackles, heaving to run out the gun. Meanwhile, the gun captain pricked the bag of powder with the priming iron, and then poured gunpowder from his powder horn into the firing pan. The six guns were elevated using crowbars and hand-spikes to fire at the corsair's rigging. And now they waited, the smell of slow matches burning in their tubs beside each gun. The gun crews were ready, the gunner waiting for Sterett's command.

Below the gun deck, Sterett knew that the carpenters were checking the main pumps, as well as the head and cistern pumps, making sure they were all in good working order. They would also look over their own tools—shot plugs, mauls, and oakum—to be ready to fix any holes punched through the hull by the enemy. In the armory, pistols, cutlasses, boarding axes, and pikes were removed and taken to the quarterdeck, ready in case they were needed. Other men hung fire buckets on the capstan. Meanwhile, the marines readied themselves, hauling muskets, blunderbusses, and cartridges into the fighting tops. Above him, Sterett spied his midshipmen, each commanding one of the tops. Their job was to make sure the marines didn't shoot in a way that set fire to the sails. As all preparations were complete, the ship fell oddly silent save for the creaking of oak timbers, the hissing of water against the hull, and the flap of canvas above. As two bells clanged in the forenoon watch, announcing the hour of nine a.m., all was ready for battle. In a moment, they would know if their preparations were necessary.

The *Enterprise* rapidly approached the vessel from windward. As they hove to, Sterett saw the Tripolitan ensign flying from the masthead. Sterett hung on to the rigging overhead, and as the *Enterprise* came within pistol shot, called out to the corsair's commander and asked him the purpose of his cruise. The commander replied that he had slipped out of the harbor at Tripoli, and was cruising for Americans, but that, unfortunately, he had not found any yet. By way of reply, Captain Sterett nodded to a waiting midshipman, who pulled hard on the halyard, sending the American colors up the mainmast. As the Stars and Stripes fluttered in the breeze, the corsair commander swore and shouted orders to his men, who, Sterett could see, were also manning their guns. They, too, had been watching and waiting for their captain's orders.

As the *Enterprise* moved past the corsair, Sterett gave the

order to fire. Marines, who had lain waiting for the word,
stood as one man. As their commander, Lieutenant Enoch
Lane, barked orders, the men carefully took aim. Then, as
Lane's sword swept down, the marines fired, sending a rattling hail of lead into the Tripolitan cruiser. The marines
aimed for the gunners and officers, aiming to reduce the
enemy's ability to fight. As the two ships sped apart, however, a great roar rose from the corsair vessel as she managed
a partial broadside. Balls whistled overhead, and splashed
into the water around the *Enterprise* but, miraculously, did
little damage.

Sterett ordered his lieutenants, David Porter and Richard
Hawson, to take the ship about and fire on the enemy. Mindful of the weather gauge, he instructed the helmsman to
come about so that they would stay to windward of the
Tripolitan vessel. Keeping to windward meant that he could
control the flow of the battle, deciding when to attack, and
when to withdraw. The Tripolitan captain had provided him
with this advantage and Sterett did not intend to give it up.

Belowdeck, the gun crews understood what the captain
had in mind and moved across the gun deck to the port side
guns. Beside each of the six port side guns stood a captain of
the gun, second captain, spongers, a fireman, boarders, and
sail-trimmers. The captains ordered tampions out, and a
crewmember of each gun removed the bung that kept water
out of the muzzle. Next, the gun crew hooked tackles to each
gun, to allow them to run the gun out, and a train-tackle behind to run it inboard for loading.

On deck, Sterett watched similar preparations aboard the
enemy cruiser. They were now closing on each other, within
pistol shot. As the *Enterprise*'s prow cut through the blue waters, the helmsman steered a parallel course that would take
the sloop alongside, giving her port guns ample opportunity
to shatter the corsair. As they came alongside, Sterett gave
the word, and the *Enterprise* loosed a broadside into the men
who packed the rails of the Tripolitan vessel.

Six guns erupted in flames and smoke as half a dozen six-
pound shots tore at the xebec's sails and smashed into her

hull. Meanwhile, Sterett heard the accompanying roar from the enemy ship as she fired a ragged broadside in return. But because the *Enterprise* had fired first, she had been shrouded in smoke, which had obscured the Tripolitan gunner's view. Once again, the Tripolitan volley had passed over them, only cutting some cords and rigging. Sterett surveyed the deck, seeing little damage and miraculously no wounded. Meanwhile, the marines under Lane were steadily firing and reloading, firing and reloading into the thick smoke in the direction of the enemy cruiser.

Suddenly through the smoke, the Tripolitan cruiser loomed large and Sterett saw her name painted on her side: the *Tripolino*. He immediately realized what the enemy captain had in mind: He was attempting to lay his ship close enough to board the *Enterprise*. Barbary pirates were known to dislike long-range gunnery. Instead, they preferred to close and board, relying on numbers rather than skill.

As the ships came closer together, Sterett ordered his men to repel the boarders. The marines took aim at the pirates who were crowding the waist of the ship armed with swords, cudgels, knives, and scimitars in readiness for hand-to-hand combat. As the ships came close, grappling hooks were thrown toward the *Enterprise,* but the Americans were ready. Lane's marines let loose a deadly volley, and a file of pirates was seemingly plucked from their positions and thrown to the deck. As the *Tripolino* bore away, Sterett pursued, and with guns loaded again, fired a deadly broadside, holing the xebec and smashing her masts and rigging.

The *Tripolino*'s guns went silent, and suddenly, the smoke cleared to reveal an officer aboard the xebec hauling down her colors; they were surrendering. The American gunners and crew raced onto the deck in readiness to board, and as they approached the shattered *Tripolino*, gave three cheers as a mark of their victory. As the *Enterprise* came within pistol shot, the enemy ship appeared lifeless; no men could be seen on deck save the captain and his lieutenant.

Just as the ships were about to touch, the Tripolitans hoisted their colors, and a mass of men rose from the deck

and fired into the throng of Americans crowding the deck of
the *Enterprise* in eagerness to board. Sterett swore; he had
fallen for the ruse. The Tripolitans had only meant to lure the
Enterprise close, to try and board her. As musket shots whistled overhead, Sterett ordered his crew back to the guns and
ordered his sailing master to wear away from the cruiser.

The two ships separated as Sterett waited for the signal
that his gunners were ready. Finally, he heard the familiar cry
of the division officers and gave the order: fire. Six iron shots
belched from the *Enterprise,* smashing the Tripolitans'
cruiser's masts and rigging and holing her above the waterline.

The enemy captain, however, would not give up, and seeing his opportunity as the *Enterprise* reloaded, steered for
the *Enterprise* in another attempt to board her. Sterett knew
his gunnery must be taking its toll aboard the enemy ship,
but still he saw men line the waist, weapons in hand, ready to
board. As they came closer, grappling hooks once again
sailed overhead and several clattered on deck. But Lane's
marines were ready, and fired into the massed ranks of the
boarders, again thwarting their attempt to board the *Enterprise.*

The two ships drifted apart and through the swirl of smoke
Sterett saw the colors again come down. They were surrendering. This time, however, his crew did not race onto the
deck or give three cheers. No, he would wait and see if this
was yet another ruse. Sterett kept his sloop away from the
Tripolino, watching, but saw only carnage and death aboard
the enemy. Yet as he watched, the commander of the xebec
again steered toward the *Enterprise.* Sterett realized in an instant what he was trying to do: get close enough to attempt to
board one last time. Sterett, angered by the duplicity of the
pirates, ordered his gunners to hole the ship below the waterline and sink her. The *Enterprise*'s gunners, bent on revenge,
fired broadside after broadside into the *Tripolino,* whose rigging and sails were cut to ragged tatters, and whose hull was
holed with six-pound shot.

Finally, seeing that all hope was lost, the enemy captain
hauled down his colors. Sterett yelled across the short dis-

tance between the vessels that if the captain wished to surrender his ship, he would have to come aboard the *Enterprise* or send some of his officers. The two ships, silent save for the creak and groan of rigging and the ripple of water, slid beside each other, the crew of the *Enterprise* waiting beside their guns, the marines ready to fire, the *Tripolino* oddly silent, with only a few men standing on deck.

The enemy captain cried out that his ship's boat was smashed and would not float, so Sterett ordered Lieutenant Porter to take an armed boat and seize control of the *Tripolino*. A moment later, Porter climbed into the boat and ordered the oarsmen to row quickly toward the *Tripolino*. The crew was armed with pistols and cutlasses in case this was another ruse.

As the launch moved across the narrow space between the vessels, Sterett watched for any sign that the pirate captain would again trick him. When the boat touched the side of the *Tripolino,* Porter grabbed hold of the lines, climbed aboard, and saw a dreadful sight: The deck was littered with dead and dying men, and the planks were slippery with blood. The captain, Admiral Rais Mahomet Rouse, himself wounded, handed Porter the colors and his sword. The battle was over.

Watching the surrender, Sterett ordered his men to board the *Tripolino,* which was now listing and taking on water. Stepping aboard, he, too, was repulsed by the carnage. Porter quickly gave him the tally: twenty dead, including the surgeon and second officer, and thirty wounded, including the captain and first lieutenant. Sterett asked for the butcher's bill aboard his own ship and was stunned by the answer: none. In a battle that had lasted three hours, the *Enterprise* had taken the larger vessel without a single casualty. Nor, he found, had they suffered any significant damage. Sterett realized that he had just won a victory that would resonate throughout the Mediterranean, and the world.

Wasting no time, Sterett ordered his surgeon to tend to the enemy wounded. Meanwhile, he set about following Dale's orders, which he had read and reread these many days:

"heave all his Guns over board Cut way his Masts & leave him In a situation, that can Just make out to get into some Port." Since the United States had not officially declared war against Tripoli, and because Jefferson, not Congress, had ordered out the fleet, Sterett knew that he could not make the *Tripolino* a prize. So, amid the cries of the wounded, his crew swarmed over the corsair, disposing of the dead, washing the deck, and clearing the wreckage. The steady chop of axes indicated that his men were taking a keen interest in Dale's orders; minutes later, a loud crack and orders to stand clear preceded the masts toppling overboard. Men belowdeck added to this cacophony of noise by throwing overboard powder, cannon balls, small arms, swords, and the guns. They would leave the corsair a toothless hulk, just capable of floating to port.

Hours later, aboard the *Enterprise,* Sterett watched as the shattered *Tripolino,* no longer sinking, its holes plugged, sailed away under a jury-rigged mast, a small square of canvas snapping and fluttering in the breeze. He watched as Rais and his remaining men set sail for the south, to tell his master, Yusuf Karamanli, what had befallen them in their first run-in with the Americans. Sterett hoped this would teach the Bashaw a lesson he would not forget.

Joseph Gavino kept a sharp lookout over the two Tripolitan corsairs anchored in Gibraltar Bay. It was now August 7, and they had been bottled up by the *Philadelphia* for more than a month. He had heard reports that they were running out of food. And the day before, he had heard from a reliable source that they had swept the bread room and served the contents of the dustpans to the crew for supper.

A knock at the door brought a messenger, who told him that the crew of the Tripolitan brig had mutinied. Gavino walked quickly down the cobblestone streets of the fortress, arriving at the shore and watching as the Tripolitan small boats arrived. Gavino saw another boat arrive carrying an officer, who argued with the crewmembers, begging them to return. Gavino overheard him promising that Admiral Reis would find them food. After much haggling, the officer promised them three days' provisions, and the disgruntled crew agreed to return to their brig. Clearly, the admiral was having difficulty holding his crews together in the face of the U.S. blockade. Gavino knew this with even more certainty when, after the crew had returned, he saw small boats plying between the brig and the *Meshouda,* carrying the former vessel's guns over to the flagship. Reis no longer trusted the crew of the brig.

After watching the activity aboard the Tripolitan vessels, Gavino turned his attention to the American vessels anchored in the harbor, the *Louisa* and the brig *Jason Stuart.* The activity aboard these merchant ships indicated that they were preparing to depart. Gavino watched as crewmembers raced up the shrouds and dangled from the yards as officers below ordered them to bend sails. Meanwhile, a drum beat the time as the men heaved against the capstan bars, and the anchor was slowly drawn from its resting place in the bay mud.

Gavino glanced over at the *Meshouda* and saw similar activity, crewmembers crowding the yards as the sails were unfurled. Did Reis mean to follow them and take them? If so, he would not be able to send a dispatch boat to the *Philadelphia* in time to stop the corsairs from taking the merchantmen as prize. Gavino realized that the only way to stop them would be to prevail upon the British authorities to detain the *Meshouda.*

Out of breath from his hurried journey back to the consular house, Gavino sat at his desk and quickly penned a note to Admiral Saumarez, who had just won a resounding victory against the French fleet off Cadiz three weeks prior. He asked the British officer to detain Reis for twenty-four hours. Gavino stuffed the message into an envelope, sealed it, and dispatched a messenger to the admiral.

Later that afternoon, he received a response from the admiral indicating that Reis would be dealt with. Resting easier, Gavino watched as the two American ships, bound for the Atlantic and home, left the bay unmolested and sailed out into the Strait. Gavino watched them round Cabreta Point, and then lost sight of them as they moved over the blue horizon into the glimmering ocean.

The following morning, Gavino wrote two notes to Captain Barron, telling him of the previous day's events and letting him know that it was common knowledge now that the *Philadelphia* was blockading the Tripolitan vessels. He wrote to Barron that he ought to keep between Tangier and Tetuan since Reis was low on provisions and would likely make a run for Tangier, Larach, or Tetuan. Left unsaid was Gavino's belief that Reis either had his own source of intelligence on the whereabouts of the *Philadelphia,* or, more likely, that the wily admiral knew the winds so well that he had known the *Philadelphia* would not have been able to remain on station and would have been carried far to the east. Gavino sealed the notes and sent them by messenger to waiting dispatch boats. One would head east, the other west, in search of the *Philadelphia,* and deliver Gavino's urgent message. The consul had done all in his power to assist in taking Reis. Now it was up to Barron.

The following morning, Gavino woke early and strode down to the harbor to learn any news he could of the *Philadelphia.* There he discovered, from vessels that had just arrived from the Mediterranean, that two days earlier the *Philadelphia* was somewhere near Malaga, a town on the Spanish coast to the east. It stood to reason, thought Gavino. The last few days the winds had been out of the west, which would have pushed the *Philadelphia* off station. He anxiously hoped that one of the dispatch vessels had found Barron and delivered his message, or better yet, that Barron was already sailing for Gibraltar.

Gavino turned his attention to the Tripolitan vessels and was startled by what he saw. Beside them were two vessels flying Moroccan colors, and standing nearby, an English King's Lugger, sixteen guns. Gavino watched as small boats ferried the crew of the brig and the *Meshouda* to the two waiting ships. What was happening was as clear as day: Reis meant to rescue his crew and send them to Morocco. If Gavino had learned that the *Philadelphia* was two days' sail from the Straits, no doubt Reis had, too. And, by the looks of it, he had cut a deal with the British, who, it appeared, would convoy the two ships across the Straits.

Gavino watched, powerless, as the loading was completed and the two vessels, convoyed by the sixteen-gun lugger, sailed out of the bay, bound for Tetuan. He glanced at the two Tripolitan vessels still at anchor in the bay and saw that there were still men aboard. Gavino sent spies to learn if Reis had left or if he remained. Later that day, they returned and reported that some eighty men and officers, including Reis, were still aboard the ships, but two hundred and seventy men had just escaped the American trap. As long as Reis had not escaped they could still claim victory. But if he somehow managed to get away, it would be a devastating defeat. Gavino waited anxiously for word from Barron, but neither of the dispatch boats arrived. He prayed that somehow the *Philadelphia* would return to station in time to take the two Moroccan vessels.

On September 1, a Greek polacre with a bowsprit lashed to its prow arrived in the roads of Tunis. She carried four guns, two facing forward, and a gun on either side of the foremast. Her quarterdeck was raised two feet from the main deck; her stern had four small window holes in it. Eaton took another look at the ship through his telescope and continued to take notes on her appearance, describing her in the letter he was writing to Captain Samuel Barron, commander of the *Philadelphia,* currently at sea blockading Admiral Murad Reis in Gibraltar.

Eaton was keenly interested in this vessel because he had heard that it had arrived from Tripoli and was on its way to Gibraltar to bring home the high admiral and his crew. Eaton dipped his pen in the inkpot, writing forcefully for the need to capture Reis and his crew:

> This would be an event so fatal to the Bashaw of Tripoli that it would at once put an end to the war. He can do nothing without the crews of these corsaires—They are many of them from the

first families of Tripoli—this circumstance, if they fall into our hands, would excite an insurrection in his Kingdom and give us the intire command of terms.

Eaton continued writing instructions to Barron about how he thought Reis could be best captured. He ended with the following warning: "I cannot but repeat, if you get possession of the English renegade, Morad Rais, it will decide our contest with Tripoli; But if he escape us and return to Tripoli it will prolong the war and be productive of incalculable mischief—"

Satisfied that he had done all he could, Eaton placed the sheets into an envelope and sealed it. He then put on his hat and strode out of the consulate toward the port. Searching through the anchored ships, he found the one he was looking for, a polacre, and hailed the vessel. Shortly thereafter, a boat left the vessel and made its way to shore, carrying her captain. Eaton greeted him warmly and together they walked along the shore and talked. Eaton handed Captain John Padwanni the envelope and instructed him to deliver it to Captain Barron aboard the *Philadelphia*. He was to leave immediately, ahead of the Greek polacre, and warn Barron of the rescue attempt. He also told Padwanni that should Barron order it, he should ready his vessel to take aboard the crew of the two corsairs, some three hundred and fifty men, and to have irons ready for them since they could easily overpower his small crew.

Padwanni nodded in understanding, thanked Eaton, and took his leave. Eaton watched as the oarsmen rowed Padwanni back to his vessel. Eaton knew he could trust Padwanni, but he also knew that Murad Reis was a wily sea dog. Barron would be tested, but he must know the importance of taking Reis, and therefore, he would not fail. Eaton walked back to the consulate knowing that he would remain anxious until he heard of Reis's capture.

As Eaton waited for word from Gibraltar, he spent time getting to know Hamet Karamanli, who was in exile in Tunis.

Hamet was the second of three sons born to Ali Karamanli. Hassan was the eldest, Hamet the middle brother, and Yusuf the youngest. Yet, as Hamet explained, Yusuf was also handsome, ruthless, and ambitious. From Hamet, Eaton learned that when Yusuf was sixteen, he declared that he, not Hassan or Hamet, should rule Tripoli. Hassan ignored Yusuf's declaration, but Hamet did not, allying himself with Yusuf and denouncing Hassan's right to rule.

By 1790, Hassan had taken the throne. His father was still alive, but had decided to hand over power to effect a smooth transfer, and thwart his youngest son's ambitions. Yusuf, who was twenty, decided to act. Ostensibly seeking to end their estrangement, he had invited Hassan to their mother's apartment. Yusuf came unarmed, and asked their mother to take Hassan's sword. After she helped her oldest son unbuckle his weapon, Yusuf asked his servant for the Koran, to validate their reconciliation. This was the signal for the servant to hand him two pistols, with which he shot Hassan. Their mother watched this scene of horror. As Hassan tried to get his sword, Yusuf shot him again. Hamet recounted Hassan's last words to his mother: "Mother, is this the present you have reserved for your eldest son?" As Hassan lay on the floor, Yusuf ordered his bodyguards to finish off his work, stabbing Hassan hundreds of times as his mother and his wife, who had hurried in at the sound of gunshots, watched. Afterward, Yusuf celebrated with a feast.

Hamet explained to Eaton how he had come to be an exile in Tunis. After Hassan's death, Yusuf allowed Hamet to take the throne. Together they fought against a squadron of Turkish pirates led by Ali-ben-Zool, who captured Tripoli in 1793 and forced them to flee to Tunis. There, they raised an army and, in 1795, marched back and recaptured Tripoli. Sultan Selim III, the ruler of the Ottoman Empire, declared that the true rulers were the Karamanli family.

Although technically independent from the Turks, each of the Barbary States owed allegiance to the Ottoman Empire. Here, explained Hamet, he made a mistake. He was not in Tripoli when Selim III sided with his family. Instead, he was in the country. Yusuf, however, was in town and assumed the throne. Hamet went into exile in Tunis, where Eaton found him and took him under his wing.

Yusuf did not forget Hamet though. Observing the saying that it was wise to keep one's enemies close, Yusuf had offered Hamet the governorship of Cyrenaica, to the east of Tripoli. His capital would be Derna. He had sent a forty-man escort to bring Hamet back and escort him to his new territory. But Eaton told Hamet that his brother likely meant to kill him and offered Hamet money to stay, which he accepted. Never mind that Eaton borrowed the money from Hadgi Unis Ben Unis, the commercial agent of the Bey. The expense, Eaton and Cathcart believed, was well worth the cost as they drafted their plan to replace Yusuf with Hamet Karamanli, the rightful Bashaw of Tripoli. If only they could get Jefferson and the Navy to agree, they would see the war to a swift conclusion and send a powerful message to the remaining Barbary despots.

Four days after the Greek polacre had left for Gibraltar, Eaton took a jolly boat to the *Grand Turk,* which was rocking gently at anchor in Tunis. As Eaton's boat approached, he saw that all hands were busy preparing the vessel for their homeward voyage. Eaton made his way up the side, and Captain Laughton gracefully offered him the use of the great cabin. Eaton sat down and began to pen a note that Laughton would carry to the secretary of state. The contents of the dispatch were so sensitive that he could not write it on land nor entrust it even to a British packet ship. In this note, Eaton laid out the bold, daring plan that he and Cathcart were working on to end the war if Reis were not captured or the naval blockade did not force the Bashaw to sue for terms.

Sir, The inclosures which I have the honor herewith to forward will inform Government, as accurately as I have the means, of our actual position and future prospects in regard to Tripoli—one circumstance only omitted, which is a project in concert between the rightful Bashaw of Tripoli, now in exile in Tunis, and

myself to attack the usurper by land while our operations are
going on by sea.

Eaton continued to write, telling the secretary of state that
the people of Tripoli were unhappy with the Bashaw and that
they were ripe for a revolt. Sending Hamet to Tripoli would
trigger that insurrection.

The idea of dethroning our enemy and placing a rightful sovereign in his seat makes a deeper impression on account of the lasting peace it will produce with that regency, and the lesson of
caution it will teach the other Barbary States.

Eaton sat back and thought over the plan. He had spent almost three years among the Barbary pirates now and knew
the games they played. Treachery, intrigue, deceit—these
were their watchwords. The United States might very well be
fighting a just war, but to win the war, it would have to adapt
to the rules of the pirates. They would also have to use guile,
deceit, and treachery. The plan, Eaton knew, might meet with
raised eyebrows in Washington, and would certainly meet
with disapprobation by the stiff group of naval officers sent
to carry out the war. But Jefferson himself had said that force
must be repelled by force. And that meant that if the pirates
used treachery, then the United States must also use it. Satisfied, Eaton sealed the envelope and handed it to Captain
Laughton. All he could do now was wait, and hope that Reis
had not escaped the trap.

On September 13, Gavino watched as Murad Reis and
eight officers boarded a British vessel bound for Malta and
thence on to Tripoli. The British had again sabotaged America's plans. Just as the British consul to Algiers had opened
the Atlantic sea-lanes to Algerian corsairs in 1795, so the
British had now prolonged the war. Of course, all Gavino
could do was make an appearance at Governor House and
politely protest. As Gavino knew, the head of the government
did not always control the hands; internal politics, most

likely, were also at play. Still, it was a duplicitous action on the part of the British, and showed Americans that while they were ostensibly on good terms with their former masters, they would have to watch King George III. It also meant that relying on the use of Gibraltar as the main American base was foolish. Not only was it nine hundred and forty nautical miles from Tripoli, but the British controlled it. If America was serious about fighting the Tripolitans, they would not only have to send more ships and men to the Mediterranean, but also establish their own naval base.

Gavino walked down to the waterfront and saw that the two Tripolitan cruisers had been laid up on the mole. It was an important victory, but sadly hollow, he realized. For the real prize had slipped their trap. Gavino tried to put the news in the best possible light as he penned a note to the secretary of state, which he would send with the next American ship sailing into the Atlantic. At least the two Tripolitan vessels were still in the bay. Their yards had been struck, along with their topmasts, and only about twenty men remained to take care of the vessels. Tripoli's two best warships were effectively out of the war. But it was now a hollow victory. As Eaton had noted, the war, which could have been won had they captured Reis, would now last longer, cost America more money, and cost more American lives.

It was pitch-black as the small boat rowed him toward the familiar, ochre-colored shore. High Admiral Murad Reis, along with his eight most trusted officers, sat huddled in the small boat, silent, with no lanterns to indicate their position to the blockading Americans. Reis felt the tug of the oars as the crew dipped their long paddles into the waters of the Mediterranean and pulled them closer to the shore.

Above, the pinpricks of stars shone like diamonds set in black velvet. A warm breeze blew off the land, carrying with it scents from the Sahara. Reis heard the crash and roar of the surf, and then the boat bucked and passed through the surf line, its bottom grinding along the sand, touching the shore. As he and his officers stepped from the boat onto the wet

sandy beach some forty miles to the east of Tripoli, they
bade farewell to the boat crew and began the final stage of
their journey. It would take several days to reach the city, but
that was no matter. Reis felt the glow of satisfaction: In spite
of a months-long blockade, he had managed to elude four
American warships and escape. And he had also gained valu-
able intelligence. He had learned about his enemy, and what
he now knew was that the Americans were new to war, and
unfamiliar with the enemy they faced. He also knew that
they would soon return home, their provisions finished, the
terms of service for their sailors up. And then, thought Reis,
he would exact revenge.

Jefferson sat at the table, set in the center of the long, spacious cabinet room. It was his favorite room in the White
House, which he had filled with his most treasured things.
Jefferson glanced to his right and eyed Dick, who spent
many a night with him, perched on his shoulder. He took a
piece of bread from the plate before him and put it into his
mouth. The mockingbird hopped off his shoulder and onto
the table, taking the offering from the president's lips, then
began to walk to and fro, amid the papers and reports. Jefferson liked his company. The White House was spacious and
empty, except for Dick and Jefferson's secretary, Meriwether
Lewis. It was quiet, too, good for working, but a lonely
place. Jefferson was used to being by himself; his wife,
Martha, had died in 1781 and he had never remarried.

Glancing toward the window recesses, Jefferson's eyes
rested on the plants—roses and geraniums—that he tended
with the tools he kept in the drawers of the table. The walls
of the room were covered with maps and charts, and lined
with bookcases filled with volumes he had purchased in
France and England. Jefferson glanced at the map of Europe,
and his eyes focused on the Mediterranean, and within, on
the Barbary State of Tripoli.

He needed to appoint a new commodore for the Mediterranean squadron. Dale was expected back soon, since his
crews had signed a term of service for only one year. And,

Jefferson had to admit, Dale had not applied enough force to repel the Tripolitans. Jefferson recalled the dispatches and letters received over the last year. Some, such as the news that Dale had found Murad Reis in Gibralter, along with the *Meshouda,* the best ship the Tripolitans possessed, had vindicated Jefferson's decision to send the squadron in spite of the lack of authorization from Congress. The news of the action between the *Enterprise* and *Tripolino* had also made him rest easy. But then Jefferson had received troubling news: Murad Reis had slipped the trap. Although his vessels were still blockaded in Gibralter Bay, the crews and, more important, the high admiral, had been given safe conduct to Tripoli by the British. Murad Reis would fight another day.

Jefferson's first choice to replace Dale had been Captain Thomas Truxtun, who had won a series of brilliant actions against French privateers in the Caribbean during what historians were now calling the Quasi-War. He was a fighter and could win battles, but when offered the position, he had told Secretary of the Navy Smith that he required a captain to serve beneath him on the flagship, as was the custom in more established navies. And Truxtun had then made a fatal mistake: He had "begged leave to quit the service" if his request was not met. Secretary Smith had not blinked, and had accepted Truxtun's resignation. Truxtun, as he had no doubt learned, was far better equipped to fight ships than politicians.

Jefferson had next briefly considered Edward Preble, but his ill health prevented him from accepting the commission. Instead, Jefferson turned to Richard Valentine Morris. Jefferson was well acquainted with Morris's father; Lewis Morris of Morrisania, New York, had been a member of the Continental Congress and a signer of the Declaration of Independence. And Richard's elder brother, Lewis Robert Morris, had done Jefferson a service as a Federalist member of the House during the contest over the presidency. When the outcome of the election was left to a vote in the House, the members had cast ballots thirty-five times without reaching a decision. Finally, on the thirty-sixth ballot, Lewis had withheld his vote, allowing Jefferson to defeat Aaron Burr and become the third president of the United States.

Richard Valentine Morris had served as a captain during Adams's administration and was next on the navy's list. He had accepted the offer, but Jefferson was troubled by his request to have his wife accompany him on the voyage. Officers sometimes brought their wives with them on long cruises, but against the Barbary pirates, to bring a woman into that sort of danger was difficult for Jefferson to understand.

Morris's request was especially hard for Jefferson to comprehend in light of the fresh intelligence brought by Dale on April 14 when the *President* had arrived in Hampton Roads. Dale had delivered to Secretary Smith troubling letters from James Simpson, U.S. consul in Tangier, Morocco. Although the United States had signed a peace treaty with Muley Soliman, emperor of Morocco, the Moroccans had assisted Tripoli in extracting its crew from Gibraltar. And now Jefferson learned that Soliman had asked Dale for a passport to allow the *Meshouda* to return to Tripoli. In addition, Soliman had ordered his corsairs to ready for sea, and was sending grain boats to Tripoli, in open defiance of the American blockade. The line from Dale's letter that concerned Jefferson the most was the following:

> You will see from Mr. Simpsons letters the extraordinary request of the Emperor of Morocco, by such a request and his ordering his corsairs to be got ready for sea with all possible Dispatch, also his sending a man to Gibraltar to purchase some small Vessels that would answer for corsairs, I am fearful that the [Emperor] intends to take a decided part in favour of the Bey of Tripoli Should that be the case he Has it in his power to do our trade (going into & coming out of the Mediterranean) more Injury than the other three Barbary Powers put together . . .

To ensure that Morris prosecuted the war as Jefferson wished, Secretary Smith had provided the new commodore with specific instructions. Rifling through the papers on his desk, Jefferson found Smith's orders and scanned the letter, finding the second to last paragraph in which Smith laid out what was expected of Morris:

"The most effectual plan for accomplishing the great object of maintain[ing] a Squadron in the Mediterranean, which is the protection of our commerce, will be to keep the enemy in Port by blockading the places out of which they issue. Convoy must be given to our vessels as far as it can be done consistently with this object."

After much delay, the new commodore had departed Norfolk on April 27, 1802. He would join a growing American fleet. The *Philadelphia* and *Essex* were in the Mediterranean. The *Constellation,* commanded by Alexander Murray, was on its way. The squadron would be further bolstered by the *Chesapeake,* which would serve as Morris's flagship. Later, three more frigates, the *Adams,* the *New York,* and the *John Adams,* would be sent. These additional ships, Jefferson believed, would provide the United States with enough force to defeat Yusuf Karamanli and end the war.

It was growing late. Jefferson rubbed his eyes, and snuffed out the lantern. He stood, stretching his six-foot-two-inch frame, and walked upstairs. Faithful Dick followed, hopping up the stairs behind him.

Time would tell whether he had made the right choice in offering command of the Mediterranean fleet to Morris. He had wanted Truxtun, who had stood on privilege, and Preble, who had been sick. Morris was his third choice, and though a capable seaman, he was untested as a fighter and diplomat, two skills Jefferson now realized were required to defeat Tripoli.

Jefferson climbed the last of the stairs and entered his bedroom. The war had been going on now for one year. As he readied himself for bed, he hoped, fervently, that it would not last two.

VI

A BADLY LED WAR

At six o'clock on the morning of May 25, 1802, Captain Bainbridge stood on the quarterdeck of the U.S.S. *Essex* and watched as his orders to weigh anchor and make sail were carried out. As men strained against the capstan bars, winching in the anchor chain foot by foot, other sailors ran up the ratlines and began to unfurl the sails, which began to flap and fill in the breeze.

By four bells in the first watch, which signaled the hour of ten a.m., the *Essex* passed Cabreta Point. Bainbridge scanned the sea-lanes, and saw a glimmer of white on the southern horizon near the ochre shore of Tangier. The lookout hailed the deck, indicating that he spied a frigate under full sail, standing to the east, and that she was signaling. Bainbridge turned to his signal officer, but he shook his head; he could not distinguish her flags. Bainbridge ordered the signal officer to make the private signal. The frigate responded by hoisting the correct flags in response. She was American.

An hour later, at six bells in the first watch, the *Essex* approached the frigate and the crew cheered. She was the *Chesapeake,* with Commodore Morris aboard. Receiving the commodore's signal to repair aboard, Bainbridge donned his best uniform and hat and made his way across the narrow gap of blue sea to meet the new commodore.

Ushered into the great cabin, Bainbridge was surprised by the picture of domestic harmony that greeted him. Commodore Morris sat on a match tub. Beside him, seated in a chair, was his wife, reading a book. Between them was their son, Gerard. To either side of the family were nine-pounders, ready for action. Behind the family on the bulwark were fixed battle-axes in the form of a half moon and a row of shot in the shot locker. It was a strange scene, one Bainbridge could barely fathom. Why had the commodore sailed to war with his family? Bainbridge made his greetings, and then took the proffered chair as Morris told him of their difficult passage. Bainbridge listened to why it had taken two months to reach the Mediterranean. They had been held up in Norfolk for some time, awaiting favorable winds, finally leaving on April 27, a month after their scheduled departure. Then, Morris recounted, four days into the voyage, the flagship sprung her mainmast, which was rotten three inches in all around. A shameful neglect by the carpenter at Norfolk, Morris insisted, not to have discovered the defect during his inspection.

They had had to jury-rig a main topmast, which, Morris told him, had slowed their passage. And during additional examination, they had found other rotten spars. Morris also complained that the ship had been very uneasy during her crossing on account of a poorly stowed ballast, which he claimed was injudiciously placed. Bainbridge did not comment on the obvious, that the captain was responsible for his ship, and therefore should have checked the masts and ballast prior to leaving Norfolk. Indeed, the new commodore had been in Hampton Roads almost a month after being issued orders, so he would have been able to effect any changes prior to venturing into the Atlantic.

After hearing of the commodore's woes, Bainbridge provided Morris with an understanding of the situation in the Mediterranean. The *Enterprise* had arrived in the Mediterranean in early spring. The *Constellation* had arrived in Gibraltar on May 5, but had sailed for Tunis; Captain Murray had left dispatches with Joseph Gavino, the U.S. consul at Gibraltar. The *Philadelphia* had already departed for the United States, bearing dispatches from Captain Murray. Bainbridge also told Morris that Morocco had become increasingly bellicose and had made two demands on the

United States. First, the Moroccan emperor had demanded that the *Meshouda* and the Swedish brig, which Murad Reis had abandoned in Gibraltar Bay, be given to Morocco. Under what legal grounds Bainbridge was unaware. He only knew that in 1785, the *Meshouda* had been the Boston brig *Betsey,* which the Moroccans had captured and then released back to the Americans. In addition to the vessels, the emperor wanted passports to send wheat shipments to Tripoli. And, as if to make his point that he was serious about both demands, he had sent agents to Gibraltar to purchase additional corsairs.

Morris thanked Bainbridge for the news and told him that he had heard much the same prior to his departure, and that the *Adams, John Adams,* and *New York* would arrive on station shortly. He also told Bainbridge that he planned to distribute his force to deal with the twin menaces of Tripoli and Morocco. Thanking Bainbridge, he dismissed him. He needed to get to Gibraltar, repair his ship, and provide his wife and son with the comforts only afforded on land. He would also have to wait in Gibraltar for reinforcements to arrive; he couldn't possibly leave Morocco unguarded.

On May 24, Eaton received a note from the prime minister summoning him to the palace. When he arrived, he learned that the Bey was interested in mediating a peace between the United States and Tripoli.

Eaton replied that Tripoli had violated their treaty, and the United States would find it difficult to negotiate with a ruler who had done so.

"If the Bey of Tunis would act as mediator between the parties, and take upon himself the guarantee of the peace on the part of Tripoli, would it remove this difficulty?" asked the minister.

"We have great reliance on the good faith, equity, and magnanimity of His Excellency the Bey of Tunis," replied Eaton, wondering why the Bey was suddenly interested in peace. "And should be very secure in his responsibility; but is it certain, that this Bey would take upon himself the guarantee of a peace on behalf of Tripoli?"

"Yes," said the minister. "But if you talk of retractions and indemnities, it would be idle to talk of peace. On the contrary, according to all custom, you must make the Bashaw a small present, though he would be willing to put up with something less than what he at first demanded."

"We were not the first to violate the peace," replied Eaton. "We are not the first to demand it. If Tripoli be solicitous for it, she must abandon the idea of imposing conditions; she will most certainly never receive a caroube in consideration of her friendship. We do not set any value upon it."

"Nay," replied the minister, "but if you place no value on her friendship, the security of your commerce in this sea, and the saving of the expense of armaments, are objects of consideration, in which you consult your own interest."

"We never supposed our commerce in this sea more secure than at present," replied Eaton. "Notwithstanding the war with Tripoli; and, as to the expense of armaments, we accumulate nothing on that score from making the Mediterranean the maneuvering ground of our seamen. We shall probably always have a squadron in this sea."

"But Tripoli is very poor," said the minister, trying a new tack. "She cannot subsist without the generosity of her friends; give something then on the score of charity."

Eaton would have none of the minister's arguments. "Tripoli has forfeited her title of friend. Besides, there is a vast difference between the beggar who seizes my horse by the bit and, with a pistol at my breast, demands my purse, and him who, with one hand pressed to his heart, and the other hanging with his hat, asks charity for the love of God. The former merits chastisement; the latter excites commiseration. I leave you to apply the figure."

"I feel it," said the minister. "But the Barbary Regencies never make peace without presents."

"It is high time, then, that there should be a precedent," responded Eaton.

"But you say you are disposed for peace?" asked the minister.

"Yes," replied Eaton, "but you are not to understand me that we either wish or will accept it on dishonorable terms."

"There can be nothing dishonorable in making a small voluntary present to Tripoli," said the minister, again trying to get Eaton to budge.

"Drop the subject, if you please," replied Eaton. "Tripoli is not in a right position to receive expressions of our hospitality. Nor am I vested with powers to negotiate. I can only express to you the general, but fixed, sentiment of my government and country, that we prefer peace to war, if we can have it on honorable terms; and you are at liberty to express this sentiment to Tripoli. Otherwise, four or five years of warfare with that state will be but a pastime to our young warriors."

"I shall send off a cruiser," said the minister, "with the result of this interview." And with that the discussion ended. As Eaton left the palace he knew that the Bey would never have proposed this by himself. Instead, he must have received a plea from Yusuf. Very well, thought Eaton, if the navy could apply further pressure, perhaps Tripoli would sue for peace.

May slipped into June as the *Chesapeake* rode gently at anchor in Gibraltar Bay. The mast was repaired, but Morris felt that it was his duty to remain in Gibraltar, in case Morocco made any new demands. Reinforcements were on their way, and they would no doubt carry dispatches from the secretary of the navy. Perhaps his orders had changed? Indeed, he could not leave until another ship arrived to watch over Morocco. Morris hoped the ship would arrive before July. In the meantime, he still had not heard from Murray, but presumed the *Constellation* was blockading Tripoli. After all, he had not heard of any piratical acts during the past two months. The Mediterranean was safe for the time being, and as long as he was anchored in Gibraltar Bay, no pirates would enter the Atlantic.

Meanwhile, seven hundred and fifty-three nautical miles away, the *Constellation*'s anchor chain rattled through the hawseholes, and settled in the soft mud of the Goulette. Captain Murray, dressed in his finest uniform, descended to the waiting barge and was rowed to shore to pay his respects to Hamouda Bashaw, Bey of Tunis, and call on William Eaton. Murray's rise to captain a warship had begun at an early age. In 1773, at the age of eighteen, he had become master of a small merchantman. During the Revolutionary War, he fought with his native Marylanders at Long Island and White Plains. Later in the war, he became a privateer before joining the Continental Navy, where he became a lieutenant in 1781. Now, at the age of forty-seven, he was a seasoned veteran.

Several hours later, Eaton and Murray sat in the consulate and Eaton expounded on his plan to overthrow Yusuf and replace him with Hamet. As Murray listened, Eaton told him the history of Yusuf's rise to power and the plan Cathcart and he had developed to unseat Yusuf. Furthermore, Eaton explained, Hamet had left Tunis for Malta in March. There he awaited the arrival of the American squadron. Eaton told Murray that they could set the plan in motion by conducting Hamet to Derna, the easternmost city in Tripoli, where his following was strongest. There Hamet would overthrow the governor and begin the long march to retake the throne. All that was required was for Murray to deliver him to Derna.

After Eaton had finished, Murray told Eaton that quite frankly he had no orders that would allow him to take Hamet to Tripoli. Furthermore, his orders did not include shelling Tripoli or any towns. His instructions, he told Eaton, were to make war only against Tripoli's cruisers. Eaton was astonished. Surely, he reasoned, since Tripoli had declared war against the United States, this meant that the United States could wage war not only against the enemy vessels but also against the entire state. Did not the principles of the laws of nations and maxims of war indicate that this was so? Furthermore, argued Eaton, even if Murray's orders were correct, and he was only authorized to attack enemy shipping, surely those same orders did not prohibit Murray from cooperating with the rightful Bashaw to seduce the rebel Yusuf and bring about a lasting peace at much lower cost than continuing this expensive naval action.

While Eaton and Murray argued over how to wage the war, two enemy cruisers sailed up the coast from Tripoli, and passed the Bay of Tunis, heading west, in search of American shipping. Murad Reis was seeking revenge.

Captain Andrew Morris stood by the wheel of the brig *Franklin* as she cut through the moderate swell bound for Gibraltar. Eight days earlier, he had loaded his cargo at Marseilles, and was looking forward to clearing the Straits of Gibraltar and delivering his cargo to the West Indies. After that, he would return home to Philadelphia. As he braced himself against the rolling waves, he spied the lights of Cape Palos to starboard. They were now only a few days away from the Rock, and the relative safety of the Atlantic. The Mediterranean, however, had become much safer in the past year, ever since the squadron had arrived. The Tripolitan corsairs had been pretty well bottled up by Dale. And he had heard news that a new commodore had arrived, bringing with him an even stronger squadron.

A lookout brought him back to the present; three sails on the port bow. Morris scanned the horizon. Yes, there they were, rapidly approaching. They were lateen-rigged, which was preferred by the Barbary rovers. Still, Morris was unconcerned; America was at peace with Morocco, Algiers, and Tunis, and no Tripolitans could have slipped the American trap. But as the three corsairs approached, he saw something that shocked him: the red ensign of Tripoli fluttered from the masthead.

They were boarded and the *Franklin* was taken as a prize, along with her crew. They arrived in Algiers on June 26. Fortunately, Consul O'Brien was on the lookout, and sent a message to the *reis* of the Tripolitan corsairs, asking if he could ransom Captain Morris and his crew. Instead, the Tripolitan cruisers beat a hasty retreat and kept to shore, sailing east along the coast of North Africa, and arriving in Bizerte on

July 7, where they left the *Franklin* in the care of their agent
and proceeded on toward Tripoli.

On July 19, Morris caught sight of Tripoli, five leagues to
the southeast. His heart filled with joy when he spied two
sails: one an American frigate, the *Constellation*; the other a
Swedish warship. He had heard rumors that the Bashaw had
declared war on Sweden; the presence of a Swedish warship
confirmed this. Better still, there was an American warship.
They would soon be free.

The winds, however, were calm, and within full view of
the two frigates, a corsair, flying the red ensign of Tripoli and
the Stars and Stripes, reversed, made her way into the harbor.
Morris was shocked. Surely the frigates would give chase or
fire a warning gun? Instead, they did nothing. Morris fumed.
The frigates could have taken the corsair, or driven her to
shore far from the protection of their batteries. Instead, five
hours after they had first sighted the enemy citadel, Morris
and his crew were paraded through the streets of Tripoli and
taken to the Bashaw under the eyes of the U.S. Navy, which
was supposed to have protected them.

Meanwhile, in the Bay of Gibraltar, the arrival of the
Adams finally allowed Commodore Richard Morris to sail
east. On August 17, almost two months after his arrival in the
Mediterranean, Commodore Morris ordered his crew to
weigh anchors and make ready for sea. As the men stamped
and strained on the capstan bars to the beat of drums, and
other crewmen unfurled the sails, Morris saw that the *Enterprise* was also readying for sea, as he had instructed. The
Adams would remain in Gibraltar, continuing the blockade
of the Tripolitan corsairs in Gibraltar Bay, and watching over
the emperor of Morocco, who continued to press his demands to take the Tripolitan vessels out of the bay and ac-
quire passports to allow grain-carrying vessels to enter
Tripoli.

It was a beautiful summer day. The sun shone on the wide
expanse of water, crowded with ships of the British fleet, as
well as those of Spain. Near their anchorage were also nine

Swedish and eleven American merchantmen also readying
for sea. As Morris paced the windward side of the quarterdeck, he thought over his plans. Given the capture of the
Franklin, he intended to sail for Leghorn, a distance of approximately eight hundred and forty nautical miles, convoying these merchantmen to ensure that Tripolitan corsairs
would not take another ship. Once at Leghorn, he would
carry James Leander Cathcart, the former U.S. consul to
Tripoli, to the enemy capitol to determine if the Bashaw
could be persuaded to take the path of peace. The emperor of
Morocco's threats of war had worried Jefferson, who had decided to hedge his bets. The secretary of the navy had instructed Morris to continue prosecuting the war, but at the
same time, as a contingency, to send out peace feelers. It was
a prudent course of action, thought Morris, who watched as
his convoy began, one by one, to head out of the bay and east,
toward Leghorn.

More than four hundred nautical miles to the southeast,
William Eaton fumed. As far as he could ascertain, nothing
was being done to bring the war to a decisive conclusion.
Dale had been ineffective, having bottled up two of Tripoli's
finest warships, but letting her crews, and the admiral, escape. That had been a black eye on America's reputation. The
only saving grace had been Sterett's thumping of the
Tripolino, which had occurred more than a year earlier. As
Eaton sat at his desk, he glanced outside, at the sun-drenched
buildings. August was a very hot month in Tunis, and the
heat was punishing. Eaton, however, felt his own blood boil
as he wrote a letter to Secretary of State James Madison,
criticizing the commanders who were supposed to be prosecuting the war against the Bashaw. He dipped the nib of the
pen into the inkpot and then began to write, forgetting, as he
so often did, that he was a diplomat.

> Our operations of the last and present year produce nothing in
> effect but additional enemies and national contempt. If the same
> system of operations continue, so will the same consequences.
> The obstinate posture and affected indifference to menace,

which have hitherto been my talismen in lieu of solid argument
here, no longer avail. The Minister puffs a whistle in my face,
and says; "We find it is all a puff! We see how you carry on the
war with Tripoli!"

Eaton wrote on, describing his circumstances so that
Madison would understand his last lines:

I am constrained therefore, not less by a regard to the interest and
honor of my country than to my own individual interest and
honor, to request the President will permit me to resign the trust
I have the honor to hold under the government of the United
States; unless more active operations shall be resolved on
against the enemy; in which case it would gratify me to remain
on this coast till the issue be determined.

Eaton sat back, and wondered if the letter would prompt
any action. He desperately wanted to know what Madison
thought of the plan to install Hamet on the throne in place of
Yusuf. Cathcart had initiated the scheme, but Eaton was now
deeply involved in the plan, and had helped Hamet get to
Malta, there to await an American ship that Eaton hoped
would take him to Derna, allowing him to begin his long
march on Tripoli. Yusuf, however, who had spies everywhere, had learned of the plan, and had now offered Hamet
the governorship of Derna, effectively co-opting their plan.
And yet Yusuf's actions also meant that he felt threatened by
his brother. If Hamet accepted the governorship, his brother
would try to kill him. No, he would only be able to return as
sovereign, and then, backed by American arms and money,
he could march on Tripoli by land while the U.S. Navy
pounded the city from the sea. Eaton fervently hoped that his
letter to Madison would jolt Washington into action and
thereby bring the war to a speedy conclusion.

In Leghorn, Cathcart, too, ruminated over this plan. He,
too, sat at his desk and wrote to James Madison, hoping that
with the pen he would be able to move the secretary of state
toward action, since no action, it appeared, would come from

the naval forces that had been in the Mediterranean now for more than a year. Cathcart knew that Yusuf was weak. He may have overthrown his brother, but he was not secure on the throne. Each time Yusuf left for his countryseat, he took all of his treasure and jewels with him in chests mounted on mules, and was accompanied by three to five hundred men. Cathcart knew that Yusuf not only worried about the residents of Tripoli, who viewed him as a usurper, but also about Sultan Selim III in Constantinople. Although technically independent from the Turks, each of the Barbary States owed allegiance to the Ottoman Empire. In private, the sultan had complained of Yusuf's arrogance. As a result, Cathcart believed that the sultan would side with the United States if they tried to restore Hamet to the throne. Cathcart laid out additional arguments for helping Hamet, and finished his account. As he sealed the envelope, Cathcart hoped that the president would back the plan to install Hamet on the throne. Because Cathcart, like Eaton, had watched as U.S. naval commanders, who were ignorant of the customs and guile of the Barbary pirates, persisted in poorly executing the war.

James Madison, however, had taken all the time he needed to think over Eaton's and Cathcart's proposal. Writing from his home in Montpelier, Virginia, Madison knew that Jefferson wanted to win this war, and if the navy was ineffectual, as it had been, and if Commodore Morris was unable to defeat Tripoli, which many thought true, then Madison knew it was up to him to provide an additional means of usurping Yusuf Karamanli. He sat down at his desk, and wrote his response to Eaton's letter.

> Sir, Not having your last letters with me, I cannot refer to their dates, nor particularly to their contents. The most important part of them, communicated the plan concerted with the brother of the Bashaw of Tripoli, for making use of him against the latter, in favor of the United States.

Madison thought carefully about what he was about to write, since he knew that the U.S. Congress had not declared

war on Tripoli, and furthermore had not authorized military
action against the Barbary State. He would have to walk a
fine line, and so he wrote the following:

> Although it does not accord with the general sentiments or views
> of the United States, to intermeddle in the domestic contests of
> other countries, it cannot be unfair, in the prosecution of a just
> war, or the accomplishment of a reasonable peace, to turn to
> their advantage, the enmity and pretensions of the others against
> a common foe.

Madison ended the letter by stating that Commodore Morris had in his possession $20,000 that could be used to begin
the plot. He signed his name, then carefully folded the sheets
of paper and inserted them into an envelope. It would be
many months before he heard the results, but he knew that
Eaton, given free reign, would act immediately.

Meanwhile, Eaton waited. Then, on September 5, the *Constellation* hove into the road of the Goulette, and the American jack flew up the fore topgallant masthead, a signal he
knew meant that Murray wanted to speak to him. Since Eaton
was already at the port, he answered the signal with his own
from a vessel he owned and operated, the *Gloria,* then
hoisted his large frame into a jolly boat and was rowed to the
waiting frigate. But as Eaton approached, he saw the *Constellation*'s sails fill, and the great ship stood out to sea. At
anchor near the frigate was a French warship, and Eaton saw
that a boat from the *Constellation* was leaving her. Eaton ordered his crew to row to the French vessel, where he found a
letter from Captain Murray. Eaton thanked the French admiral, clambered back in the boat, and returned to the consulate
to read its contents.

What he read set his blood boiling. Murray's letter indicated that he had blockaded Tripoli, but was forced to leave
station because he had run out of stores and also needed to
repair his ship. Here it was, September 5, and Eaton had only
just heard from one of the American frigates on station in the

Mediterranean, and had not even seen the commodore. Eaton certainly understood Murray's predicament; he was but one ship in the squadron, and no one had relieved him these many months. Instead, he had heard that Commodore Morris was busy convoying American merchantmen around the Mediterranean, and stopping for long rests at each major port where, if the rumors were true, his wife and he dined with the royalty and spent time on shore.

America would not beat the Barbary without sufficient energy, and that was lacking. Furthermore, he disagreed entirely with Morris's approach of guaranteeing the security of American merchantmen by convoying them. The only way to guarantee the safety of American shipping in the Mediterranean was to defeat Yusuf.

Three days later, the *Constellation* again appeared and hove to in the road of the Goulette. Again she signaled that she wanted to speak with Eaton. This time, assured that she would not anchor, and fearing that there was no time to gain the Bey's permission to reach her, Eaton rushed to the Castle of the Goulette, bribed the commandant, and set off in a jolly boat. A cannon shot from shore, he rendezvoused with the flagship's small boat, where a naval officer handed Eaton a packet of dispatches. Eaton accepted them and rowed back to shore, where he learned that the true reason Murray had left Tripoli was that the *Constellation*'s rudder-irons were badly damaged. Murray needed to get her to a port with the proper facilities to effect a repair.

To avoid going back to Tunis and alerting the Bey that he had received dispatches without asking permission, Eaton spent the night with the Danish consul at his garden in the ruins of old Carthage. The following morning, Eaton covered his tracks by sending his dragoman to the palace to seek permission to go aboard the frigate. Eaton received his answer later that day: "Tell the American Consul I will not suffer the ships of war of his nation to cruise in my harbor—If they enter here they shall anchor, their commanders come ashore, according to custom let me know their object and their wants—and pay me and the neutrality of my port the respect due to a sovereign."

To Eaton's mind, however, the Bey did not show Eaton's country's ships the respect they deserved. And Eaton, in the service of America, let the Bey know this. Taking up pen and paper, he replied:

> But so long as he refuses the usual salute to our flag, and with-holds the customary present of provisions to our ships of war, as has hitherto been the case, if he expects gratuitous compliments he must be disappointed. I would take care never to invite an-other Commander on shore until I should have assurance that he would receive the distinctions usually shown those of other sovereign powers in friendship with him.

Meanwhile, in Tangier, Consul Simpson finally acceded to the demands of the emperor of Morocco, Mulay Soliman, and presented to him the former Tripolitan cruiser, the *Meshouda*. While Simpson knew that Eaton might think this weak, it served a dual purpose: The *Meshouda* was originally the Boston brig *Betsey,* which the Moroccans had captured in 1785 and returned to the United States. Later, the ship had been seized by Tripoli, and taken into service. According to the emperor's logic, the ship belonged to Morocco. More-over, the vessel had laid at anchor in Gibraltar for more than a year, guarded during that time by an American warship lest the Tripolitans tried to rescue their ship. That tied up American sea power, and weakened America's ability to blockade Tripoli. By giving the ship to the emperor, the United States would be able to free up a warship to blockade Tripoli and re-move the potential threat of war with Morocco.

By accepting the deal, the emperor had agreed to respect the blockade, so America once again had an ally to the west, and was at war with only one Barbary State. But Simpson knew that giving the ship to Morocco also sent a message to the other Barbary States: The United States, in spite of her new warships and presence in the Mediterranean, still treated with pirates.

From his exile far to the north, Cathcart was angered by the way in which the naval commanders were waging this war. On October 3, when the *Constellation* arrived in port from a brief blockade of Tripoli, Cathcart found that Murray's heart was not in the task. Murray had told Cathcart that since the United States was too weak at present to fight the Barbary pirates, it should instead purchase peace. He told Cathcart that in two years' time, when the government had more energy than at present, the United States could go to war. Cathcart was angered by Murray's Federalist views, and the insinuation that Jefferson's Democratic-Republican administration was the reason no American naval commanders had the courage or perseverance to take the fight to Tripoli. However, what Murray said was true. Cathcart had to admit that Richard Morris was an example of the ineffectual commanders Jefferson had sent to the Mediterranean. Morris had been on station now for more than four months, but had still not appeared before Tripoli. And it was now too late in the season to accomplish anything. Soon the North African coast would be buffeted by storms, making a blockade dangerous. Further action would have to wait until the spring.

On October 12, nine days after Murray arrived, Morris, too, arrived in Leghorn, fifty-five days after departing Gibraltar. Seated in Cathcart's home, Morris told him that calms and easterly winds had delayed his arrival. Cathcart told Morris that he felt that even though it was too late in the season to blockade Tripoli, he nevertheless believed that Morris should proceed immediately to Tunis to gather intelligence and let the Bey of Tunis know that the United States was watching. Cathcart also believed in putting up a bold front, to stop the insurrection mounted by Morocco from spreading. He also urged Morris to then sail to Tripoli, only a short distance from Tunis, and send a signal beckoning the Danish consul, Mr. Nissan, to come aboard to determine if the Bashaw would agree to a truce.

If the Bashaw would agree to a truce, then, Cathcart explained, Morris could gather intelligence by sounding the

roads close to the rocks. Cathcart was convinced that there
was enough water for the frigates to bring to bear their
broadsides on the town, half a gunshot from the rocks. If the
negotiations were abortive, then Morris could give the
Bashaw several broadsides. Cathcart knew that the Barbary
pirates respected force and its use. American frigates, drawn
in a line and sailing on Tripoli, would show the Bashaw that
he was not dealing with a weak power. Furthermore, ten
shots lodged into his castle would ensure peace for a century,
or at least during the Bashaw's lifetime. Cathcart urged Morris to act, and told him he was ready to accompany him at
any time.

Murray briefed Morris about his blockade of Tripoli, and
told the commodore that in spite of the blockade, grain and
wheat were cheap and plentiful. Cathcart knew that this was
because the American vessels sent to blockade the harbor
drew too much water, and that shallow-drafted feluccas ran
along the coast from Tunis, entering and leaving Tripoli at
will. Still, Morris saw this as a sign that he could offer something to the emperor of Morocco, something that would keep
the Moroccans from declaring war. He authorized Captain
Murray to instruct Mr. Simpson to grant passports to Moroccan vessels bound for Tripoli, laden with wheat.

Where was Morris and where was the fleet? Eaton dipped
his pen into the inkpot, and continued writing his urgent note
to the commodore. Yesterday, November 8, he had learned
that Murad Reis had made use of his freedom and was readying a squadron of corsairs for sea. The squadron included
two xebecs of ten and fourteen guns, and a kirlanghie of
fourteen guns. Already departed and cruising for Americans
was another fourteen-gun xebec. According to Eaton's spies,
these three ships would be followed by a kirlanghie and polacre of eighteen guns apiece. Most alarming, however, was
the rumor that they intended to pass through the Straits. To
prevent the Americans from stopping them, they planned on
disguising themselves, forgoing their typical Moorish dress
of short blue jackets, overalls, and hats in order to decoy

themselves as American vessels. Once out in the western Atlantic, they would rely on this subterfuge to lure American merchantmen until they were close enough to board. Eaton finished the letter, and stuffed it in an envelope, hoping it would not have far to travel to find its recipient.

Morris had read Eaton's letter upon his arrival in Malta on November 20, which seemed like ages ago. The commodore stood on the quarterdeck of the *Chesapeake* as it rode at easy anchor amid the British men-of-war and merchant ships anchored in the harbor at Valetta. Christmas had passed and now it was the middle of January. Morris was torn between the need to take Cathcart to Tripoli, as ordered, to learn if the Bashaw would agree to a truce, and his desire to stay by his wife's side. She was pregnant, and the baby was due at any time.

Morris paced the deck and watched as boats plied to and fro between the *Chesapeake* and the *New York*, which had just arrived in company with the *John Adams*. The boats were taking his baggage to the *New York*; he was transferring his pennant to the *New York* since the *Chesapeake* was ordered home. He wished the transfer was complete; he was in a hurry to return to shore and get back to his wife. As he paced, he tried to reconcile the various demands placed on him. He had been ordered to take Cathcart to Tripoli. There was no denying that. And Eaton had sent letter upon letter asking him to come to Tunis. An officer appeared in his peripheral vision and saluted. Morris stopped pacing and the officer presented the following information: Spies had reported that a vessel in the harbor, the imperial polacre *Paulina,* was loading for Tripoli.

Morris nodded and asked the officer to send word for Captain Sterett. Morris went down to his cabin and began to write up his orders. A knock at the door announced the arrival of Sterett. Morris handed him his orders: shadow the *Paulina,* and when she was outside the jurisdiction of the British, seize her as prize.

* * *

Thomas Jefferson awoke at five a.m. and padded down-stairs to the Cabinet Room. He had kept the same habit since his days at William and Mary College, rising early and com-pleting his paperwork by nine a.m. On this morning in the middle of January, he took up his pen and began to write a secret message to Congress that would change the course of the nation. While he had watched with dismay as the power he had attempted to project into the Mediterranean was not having the effect he had intended, he had also kept one eye to the west, toward the vast unknown reaches of the continent, a wild, untamed land that America would soon need as the number of her citizens increased.

Britain controlled the fur trade in this unexplored domain and would regard any incursion as a threat to this lucrative trade in pelts and furs. That was why what Jefferson was about to propose to Congress must be held as a closely guarded secret, for if the true intent of what he envisioned was known to Britain, she would try and thwart America's intentions.

Outside it was still dark as Jefferson took up his pen and began to write a letter to Congress, explaining his plan to send an expedition up the Missouri River to explore the west: "An intelligence officer, with ten or twelve chosen men, fit for the enterprise, and willing to undertake it, taken from our posts, where they may be spared without inconve-nience, might explore the whole line, even to the Western Ocean."

Jefferson's pen scratched against the paper as he contin-ued his message.

While other civilized nations have encountered great expense to enlarge the boundaries of knowledge by undertaking voyages of discovery, and for other literary purposes, in various parts and directions, our nation seems to owe to the same object, as well as to its own interests, to explore this, the only line of easy commu-nication across the continent, and so directly traversing our part of it.

Jefferson finally outlined the need for secrecy and, above all, a false cover story, in order to have any chance of success.

The nation claiming this territory, regarding this as a literary pursuit, which is in the habit of permitting within its dominions, would not be disposed to view it with jealousy, even if the expiring state of its interests there did not render it a matter of indifference. The appropriation of two thousand five hundred dollars, "for the purpose of extending the external commerce of the United States," while understood and considered by the Executive as giving the legislative sanction, would cover the undertaking from notice, and prevent the obstructions which interested individuals might otherwise previously prepare in its way.

The man he had in mind to lead the expedition was the only other occupant of the White House: Meriwether Lewis. Before becoming Jefferson's private secretary, Lewis had been a captain in the Army of the West. He knew the west, and his grandfather and Jefferson's father had mapped Virginia long ago. If anyone could pull off such a bold adventure, it would be Lewis.

At seven in the morning on January 26, Eaton was awoken by a summons from the Bey's prime minister, requesting his immediate appearance at the palace. Hastily making his way to the main hall, Eaton saw that the Bey was agitated, and soon learned why: An American warship had taken as prize the Tunisian vessel *Paulina*. The ship was laden with merchandise bound for Djerba, an island south of Tunis, midway between Tunis and Tripoli.

"This was a cargo from the Levant, belonging and consigned to one of my subjects, of the Island of Djerba," the Bey told Eaton. "It arrived in Malta. There the proprietor chartered an Imperial vessel, into which he transferred the cargo, to be carried to the port of its destination; but having two Tripolitan subjects on board, whom he was obliged to land at Tripoli, he gave instructions to the master, to shape his course first to that port, with this view: with precise orders, that if he encountered any American vessel of war, before the port, to discontinue the voyage, and proceed to Djerba; in pursuance of which instructions, the said vessel fell in with an American cruiser of two masts, was by him captured, and conducted to Malta. You are responsible for the cargo."

"I cannot call in question your excellency's veracity in this statement," responded Eaton, "but it is presumed that your information on this subject must be incorrect. It is highly improbable that a merchant of Djerba, who could not be ignorant of the blockade of Tripoli, should risk a ship to that port, laden with a cargo intended for Djerba, merely for the purpose of landing two passengers, if his intention was not to land his cargo there also; and the more so, as the port of Djerba is nearly in the direct passage to Tripoli, and but about half the distance."

The Bey hesitated a moment, then spoke: "Well, admit the cargo was intended for Tripoli, what right have you to make a prize of it?"

"A very simple one," replied Eaton. "It is long since I have announced to your excellency the blockade of Tripoli, and I have never ceased to caution your agents and subjects against making shipments to that port. If, in contempt of this advice and caution, they choose to risk their property, and it falls into our hands, it becomes, of course, good prize. By a right founded on the known and received laws of nations, applicable in such cases."

"We Barbary States, do not admit the laws of war, established among Christian nations, applicable to us," replied the Bey. "We have always enjoyed the exclusive privilege to assert our own customs. We shall exact the same privilege of you. I therefore demand the immediate restitution of the cargo in question, with damages for detention. You will communicate this demand to your commodore, and tell him to restore the cargo without delay."

Eaton explained that it would take some time to communicate with the commodore, as well as the president, and expressed the hope that the Bey would allow him sufficient time to await their reply. The Bey, however, was impatient.

"No, I will indemnify myself in a shorter and more certain way. You know I am at war with Naples and Genoa; I will order my corsairs to make reprisals on your merchant vessels entering those ports."

Eaton understood the Bey's implicit threat: Release the cargo or the Bey would break the peace and declare war on the United States. Eaton argued against opening direct hostilities, reaffirming the wishes of President Jefferson for peace and good relations with the Bey. After promising to send a letter to Morris immediately, Eaton left the Bey's chambers and returned to the consulate, where he wrote a long letter to Commodore Morris, detailing the audience and asking the commodore to come to Tunis immediately. Pen poised over paper, he realized that he would have to write something to compel the commodore to finally make his appearance before the Bey. And so, he wrote the following: "I should have an interview with you and Mr. Cathcart, and soon. Affairs of incalculable moment to the United States here, require the assistance of your counsel, and perhaps your force." Eaton sealed the letter and handed it to the captain of the dispatch boat that would set sail for Malta.

Several days later, the *Enterprise* appeared in the offing and Eaton rowed out to the vessel. Once aboard, he was ushered into the captain's cabin, where he found Captain Sterett. Morris was not aboard. Sterett handed him a letter from the commodore, which Eaton tore open and scanned the first few lines of:

Sir, I have this moment received your favor of December 30th and regret that circumstances have prevented me from calling off Tunis before this time, but from the Urgent Necessity you Express of my having a personal Interview with You—I have thought proper to send the United States Schooner Enterprize to apprize you of my Intention of calling at Tunis Bay in a few days—There is necessity of great Moment that I should appear off Tripoli . . .

Eaton breathed a sigh of relief and thanked Sterett for delivering it. Eaton realized, however, that Morris had, perhaps unintentionally, done further damage to an already strained relationship between Tunis and the United States. Instead of arriving with the entire American squadron, Morris had sent a mere sloop. This amounted to a slap in the face, and would not, Eaton feared, be lost on the Bey. Eaton hoped there would be no repercussions, and prayed for the imminent arrival of the commodore.

Eaton, in fact, waited two weeks. Finally, on February 22, he spied three sails on the horizon as the *Chesapeake, New York,* and *John Adams* stood in for Tunis Bay. Eaton wasted no time, and hurried to the palace to get permission from the Bey to take a boat out to the flagship. To Eaton's surprise, the Bey refused his request. He stated that it was customary before such permission was granted for the commodore to report his arrival at the Goulette. He had not.

Eaton left the audience chambers and decided that he would not let the Bey's refusal hinder him. Instead, he made his way to the Castle at the Goulette, told the captain that he had already received previous permission to visit the warships when they arrived, and was carried out in the *New York*'s own jolly boat, under cover of nightfall, to avoid detection. As the jolly boat touched against the flagship's steep, oak side, fours bells in the first dog watch announced the hour of six p.m. Eaton scrambled up the ladder as the boatswain's call announced his arrival.

Eaton was ushered into the commodore's capacious cabin and greeted Cathcart. After they had been offered refreshments and had taken their seats, the commodore explained that the squadron had been quite unfortunately delayed: They had sailed for Tripoli on January 30, but a strong gale had prevented them from reaching the pirate harbor. Instead, they had beat back to Malta, and then sailed for Tunis. Eaton inquired as to the health of the commodore's wife and son, and Morris thanked him, saying she was resting at a hospital in Valetta, pregnant with their second child.

Eaton told the commodore that he would require a cabin

aboard overnight, so as to avoid causing any diplomatic problems over his visit to the ship. Then he reaffirmed his reason for requesting that Morris make an appearance here. Ever since the Americans had let Murad Reis slip the trap set for him in Gibraltar, the Barbary States had seen the Americans as weak and ineffectual. Acceding to the demands of the Moroccan emperor had only confirmed this view. As a result, Eaton told Morris, the Bey had taken an increasingly belligerent tone and had decided to ignore the American blockade of Tripoli. Then the *Paulina* had been taken. The Bey was indeed angry that the ship had been captured, and demanded its return, threatening to renounce the peace treaty in an effort to win back the vessel. The Bey, Eaton concluded, needed to be shown that the United States would not be bullied; she had the warships to exert her influence in the Mediterranean, and would seize any vessel that attempted to run the blockade. Finally, concluded Eaton, although the Barbary pirates respected force, they also required careful, diplomatic handling. The Bey felt slighted by the United States since no commodore had yet paid him a formal visit. This visit was now required, especially in light of the Bey's anger over the seizure of the *Paulina*. Morris listened attentively; after Eaton had finished, he told him he would think over the matter and they adjourned for the evening.

Eaton spent the night aboard, and the following morning returned to shore with Cathcart. There, Eaton played the role of messenger, delivering a flurry of letters between the commodore and the Bey. Finally, five days after the squadron's arrival, Morris agreed to the Bey's demands for a formal visit, and so, on February 27, five days after the squadron's arrival, Eaton, Cathcart, Captain John Rodgers, and Morris took a boat to shore and asked for a reception with the Bey. The message was delivered and they waited for the reply, which was not long in coming: come back tomorrow.

Rather than return to the ship, Eaton brought Morris to the consular house, his residence. There, Morris was introduced to all of the consuls in Tunis, and also Hamet Gurgies, the agent of Hamet Karamanli. In a private meeting with Eaton and Morris, Gurgies told the commodore that Hamet was now in Derna, and could raise an army of thirty thousand. All he needed was gunpowder and money: twenty quintals of powder and $16,000. Eaton watched as Morris listened politely, then told Gurgies he would consider the matter and stood to rejoin the party. The private meeting was over, but at least Eaton had seen to it that his strategy for overthrowing the usurper had gained some visibility.

Morris and Eaton also met with Hadgi Unis Ben Unis, the Bey's commercial agent. Eaton told Morris of the difficult situation he had been in for the last twelve months, with no American force to back up his firm stance against the pirate states. He also told Morris that he had contracted significant debts in his capacity as consul as well as in his own, private commercial pursuits. Eaton told Morris that he had informed the government, and that he daily expected relief of his debts.

The following morning, they returned to the palace and were admitted to the Ambassadors' Hall. They were ushered in and shook hands all around, then offered coffee, which they drank with the Bey. When the coffee cups were cleared away, the Bey immediately demanded that the *Paulina* be brought to Tunis, where it should be decided if she were a lawful prize. Cathcart translated the Bey's words for Morris.

Morris listened to the Bey's demand, then reaffirmed his decision to send the *Paulina* to Gibraltar, where the admiralty court would decide if she was lawful prize.

The Bey was unmoved, and Cathcart translated his dire words: Unless the vessel was brought here and the property of his subjects restored, the United States would find itself in the same situation here as it found itself in Tripoli. The Bey would declare war.

Morris abandoned his position and quickly agreed to the Bey's demands, under one condition, that the Bey would examine the regular papers found on board the prize, and would waive his rights to any property that did not belong to his subjects.

The Bey nodded in agreement.

Morris would send for the papers, and once they arrived, they would settle the matter. The audience was over.

That evening, at the consular house, Hamet Gurgies returned to follow up on his request for powder and money to assist Hamet Karamanli. After he took a seat in the sitting room, the commodore told Gurgies that he absolutely refused to provide Gurgies with any money. He would, however, consent to provide him with twenty barrels of powder. Eaton and Cathcart remained silent. Gurgies thanked the commodore, and asked if he would provide him with passage to Derna aboard the *Enterprise* so that he could inform Karamanli of the commodore's decision.

No, replied Morris and stood to leave. The conference was over.

The papers from the *Paulina* arrived and over the course of several days, Hadgi Unis and Morris negotiated over the prize. Morris promised the return of the cargo that they agreed lawfully belonged to the Bey. Morris was anxious to conclude the negotiations. He had now been in Tunis for almost two weeks. It was time to return to Malta, where his wife and son were waiting for him. At nine o'clock on the morning of March 4, determined that negotiations were concluded and in the company of Eaton, Cathcart, and Rodgers, along with other officers, Morris proceeded to the mole, where they would board a Moorish sandal to carry them across the lake to the Goulette.

As they walked, Eaton and Cathcart told Morris that in the Barbary States, it was customary to take leave of the Bey. But Morris was in a hurry, and told them he intended to leave immediately, their business with the Bey concluded.

Hadgi Unis followed them and when they reached the mole, he presented Morris with an obligation from Mr. Eaton, for $34,000. Morris was outraged, but Hadgi Unis explained that Eaton had told him he would pay the debt as soon as the American squadron arrived. Had it not arrived? As they had discussed, Eaton owed the Bey money, which he now intended to collect. Furthermore, explained Hadgi Unis, Eaton had told him that the commodore was responsible for the debt, and that he would have to hold the commodore as security until the debt was paid.

Eaton was outraged. He had never promised that the commodore would pay the debt. Never. Only that he hoped he would be able to pay off the debt once the squadron arrived. While Hadgi Unis and Eaton argued, guards allowed the minor officers to board the sandal, and return to the fleet. Eaton, Cathcart, John Rodgers, and Morris walked back to the consular house, effectively under arrest.

Once inside, Morris angrily told Eaton to go to the palace and find out if the Bey had detained them, and if so, under what circumstances. Eaton hurried off, and returned a short time later with the answer. Yes, they had been detained by the Bey, and as to the reason, the Bey would discuss it with the commodore on the following morning. But both Cathcart and Eaton realized that Morris had been detained, in part, because he had not paid his compliments to the Bey upon his departure. And the Bey, a despot, wished to let the commodore know this, that the commodore could not come and go without his permission. They would have to wait until the following morning to learn how they could extricate themselves from the clutches of the Bey.

At eight a.m., Cathcart, Rodgers, Morris, and Eaton were admitted to the palace. The audience began with Hadgi Unis presenting Eaton's bond, and requesting payment from Morris. Hadgi Unis told the assembled men that Eaton had promised that he would pay his obligation upon the arrival of the squadron.

Eaton again contradicted him, stating that he only hoped to pay the bond when the squadron arrived. He had made no promises.

Morris intervened, telling Hadgi Unis that it was extraordinary that he had only been told of Mr. Eaton's debt just as he was about to embark.

The Bey interjected, stating that he had not mentioned it in their audience in the hopes that the matter would have been terminated without his intervention. His agent, however, had come to him, seeking justice, and the Bey had promised to speak to Morris on his behalf. When he learned that Morris was about to embark without settling the debt, his agent's actions had been perfectly correct. Would you like to have heard that your consul was imprisoned for debt, the Bey asked Morris?

Morris promised to pay the debt that day, or the next, if the weather prevented a boat from reaching the squadron.

Eaton was angry. He said he had never promised that the commodore would assume his debt. On the contrary, he had some property of his own, and with some relief from the government he hoped to make all square. Eaton turned to the Bey and demanded to know if he had ever deceived him.

The Bey responded: "No, you have a good heart but a bad head. Those entrusted with the guidance of important affairs must have a great deal of forbearance. I am obliged to exercise it myself, and recommend it to you."

"No wonder that my head is bad when I am surrounded by imposters," replied Eaton. "Your agent among other things informed me that you would never permit Mr. Cathcart to land in your territory, though now you send for him expressly, and your prime minister has robbed me of my property. Otherwise, I should not at this moment be convened before your excellency."

Cathcart, who had been translating, requested that the Bey now find another translator. The Bey refused, so Cathcart continued as the tension in the room built to the cracking point.

"You are mad," the minister told Eaton.

"Yes, you are mad," stuttered the Bey, in a frenzy, twirling his whiskers nervously. "I did not intend to injure you, but since you have yourself begun, I will turn you out of my kingdom." The Bey turned to Cathcart.

"Tell the commodore that this man is mad, has beat my people. My jew money counter, Famin, Hargreaves, and the Dutch consul. I won't permit him to remain here."

"Let him take him away," said the minister, "and leave one of his officers here, until another consul arrives."

"I thank you," said Eaton. "I long wanted to go away."

Morris listened to this interchange, then asked Cathcart to confirm the Bey's wishes. "Ask the Bey if he is really determined to send Mr. Eaton out of his dominions."

"Yes, he shall no longer remain here," replied the Bey.

"Tell him I do not have the power invested in me to change a consul, but that as he has a right by treaty to have the consul changed, I will leave an officer in Mr. Eaton's place until the will of the government is known. Ask him if there is any further impediment to my going aboard," replied Morris.

"None," replied the Bey. "Settle with Hagdi Unis and I wish you a good voyage."

Robert Livingston, the minister to France, resented the intrusion of James Monroe in the sensitive negotiations he was carrying out with the government of France over ceding New Orleans and the Floridas to the United States. Britain and France were currently at peace, having signed the Peace of Amiens. Yet a resumption of the war was on the horizon.

It was true that the French had held stubbornly to the notion that they would expand the French empire to encompass not only their European territory but also the Americas. Livingston also knew that Napoléon wished to use New Orleans as the capital of his territory in the Americas, and that a fleet of French veterans had departed to occupy the town and reaffirm its ties with France.

Talleyrand, his opposite in the negotiations, knew Monroe was on the way, and was using this to delay negotiations. Livingston, however, did not give up. He kept bombarding Napoléon, Talleyrand, and all French officials he thought could sway the negotiations in his favor to accede to his demands. He felt that he was close to a breakthrough, and did not want to let Monroe steal his work.

On April 11, Livingston left his apartment and made his way to yet another audience with Talleyrand. The French minister greeted him and asked him a question that caught him off guard.

"Would the United States wish to have the whole of Louisiana?"

Livingston misunderstood the question, and replied: "No." The United States was only interested in New Orleans and the Floridas, and, if possible, the country above the Arkansas River.

Talleyrand told Livingston that without New Orleans, the rest of the territory wasn't much use to France. "What would you give for the whole?" he asked.

Livingston was not prepared for the question so he suggested 20 million livres.

Talleyrand shook his head. The sum was too low. He asked Livingston to think it over and come back on the morrow.

Little did Livingston know that the French fleet sailing for New Orleans had been diverted to put down a rebellion in Santo Domingo, and the army of French veterans had been defeated. Napoléon, mindful that the war between France and Britain was about to resume, needed money most of all, and did not want to divert resources to defend his far-flung empire. He had instructed Talleyrand to make a deal with the United States for the entire Louisiana Territory.

Monroe arrived in Paris on April 13 and together he and Livingston worked out a deal whereby the entire Louisiana Territory was ceded to the United States. The treaty was signed on May 2. For $16 million, the United States received Louisiana, New Orleans, and an inchoate claim against the Floridas. While the war against the Barbary pirates was going nowhere, America had just doubled in size. It was a stunning diplomatic victory.

Jefferson sat at the long table in the Cabinet Room; Dick stood before him on the long, broad table, pecking at a few crumbs. The president was in low spirits. It was now May and the reports from the Mediterranean that had made their way to his desk were troubling, not so much for the events they described, but for the lack of them. As Jefferson studied the dispatches, he concluded that Commodore Morris's conduct would require an investigation. Given his orders, his inaction was incredible. Instead of blockading Tripoli, he had convoyed merchantmen and spent an inordinate amount of time ashore in various harbors. Perhaps he had mistaken the object of his mission. After all, he had given Morris great latitude in the belief that Morris's ambition would guide him to distinguish himself. Jefferson also knew that Morris's failure would be laid at his own feet. He had heard the gossip around town—Morris was a political appointee. Jefferson would have to do something soon.

Across town, the secretary of the navy was equally disturbed by Morris's performance and lack of communication. As report after damning report was placed on his desk, he received nothing, not a single word, from the commodore. Taking up pen, the secretary wrote to Morris with a touch of sarcasm:

> I have not heard from You since the 30th November 1802, but I will not permit myself to suppose that You have not written since that period, yet it is a subject of serious concern that we have not heard from You. I presume it would be superfluous to remind You of the absolute necessity of your writing frequently and keeping us informed of all your movements.

The secretary sat back. If he did not hear any positive news from that quarter soon, something would have to be done about it. Jefferson was already calling for a change. He found that he could no longer argue against it, especially since he had heard nothing, in more than a year, that had warranted giving Morris command of the squadron and responsibility for conducting the war. Where Dale had been energetic and capable, Morris had brought ridicule and shame on America.

Several days later, on May 8, Jefferson held a cabinet meeting. He appeared gloomy and despondent over the lack of news from the Mediterranean. The president sat before his cabinet and asked the question that was on his mind: "Shall we buy peace with Tripoli?" To a man, the cabinet voted in the affirmative. It was a damning indictment of his decision to go to war, and of the navy's conduct.

* * *

The *Perseverance* arrived in Boston on May 5 after a lengthy passage from Gibraltar. As he set foot on the dock, Eaton reviewed his next steps. He would, of course, head first for Brimfield, to see Eliza. But after his matrimonial duties had been executed, he would travel down to Washington. There was the matter of his accounts, which needed to be settled; he would not pay for diplomacy out of his own funds. But more important, Eaton was impatient to tell the president and secretary of state about the war's progress and urge them to take stronger action against Tripoli. And lastly, he intended to provide a full report on Morris's tenure as commander of the squadron. The United States could not win against Tripoli if men like Morris were in charge. Eaton vowed to see to it that the man was replaced.

Meriwether Lewis bade good-bye to Jefferson on July 4, 1803. News of the Louisiana Purchase had reached Washington that day, and it was time for him to join William Clark and begin their westward journey, before winter set in. He looked forward to returning to the West, where he had served in the First Infantry. He knew the Ohio well, and had explored the interior, but this new territory, which doubled the size of the United States, beggared the imagination. As he said his farewells and gave one last look around the White House, Meriwether climbed onto his horse and set off, west, for St. Louis, where the great adventure would begin.

VII

Disaster

Bainbridge scanned the dark sea, searching for anything that would give away the enemy cruisers—a lantern through an open gun port, a lighted torch. It was August 26, 1803, as he stood with a group of his officers aboard the *Philadelphia*'s quarterdeck. The bell clanged four times, signaling the hour of eight p.m. As the bell sounded, the first-watch men took up their stations and the last dog watch went below. When the change of watch was completed, the ship again became silent; the only sound was the steady creak of the timbers as the ship bucked in the moderate chop, the flapping of canvas in the fresh breeze, and the hiss of water against the ship's side as she steered a course for Cape de Gatt.

The *Philadelphia* had only recently arrived on station, having spent several months in the yards being overhauled and refitted. She had arrived in Gibraltar two days ago, when Bainbridge had learned that two Tripolitan cruisers had been sighted off Cape de Gatt. He intended to find them before they found any American merchantmen.

Suddenly, a lookout cried out from the tops: sail ahead. Bainbridge ordered the frigate to steer for the sail, and in the inky darkness abreast of Almeria Bay, they came upon two ships, one carrying only her foresail, the other a brig. Bainbridge peered at the two ships, which appeared to be merchantmen. As they approached the first ship, Bainbridge examined her closely and saw the square outline of gun ports, closed to make her appear as though she were a merchantman. Convinced that she was a Barbary warship, but uncertain as to her origin, Bainbridge hailed the vessel and told the captain to send over his vessel's passports.

The seas were running high, so it took some time, but finally a small boat made its way across the choppy waters and reached the side of the *Philadelphia*. A Barbary naval officer clambered up the cleated steps set into the *Philadelphia*'s hull, and presented his papers. Bainbridge and his officers examined the passports. She was the twenty-two-gun Moroccan *Mirboka*, carrying a hundred men, commanded by Captain Ibrahim Lubarez. Bainbridge examined the piece of paper with care, looking for any signs of forgery. However, all he saw was the passport authorized by James Simpson, U.S. consul to Tangier, and addressed to the commanders of all United States armed vessels to treat the *Mirboka* as a friendly vessel. Affixed to the paper was the consular seal, the impression in the wax sharply defined and in good condition.

Bainbridge kept the nationality of his own vessel and that of his crew secret as he interrogated the officer. What was the nationality of the brig they had also sighted? The officer, not knowing he was speaking to an American naval officer, presented Bainbridge with the ship's passport. Bainbridge examined it closely and saw that she was the American brig *Celia*. The officer quickly explained that they had boarded her, but had not detained her crew, and that she had sailed with them for three or four days.

Bainbridge looked sternly at the officer. If they had not detained her, why was she sailing under low sail with a Moroccan cruiser? In addition, why had the officer presented her passport? Morocco and the United States were ostensibly at peace, but that did not fit what he saw with his eyes.

There was only one way to tell if the Moroccan was telling the truth. Bainbridge turned to his first lieutenant, David Porter, who had recently transferred to the *Philadelphia* from the *New York*, and ordered him to take a boat to the *Mirboka* and learn if she had any American prisoners on board. Porter saluted, clambered into a waiting boat, and made his way across the wind-tossed water separating the two vessels. Bainbridge watched as the boat reached the side of the corsair and Porter clambered on deck. Bainbridge saw him gesturing to the American frigate, and pointing to the hatch, indicating his desire to search the vessel. The lieutenant turned to Bainbridge and shouted across the gap, his voice muffled by the wind. The captain had refused to allow him to search his ship.

Bainbridge's suspicion increased. He ordered a boat of armed men to assist Porter. As another boat was lowered into the water and sent across to the corsair, filled with men carrying pistols and cutlasses, Bainbridge saw that this had the desired effect. The captain stepped aside and let Porter and his men go below.

Long minutes followed. Finally, Porter reappeared, followed by several men whom he helped into the cutter, and crossed over to the *Philadelphia.* As Porter and the men clambered on deck, Bainbridge asked them who they were. One of them stepped forward and saluted; Captain Richard Bowen of the American brig *Celia,* he announced, and told Bainbridge the others were members of his crew. Bowen explained that the *Mirboka* had captured them a week ago. When he had asked on what grounds, Captain Lubarez had told him that Morocco had declared war on the United States.

Bainbridge ordered all Moorish officers aboard the frigate, and ushered Captain Bowen and his men below. Seated in his cabin, Bainbridge asked Bowen to recount his ordeal. Bowen sat in the proffered chair, and began his story. On August 6 he had sailed from Barcelona for Malaga with a cargo of four thousand barrel staves and ballast. On August 17, under light airs, they were captured two leagues from shore and about eight leagues east of Malaga. The Moroccans took his crew, apart from his mate, aboard the *Mirboka,* put thirteen pirates aboard the captured brig, and set sail for Tangier. Each time they spoke with another ship, the Americans were locked belowdeck to keep them from speaking. Porter had found them deep in the hold.

Bainbridge had only arrived on station several days earlier, and was surprised at the change in relations with Morocco. Certainly war had been threatened, but this was unexpected, and his orders from the secretary of the navy made no mention of the threat. Moreover, Bainbridge was under command of the new commodore, who even now was sailing for the Mediterranean in the newly overhauled *Constitution*. It was more than likely that he, too, was unaware of this new threat to American commerce.

On deck, Bainbridge was watching as his men struggled to transfer prisoners from the *Mirboka* to the *Philadelphia* when Lieutenant Porter told him that the brig had disappeared. Bainbridge searched the seas all around, but could not see the brig, which had slipped away in the confusion of taking control of the *Mirboka* and transferring her prisoners. It was a damnable piece of luck. They would have to find her, and bring her back to Gibraltar.

The following morning, Bainbridge stood on the quarterdeck and saw not one sail on the horizon, but many. But which was the *Celia*? All day along, the *Philadelphia* chased down ships, trying to find the lost brig. Finally, at four p.m., they made her out as she crept around Cape de Gatt from the east, close inshore for Almeria Bay. She was well ahead, but as the evening turned to night, the wind freshened, giving the bigger frigate the clear advantage. By midnight, the *Philadelphia* finally came within hailing distance and the *Celia* hove to; the pirate crew was clapped in irons. The three ships set sail for Gibraltar, where Bainbridge hoped to find the new commodore, Edward Preble.

Edward Preble was seated in his cabin aboard the *Constitution* when he heard a knock on the door. The officer on duty announced that they had sighted three strange sails to the east. Preble stood and made his way to the windward side of the quarterdeck, where he was handed his glass. An officer pointed in the direction of the sighting, and Preble peered through the telescope. There, by Cape Saint Maria, were the vessels, three towers of white canvas rising above the blue ocean. Snapping shut the glass, he ordered the helmsman to close on the ships. He also gave his executive officer instructions to clear the ship for action.

Preble was born in Falmouth, Maine, in 1761. He was a farmer, but at the age of sixteen he ran off to join a privateer out of Newburyport, and never looked back. In 1779, his father got him a midshipman's warrant in the Massachusetts state navy, where he fought against the British on the *Protector*. On his second voyage, he was captured and thrown into the prison ship *Jersey* in New York. There, he became ill, and only survived after he was paroled as a result of his illness. Later, he was released, and went back into the navy, where he served as a lieutenant aboard the *Winthrop*.

In 1783 the war was over and Preble was twenty-two years old. He worked his way up in the merchant marine, eventually owning his own ship. But the navy didn't forget him, and made him a lieutenant in 1798. He became a captain in 1800. Preble was known as a disciplinarian, a captain who ran a tight ship. On the outside, the forty-two-year-old commodore was weak, a result of tuberculosis, yet inside the fire burned with a rare intensity. He was the sort of man Jefferson needed to bring the war to a conclusion.

Against a backdrop of running feet, the whistle of the boatswain's call, and shouted orders, Preble thought over the news he had received on September 4, three days earlier, when he had detained the brig *Jack,* off Cape Ann. Captain Haskell had told him that the *Philadelphia* had left Gibraltar ten days prior in pursuit of two three-masted Tripolitan cruisers, which had stopped at Algiers. The *Philadelphia,* said Haskell, had headed for Alicante, where they were reportedly cruising. Could they have slipped through the Strait? Preble intended to find out.

Beneath his feet, he felt the deck buck and heave as the frigate's speed increased and they closed on the vessels. As they approached, he saw that one of them flew the French tricolor. Preble could not identify the nationality of the other two, but one of them was clearly steering toward them.

At one-thirty p.m., Preble ordered the *Constitution* to tack, and cleared the ship for action. The approaching vessel responded by hauling a red flag up the halyard. She was Moroccan. Preble felt disappointed, but after beating into the wind for almost an hour, he intended to follow through and determine her intentions. The United States and Morocco were at peace as far as he knew, but tensions had run high over the past two years, and Preble intended to sound out any potential threat.

At two-thirty the two ships came within hailing distance, and Preble ordered the sailing master to shorten sail and send a boat to board the cruiser. A short time later, the officer shouted across the narrow gap of water separating the two ships that she was indeed a Moroccan vessel, and carried a passport signed by the U.S. consul to Morocco, James Simpson. During this interchange, Tobias Lear, the newly appointed U.S. consul to Algiers, stood beside Preble and told him that he knew Simpson's handwriting and would gladly validate the officer's claims. Preble, who did not trust any of the Barbary pirates, even those ostensibly at peace with the United States, decided to send Lear over to see for himself.

Jefferson had appointed Lear not only to take over from Richard O'Brien, who was retiring from government service, but also to reopen negotiations with the Bashaw of Tripoli to determine if there was a peaceful means of ending the war. Lear was a trusted, experienced diplomat who had been in government service since 1785, when, at the age of twenty-three, he had become George Washington's personal secretary. He had fulfilled that duty until 1799, when standing beside Washington's deathbed at Mount Vernon, holding Washington's hand, he heard him utter his last words and felt life leave the great man.

As the small boat touched against the side of the Moroccan ship, Lear adroitly clambered aboard. He was no novice to ships; his father had been a wealthy shipmaster. On deck, the captain handed him the passport prepared by James Simpson. Lear knew Simpson, and recognized his familiar handwriting as he scanned the document, which granted the thirty-gun Moroccan vessel *Maimona,* commanded by

Hadge Tacher Aumed, safe passage when encountering any American vessels.

The captain pointed to the top of the parchment, which showed a certificate signed by Simpson. The consular seal was also firmly attached. Lear nodded, handing back the passport to the captain. It was authentic and the signatures appeared to be genuine. Lear also noted that the ship had the number of guns listed on the passport, and, scanning the gathering of men who watched the interchange between Lear and their captain, noted also that the number of men listed as the crew of the vessel also appeared to be correct. Lear asked the captain whence he had sailed, and what his destination was. The captain, through an interpreter, answered that he had left Sallee twenty-three days ago, and was bound for Lisbon. He added, unasked, that Morocco was at peace with all nations.

That was a long time to have been out from Sallee, stated Lear. Why had it taken the captain so long to sail here?

The captain told Lear that he had been slowed by contrary winds, and had had to put back several times.

Lear accepted the captain's answer. It was indeed plausible. Lear asked the captain if he could see the Commission of the Emperor of Morocco. The captain nodded, barking orders to his lieutenant, who returned with the document. Lear scanned it, but saw to his dismay that it was written in Arabic. Without a man who could read Arabic, Lear had to be satisfied with the captain's words. He thanked the captain, handed back the documents, and returned to his boat. All appeared in order; the only piece of information that troubled him was the length of time the cruiser had been out of Sallee. The duration indicated that the ship may have been cruising rather than sailing directly for Lisbon, but there was no proof of that.

Four days later, Preble anxiously paced the windward side of the quarterdeck. Ever since meeting the Moroccan vessel they had been impeded by headwinds and calms. He was anxious to get to Gibraltar, but the winds, at present, were against him. As evening approached, they had only reached

Cadiz. The atmosphere was hazy, and to the southeast, Preble could just make out a sail, steering the same course as the *Constitution,* but slightly ahead of her.

At eight-thirty p.m., as darkness descended, the lookout suddenly cried out from the maintop that the ship they had sighted was close, too close, and appeared to be a man-of-war. Preble ordered the crew to beat to quarters, took up the speaking trumpet, and hailed the unknown vessel.

"What ship is that?" Preble demanded.

"What ship is that?" a voice replied.

"This is the United States frigate *Constitution.* What ship is that?" Preble again asked.

"What ship is that?" again replied the stranger.

"This is the United States frigate *Constitution.* What ship is that?" Preble again asked.

"What ship is that?" replied the stranger.

Preble grew angry. "I am now going to hail you for the last time. If a proper answer is not returned, I will fire a shot into you."

"If you fire a shot," replied the stranger, "I will return a broadside."

"What ship is that?" Preble demanded.

"This is His Britannic Majesty's ship *Donegal,* eighty-four guns, Sir Richard Strachan, an English commodore. Send your boat on board."

Preble, incensed at the impertinence of the stranger, climbed up the netting and shot back his answer: "This is the United States ship *Constitution,* forty-four guns, Edward Preble, an American commodore, who will be damned before he sends his boat on board any vessel!" Preble called down to his men. "Blow your matches, boys."

All was silent as the two ships drifted along together in the dark. Then, suddenly, Preble heard the splash of oars and saw a boat approaching. He stood waiting by the taffrail as a British lieutenant climbed up the ladder and stepped aboard. The British officer saluted Preble and admitted that he hailed not from the *Donegal* but instead from the British frigate *Maidstone,* thirty-two guns, commanded by George Elliot.

The officer explained that they had stood toward the *Constitution,* believing she was an enemy vessel, but in the dark had not realized how close the two ships were to each other until Preble had hailed them. They had replied evasively, stated the officer, to buy time; their commander had not cleared his ship for action. Preble's officers listened to the conversation with approval. Preble had demonstrated that he was a fighting officer. He would be able to handle the Barbary pirates.

The following day, his ship propelled by a westerly breeze, Preble ordered the sailing master to make all plain sail and set aloft the starboard studding sails. As they ran toward the straits, he spied Cape Spartel and headed toward the Barbary Coast. Before touching at Gibraltar, Preble intended to call on Consul Simpson. At ten a.m., as the *Constitution* hoisted her colors off Tangier, Preble ordered a gun to be fired, the standard signal for the consul to send a boat out to the warship. Standing alone on the windward side of the quarterdeck, Preble waited for the Stars and Stripes to appear, but as he scanned the flagstaffs of the consulates, he saw only the Swedish colors. For an hour, the *Constitution* plied to and fro, and then fired a gun again at eleven a.m. But still the Stars and Stripes did not appear at its designated place. Preble ordered the sailing master to set a course for Gibraltar. They would soon learn why Simpson had not answered their call.

As the deck cleared of smoke from firing fifteen guns in salute to the governor of Gibraltar, the anchor chain rattled through the *Constitution*'s hawseholes and the anchor sent ripples across Gibraltar Bay. Preble spied the *Philadelphia* riding at anchor, and sent aloft a signal asking Bainbridge to repair aboard. He hoped Bainbridge would provide him with news of Simpson, as well as a report on the result of his chase.

Preble waited for Bainbridge in his cabin, and was gratified when he heard a knock and bade Bainbridge enter. Wasting no time, Preble asked him for news. Bainbridge recounted

the taking of the *Mirboka* and how he had almost been deceived by the vessel's authentic passport. But he had thought
it odd that an American brig would sail in company with a
Moorish vessel, and upon investigation, had found her captain and crew detained in the hold of the *Mirboka*.

Preble was angry with himself and told of his encounter
with the *Maimona,* and how since Lear had certified the au-
thenticity of the passport they had decided to let her continue
her journey. Then Preble told Bainbridge of his visit to Tangier and how Simpson had not answered their gun. Given the
news that the *Mirboka* had been captured after having taken
an American brig, and now knowing that the *Maimona* had
probably been cruising for Americans in the western ocean,
Preble realized that decisive action was called for.

Bainbridge handed Preble the papers he had taken from
Captain Lubarez. Perhaps his orders, written in Arabic,
would shed some light on the situation. Preble sent for a lieutenant to carry the documents ashore and, with the utmost
dispatch, return with a translation.

They had but a short time to wait. The documents were
brought back, along with the translation, and there the deceit
of Morocco became clear. The papers included orders to capture American vessels. Preble sent word to bring Captain
Lubarez to his cabin. When he had arrived, Preble stated that
before him lay the translated copy of his orders and asked for
an explanation. Lubarez did not evade the question. Yes, his
orders were to capture American ships, but he had not known
this upon sailing from Tangier. The sealed orders, from the
Moorish governor of Tangier, Hadge Alcayde Abde-Rhaman
Hashash, were handed to him with instructions that he was
not to open them until he was at sea.

Over the course of the next two days, the threat posed by
Morocco grew clearer, while the squadron sent to bring the
conflict to a conclusion began to take shape. A boat arrived
from Tangier bearing letters from Consul Simpson. Preble
opened an envelope and scanned the pages, quickly understanding why Simpson had not sent out a boat when Preble

had fired a gun: He had been arrested by Governor Hashash, and his letter described how it was done:

> At eleven at night he again sent and desired to see me at his House, as it is no uncommon thing to do busyness with Ministers and sometimes with Governours even at that hour in this Country I readily went, when to my great astonishment the doors were immediately shut, and I was informed by a relation of the Governours that it was his Orders I should be detained.

Preble continued to read the letter, learning that Simpson had been released only after other consuls had protested his treatment. He was now under house arrest. The seizure of the *Meshouda* and *Mirboka,* Preble read, had prompted Simpson's arrest. But did the emperor know of his arrest, or was this only a local affair, managed by a rogue governor? Preble very much doubted that. The emperor would have known, but because the orders were written by Governor Hashash, the emperor could safely deny his involvement if things went badly.

While Preble digested this news, two more American warships arrived in the bay: The *New York,* Morris's flagship, had touched on its way back to the United States, and the schooner *Vixen,* commanded by Lieutenant John Smith, had just arrived after a lengthy passage from Baltimore. The *Vixen* was one of the new, smaller, shallow draft vessels constructed to the exact dimensions of the *Enterprise* to blockade the shoaling coastline of the Barbary States. The *Vixen,* like her sister ships the *Argus* and *Siren,* both en route to the Mediterranean, and the *Nautilus,* which had arrived in late July, would give Preble the weapons he needed to thwart shallow-draft feluccas, like those that Morris had attacked in the spring.

On September 14, the squadron was further enhanced by the arrival of the *John Adams,* commanded by Captain John Rodgers, who had brought in the *Meshouda* as prize. As rumors floated through Gibraltar Bay that the *Maimona* had captured four American merchantmen, Preble decided that the threat posed by Morocco demanded his immediate attention.

Preble planned a bold mission to end the threat of Morocco, and issued orders that while this mission was taking place, Tripoli would remain blockaded. Preble sat down at his desk, Gibraltar Bay glittering behind him through the graceful arc of stern windows, and began to write out the orders that would put his plans into effect.

He sent orders to Captain Bainbridge to take the *Philadelphia,* accompanied by the *Vixen,* and sail immediately for Tripoli. There they were to blockade the harbor and harass the enemy. Preble sent both ships because he knew the *Philadelphia* was too large, and drew too much water, to properly blockade the pirate harbor, and that the twelve-gun *Vixen* would allow Bainbridge to stop smaller, faster vessels such as feluccas from entering the harbor. Together the two ships could look after each other and effectively stop any enemy vessels from leaving or entering Tripoli.

On September 9, Commodore Morris stood on the *New York*'s quarterdeck when a lookout's cry turned his attention to six glimmering white sails in the distance. As they approached, Morris saw the Union Jack, flying high on mastheads of the six Royal Navy warships. The *New York* sailed near the largest of the vessels, a one-hundred-gun ship of the line with the name *Victory* painted on her stern. As they came within hailing distance, Morris called to her quarterdeck, where the British admiral, Lord Horatio Nelson, returned the greeting.

Several days later, Morris touched in at Malaga, where he was handed a packet of correspondence that had just arrived from Washington. Seated at his writing desk in his cabin, he sorted through the packet and found a letter from Secretary of the Navy Smith. Breaking the seal, Morris opened the envelope and unfolded the sheets of paper within, scanning the lines of graceful cursive:

Sir,
    You will on receipt of this, consider yourself suspended in command of the squadron in the Mediterranean station, and of

the frigate New York. It is the command of the President, that
you take charge of the Adams, and that you with her return without delay to the United States.

On October 5, the *Nautilus, Constitution,* and *Enterprise*
dropped anchor in Tangier Bay. The three ships had the firepower to destroy entirely the fortresses and guns of Tangier.
Preble had brought them here to put an end to the threats of
war from Morocco once and for all.

Preble stood on the quarterdeck and scanned the bay and
its defenses. The shallow bay was augmented by a mole,
which extended northeast into the strait, providing some protection for ships anchoring in its lee. The town of Tangier,
surrounded by walls and topped by minarets and domed
mosques, hugged the right side of the bay, just behind the
mole. An ominous, hulking gun battery anchored the landward approach to the mole and commanded the sea-lanes
into the bay. To the left of the town was a sandy beach, along
which ran a road that extended along the shoreline.

On the beach Preble spied a spectacle of epic proportions:
More than ten thousand Moors were marching along the
road toward Tangier. Amid this throng, Preble knew, was the
emperor, Muley Soliman, returning from his countryside
retreat to meet the American commodore. Preble watched as
this procession of cavalry and footmen marched toward
Tangier, accompanied by volleys of muskets. At two p.m.,
Preble watched as the Stars and Stripes rose above the consular house. An eighteen-gun volley from the battery saluted
them, which was Preble's signal to return the gesture and
greet the arriving emperor. Eighteen guns barked out the
American reply.

But before he met with the emperor, Preble issued instruc-
tion to his men to ensure that he would not walk into a trap,
as Morris had done in Tunis. To prevent any mischief, Preble
called together all of his commanders and gave the assembled men the following instructions:

"Comrades: The result of the approaching interview is
known only to God. Be it what it may, during my absence,

keep the ships cleared for action. Let every officer and seaman be at his quarters, and if the least injury is offered to my
person, immediately attack the batteries, the castle, the city
and the troops, regardless of my personal safety."

To further ensure his safety, on the following day, the
Adams and *New York* arrived, adding to Preble's already significant force.

After several days of meetings with Consul Simpson, an
audience was scheduled with the emperor for October 10. At
ten-thirty a.m. on the appointed morning, Commodore Preble, accompanied by Colonel Lear, Midshipmen Ralph Izard
and Henry Wadsworth, and Preble's secretary and ship's
chaplain, Noadiah Morris, stepped into the *Nautilus*'s jolly
boat, the commodore's broad pennant snapping in the
breeze. The boat's crew rowed them to the mole, where they
disembarked and made their way to the consular house.
There James Simpson joined them, along with two mule-
loads of presents for the emperor: silver teapots, silks,
muslins, linens, sugar, tea, and coffee. Simpson had gathered
the presents because on an imperial visit such as this, gifts to
the emperor and other officials and members of his court
were required. The mules also contained presents for members of his staff, including his chief groom, umbrella bearer,
and sword bearer.

As they walked through the winding streets of Tangier,
throngs of people stood and watched. From terraces, towers,
and minarets they edged their way forward to get a view of
the American admiral who walked through their city to meet
their emperor, who waited for them in the Kasba. As Preble
and his entourage arrived, they found the roadway guarded
by a double file of soldiers. The Americans walked between
them and entered the Kasba, finding themselves in a plaza
where the minister of state, Selawy, greeted them. His message to Simpson was a simple one: "We wish for peace," he
said. In response, Preble ordered the gifts unloaded and
given to twenty or so waiting Moors.

Half an hour later, they were ushered toward the right
wing of the castle, where a set of steps led to a doorway. To

their right, noted Wadsworth, were three crooked rows of
guards, their ranks ill dressed, their clothes dirty. They were
a slovenly group; Wadsworth was unimpressed. Then, a
small man wearing a woolen haik, or cloak, appeared from
an alleyway. Wadsworth watched as a servant placed a cush-
ion on the steps and the man sat down.

Wadsworth wondered when the parade would begin that
would take them into the emperor's ornamental chambers.
The minister, Selawy, approached and whispered, "That is
the emperor." Wadsworth hid his astonishment. The man on
the steps? The Americans quickly doffed their hats and
bowed. The emperor made a slight inclination of his head in
acknowledgment.

After each side had made its introductions, the emperor
addressed Preble and the two discussed the American seizure
of the *Mirboka* and *Meshouda.*

"Are you not in fear of being detained?" asked the emperor.

"No, sir," replied Preble. "If you presume to do it my
squadron in your full view will lay your batteries, your castles, and your city in ruins."

The emperor, taken aback by Preble's forcefulness, realized that this man was no Morris. He did not want war, and
apologized for the behavior of the governor of Tangier. He
told Preble that he had not authorized the taking of American
vessels; the governor had done this against his will. The emperor proclaimed his ignorance of Hashash's orders, and announced that he would be punished "more than to your
satisfaction."

The emperor continued, saying that he would ratify the
treaty made by his father, Muley Soliman, and would write
to President Jefferson indicating that although it was written
that the treaty would expire after fifty years, he would consider it binding for eternity.

Preble and Lear bowed, and the audience, so informal and
strange to young midshipman Ralph Izard, concluded. Morocco and the United States were again at peace, and war had
been avoided. Of added importance was the message that

was even now making its way across the waters of the
Mediterranean to Algiers, Tunis, and Tripoli. There was a
new American commodore in the Mediterranean, one that
could not be manipulated.

Bainbridge scanned the empty sea in a three-hundred-
and-sixty-degree arc, hoping to sight a sail. Seven days ago,
a gale out of the northwest had whipped the sea into a frenzy,
driving them away from Tripoli and forcing the *Philadelphia*
to find some sea room to ride out the storm. Now, eight days
later, they were returning, looking for vessels that may have
used the heavy weather to break the blockade.

Bainbridge also hoped to see the familiar sails of the
Vixen. A week before the storm, they had spoken to an Imperial brig whose captain had told them that two Tripolitan
cruisers were out looking for Americans. Knowing that
enemy corsairs preferred to hug the coast, Bainbridge had
sent the *Vixen* away to hunt off Cape Bon, a peninsula that
extended into the Mediterranean to the southeast of Tunis. If
the corsairs were returning from their hunting grounds to the
east, they would most likely touch in for provisions at Tunis,
and then sail around Cape Bon on their way home. It was
there, Bainbridge hoped, that the *Vixen* would find them, and
make them prize.

The *Vixen,* however, was also his insurance, and gave him
the freedom to sail close to the shore, where the water
shoaled and where many of the reefs were unknown. The
schooner was one of the newer, shallow-draft vessels built to
counter the speed and maneuverability of the xebecs and polacres favored by the Barbary pirates. Modeled after the *Enterprise,* she could operate in shallow water, whereas the
Philadelphia, which drew sixteen and a half feet of water,
had to be careful since she was at greater risk of grounding
herself on a reef or shoal.

The sound of two bells in the forenoon watch announced
the hour of nine a.m. Bainbridge surveyed his ship. The deck
was newly washed, the hammocks were in their places,
tucked into the netting, and Bainbridge could still make out

the faint smells of breakfast, which had been served an hour ago. He took out his telescope and scanned the ocean. They were now about nine leagues east of Tripoli, having beaten back to station. Suddenly, Bainbridge heard the cry of "sail" from the lookout, who pointed toward the shore. Bainbridge stood against the port taffrail, braced his feet against the swell, and scanned the ocean. There he saw it; a sail, standing to the westward, heading for Tripoli. Bainbridge peered at the ship through his glass. It could be one of the cruisers he had sent the *Vixen* after, trying to make her way back home.

Bainbridge ordered the *Philadelphia* to give chase. As the boatswain's whistle shrieked, the crew crowded on sail to catch every breath of the easterly wind, and the frigate began to pick up speed, throwing jets of water to either side as her prow cut through the chop. Meanwhile, the steady beat of drums told the crew to clear the ship for action and take up battle stations.

Two hours later, they could clearly make out that the ship they were chasing was indeed an enemy cruiser. They were also close enough to fire on her, and Bainbridge ordered the bow chasers cast loose. He watched as the gunner carefully pointed the two eighteen-pounders, then laid the match against the touchhole. The guns banged, sending out a cloud of white smoke, and leapt back on their carriages, which shrieked in protest. Moments later, Bainbridge saw two plumes of water where the ball had struck, just wide of the chase.

For half an hour, the bow chasers banged, one after another, as the distance between the two ships closed. The *Philadelphia* was making good speed, eight knots, as she hugged the shore, following the smaller corsair. But Bainbridge was worried about striking a shoal, and in lieu of having a local pilot on board or even a correct chart, he sent Lieutenant David Porter to the bow, along with another lieutenant and two masters' mates, to sound the depth. With three leads going, Bainbridge believed they would be able to react quickly to any sudden change in depth. At half past

eleven, about a league and a half from Tripoli, the leadsman
shouted that the depth was eight fathoms.

Bainbridge asked Porter, who had been to Tripoli before
and knew the area better than any man aboard, if they should
continue the chase, given the potential danger.

Porter responded that they were not in danger yet, and that
they still had time to fire a few more shots.

After several more shots, however, Bainbridge knew he
could not risk the frigate in this way, and also knew that at
their present rate of speed he would not be able to catch up
with the chase. He ordered the helmsman to haul offshore
and ordered Porter to climb to the top, look into the harbor,
and see if any cruisers were in port. As Porter climbed the
mizzen rigging, the ship suddenly lurched and came to a
shuddering stop. Porter gripped the shrouds tightly to prevent himself from being flung onto the deck.

They had struck a shoal. The ship had been moving at
eight and a half knots and had driven right up onto a submerged outcropping of rocks. Bainbridge ordered his leadsman to survey the water around the frigate and found that she
was stuck fast beneath the after part of her fore chains. He
ordered the ship's boat lowered and sent another officer and
leadsman to survey the surrounding water to determine
where the deepest water lay.

They could get her off, but they would have to act quickly:
The lookout announced that nine gunboats had sailed out of
the harbor; the vultures were after their prey. Meanwhile, the
vessel they were chasing, seeing their predicament, had cir-
cled back and had begun to fire on the helpless frigate. They
had very little time in which to act.

Bainbridge knew that the only way they could get her off
was to set the sails in an attempt to let the wind press them
off, but first they needed to lighten the bow. Bainbridge ordered the guns run abaft, and the bow anchors, except one,
cast into the water. After these orders were carried out and all
was ready, he ordered the sails laid back. A strong breeze
was blowing on the starboard beam, and the sea was setting
upon the hidden rocks. As the sails were laid back, rather

View of Algiers from the Sea. From an engraving by I. Clark after a drawing by Henry Park (circa 1816), as published in *Narrative of a Residence in Algiers*, by Signor Pananti (London, 1818). United States, Office of Naval Records and Library.

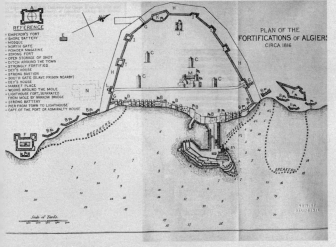

REFERENCE
- EMPEROR'S FORT
- SHORE BATTERY
- MOSQUE
- NORTH GATE
- POWDER MAGAZINE
- STRONG FORT
- OPEN STORAGE OF SHOT
- DITCH AROUND THE TOWN
- STRONGLY FORTIFIED
- DEY'S HOUSE
- STRONG BASTION
- SOUTH GATE (SLAVE PRISON NEARBY)
- MARKET PLACE
- WORKS AROUND THE MOLE
- LIGHTHOUSE FORT, SEPARATED FROM MOLE BY NARROW BRIDGE
- STRONG BATTERY
- PIER FROM TOWN TO LIGHTHOUSE
- CAPT. OF THE PORT OR ADMIRALTY HOUSE

PLAN OF THE
FORTIFICATIONS of ALGIERS
CIRCA 1816

Plan of the Fortifications of Algiers. Redrawn by James S. Murray of the Hydrographic Office, Navy Department, from a sketch by R. Rowe as published in the *Naval Chronicle* (1817). United States, Office of Naval Records and Library.

The U.S. Schooner *Enterprize* Capturing the Tripolitan Corsair *Tripoli,* August 1, 1801. From a drawing (circa 1878) by Captain William Bainbridge Hoff, U.S. Navy, in the collection of the Navy Department. United States, Office of Naval Records and Library.

Lieutenant Andrew Sterett, U.S. Navy. Reproduced courtesy of the Library of Congress, from an engraving by St. Memin (circa 1803) in its possession. United States, Office of Naval Records and Library.

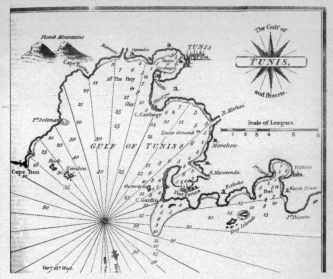

Map of the Gulf of Tunis. Reproduced courtesy of the Library of Congress from *The New Mediterranean Pilot* published by W. Heather (London, 1802). United States, Office of Naval Records and Library.

The Loss of the U.S. Frigate *Philadelphia*. Reproduced by courtesy of President Franklin D. Roosevelt from an engraving by Charles Denoon, in his collection. United States, Office of Naval Records and Library.

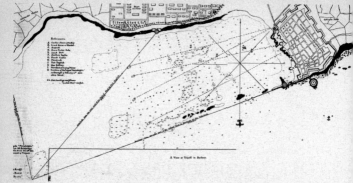

Map of the Port of Tripoli. Reproduced through the kindness of the U.S. Naval Academy Museum, from an original drawing in its collection made by Midshipman F. Cornelius de Krafft, U.S. Navy, in 1804. United States, Office of Naval Records and Library.

Map of the Mediterranean Region. United States, Office of Naval Records and Library.

The Capture of the U.S. Frigate *Philadelphia*. Published by courtesy of the New-York Historical Society from an original drawing by Captain William Bainbridge Hoff, U.S. Navy, in its collection. United States, Office of Naval Records and Library.

The Burning of the U.S. Frigate *Philadelphia*. Reproduced by the kind permission of Dr. Eugene H. Pool, from an aquatint in his possession, engraved by F. Kearney, published by F. Kearney, August 1, 1808. (Other sources say published by A. Maverick.) United States, Office of Naval Records and Library.

Captain Stephen Decatur Jr., U.S. Navy. Reproduced through the kindness of the New-York Historical Society from an original portrait by Rembrandt Peale in its possession. United States, Office of Naval Records and Library.

Commodore Edward Preble. Reproduced from the portrait by Rembrandt Peale by courtesy of Lieutenant Commander Dundas Preble Tucker, U.S. Navy, great-great-grandson of Commodore Preble. United States, Office of Naval Records and Library.

William Eaton. From an engraving by Charles Balthazar Julien Fevret de Saint Memin. Reproduced through the courtesy of the Corcoran Gallery of Art. United States, Office of Naval Records and Library.

Port of the New City of Alexandria, with the Lighthouse. From an aquatint of L. Mayer after T. Milton, published by R. Bowyer (London, 1802). Reproduced by courtesy of the Mariners' Museum, Newport News, Virginia. United States, Office of Naval Records and Library.

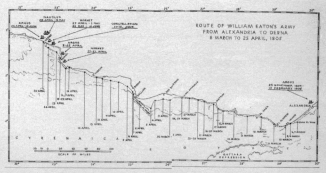

ROUTE OF WILLIAM EATON'S ARMY
FROM ALEXANDRIA TO DERNA
8 MARCH TO 25 APRIL, 1805

Route of William Eaton's Army from Alexandria to Derna, March 8–April 25, 1805. Prepared by the Office of Naval Records and Library. Based on Eaton's diary and in part on the description in the book by Francis Rennell Rodd *General William Eaton: The Failure of an Idea.* (New York, 1932). United States, Office of Naval Records and Library.

General William Eaton and Hamet Karamanli, on the Desert of Barca, Approaching Derna. From a reproduction of an old woodcut in Edward Everett Hale's *Memories of a Hundred Years* (New York, 1902). By kind permission of The MacMillan Company and Mr. Frank A. Tichenor. United States, Office of Naval Records and Library.

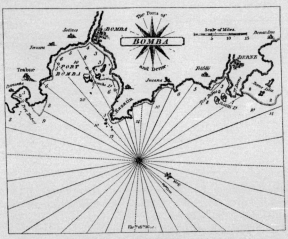

Map of Bomba and Derna. Reproduced by courtesy of the Library of Congress from *The New Mediterranean Pilot,* published by W. Heather (London, 1802). United States, Office of Naval Records and Library.

than push the frigate off the submerged rocks, the breeze canted the frigate to one side, so that the larboard sills touched the water's edge.

As the gunboats and corsair approached, the officer who had made a survey around the frigate reported that there was twelve feet of water at the bow and seventeen feet of water beneath the stern and the larboard quarter. Bainbridge thanked him for his report; if they could move the great ship toward the deep water they could get her off. Bainbridge huddled with his officers and asked for their recommendations. The answer was unanimous: They would have to lighten the ship by pumping the fresh water overboard and heaving the guns overboard. The guns on the larboard quarter could no longer be aimed at the enemy, so they were the first to splash overboard.

Meanwhile, the gunboats steadily approached the stricken ship from the frigate's stern and starboard quarters as Bainbridge watched men with axes chop at the breaching ropes securing the guns, and as fresh water was pumped overboard. The rapid approach of the gunboats prevented him from sending out the ship's boat with an anchor to warp the *Philadelphia* off the rocks since the enemy vessels would soon occupy the very location where the anchor would have to be placed. It was a moot point, Bainbridge realized; the frigate did not possess enough boats for the task.

The crash of shot brought Bainbridge up short. The gunboats were firing now, aiming for the frigate's masts and rigging. Shot whistled overhead, but since they were a ways off did little damage. Bainbridge ordered the remaining guns to return fire, but only two guns on the main deck and three cannonades on the quarterdeck could bear, and they were ineffectual. The *Philadelphia* was largely defenseless, apart from her crew of three hundred and six souls, who Bainbridge knew would repel any boarders to the last man.

Bainbridge, desperate to defend his ship and add to his firepower, ordered the stern cut away to allow the stern chasers to fire on the gunboats. But after doing so, the gunner found that the guns could not be run out far enough to avoid setting fire to the ship, and so they were abandoned.

As heavy iron shot from the gunboats whistled overhead, cutting the rigging and holing the sails, Bainbridge surveyed the frigate. In spite of lightening her, in spite of setting a press of sails abaft, she was stuck fast. He glanced up at the foremast, a great towering pillar of wood and canvas, and made a desperate decision, ordering the carpenter to cut away the mast. As the axes bit into the base of the towering mass of wood, cordage, and canvas, Bainbridge knew this was their last chance. Chopping down the foremast would lighten the ship enough, so Bainbridge hoped, that she would float off the rocks. As long as she had at least one mast she could limp away and make her way to Malta for a refit.

The steadying chopping of axes was suddenly interrupted by a crack, followed by a splintering crash as the foremast toppled overboard. As the crew cut away the rigging, freeing the ship from the deadweight of the mast, the ship rose ever so slightly. But as Bainbridge peered over the side, he was dismayed to learn that she was still stuck fast.

As the gunboats fired on the crippled frigate, Bainbridge again asked his officers for suggestions. Now, without hope, they agreed unanimously that their only course of action was to surrender. Bainbridge accepted the recommendation, but if they had to surrender, they would leave the ship unusable. He ordered the carpenter, William Godby, to go down into the forward hold and bore holes in the ship's bottom, and ordered the gunner, Richard Stephenson, to drown the magazine. Bainbridge also ordered his men to destroy anything that could be of use to the enemy and ordered Midshipman Daniel Patterson to destroy the codebook. Mr. Hodge, the boatswain, asked the captain if he could cast a stern anchor and try to warp the ship off, but Bainbridge refused. They were out of time.

As his orders were carried out, Bainbridge reflected on the misfortune that had accompanied his naval career. Only once before in the history of the U.S. Navy had a ship struck to an enemy. The commander of that ship had been Lieutenant

William Bainbridge, who had surrendered the *Retaliation* off Guadeloupe in 1798 during the war with France. Then, two years later, Bainbridge had anchored in Algiers harbor, beneath the guns of the fortress, and by doing so, had put himself in the position of having his ship, the *George Washington,* commandeered by the Bey, who had ordered him to take his ambassador and accompanying presents to Constantinople. Bainbridge knew that the loss of the *Philadelphia* would be the death blow to his future prospects in the navy. He had struck to the enemy twice now, and was the only captain to have done so. But what options did he have? Bainbridge asked himself. He did not have the right to put to death the souls under his command.

At four p.m. Bainbridge ordered the flag to be lowered. The seaman at the ensign halyard refused. An officer barked at him, threatening to run him through, but still he refused. Finally, a midshipman seized the halyards and lowered the flag. Private William Ray stood on deck, amid a group of marines and seamen, and was surprised to see the flag lowered. Only one gunboat was able to fire on the frigate, although two were getting into position to do so and several more were on the way. Even so, the gunboats were not aiming for the hull, only the sails and rigging. No one, so far, had been injured. Several of the men begged Bainbridge to raise the flag again.

Surgeon's Mate Jonathan Cowdery watched as the Stars and Stripes was lowered to the deck. The mood among the men was grim, their disapproval of the captain's actions barely contained. Had the *Vixen* not been sent to Cape Bon, they would not be in this predicament. Instead, she was three hundred miles to the west, unable to help.

As the Tripolitan small boats, crammed with pirates, approached the doomed ship, everything of value was brought on deck—clothes, barrels, and chest of provisions—and the men were given anything they wanted. Many of the men made use of the moment to put on multiple pairs of trousers and as many shirts as they could manage, knowing full well the pirate penchant for stripping the prisoners bare. Officers

brought up all hand weapons, including axes, pikes, cutlasses, pistols, and muskets, and threw them overboard.

The Tripolitans swarmed aboard as the Americans stood
mute and dejected. The pirates ran across the deck, taking
what they would from the Americans, pulling off hats and
shirts, seizing swords and weapons, and rifling through the
contents of sailors' pockets. Others raced below and returned
carrying seaman's chests, quadrants, food, and anything that
was movable. The deck of the frigate was a scene of bedlam.
As Cowdery watched, a Tripolitan officer screamed at his
men, seemingly trying to restore order. When his men did
not pay attention, the officer raised his scimitar and felled the
nearest man. Cowdery watched as a pirate carrying plunder
had a hand cut off by another officer. On deck lay several
dead pirates and others with their hands cut off, the punish-
ment in Islamic cultures for stealing.

As the Tripolitan officers restored order among their men,
one called out to the Americans, ordering them to the waiting boats, which would carry them to shore. Near Cowdery,
a Tripolitan officer took him by the arm and told him he must
go, urging him toward the railing. Cowdery asked if he could
take his assistant, a mere boy, with him. The officer shook his
head. Then Cowdery picked up his small trunk, which contained his best clothes, and tucked it under his arm. Again,
the Tripolitan officer shook his head, indicating that he could
not take the trunk. Cowdery set it down and walked to the
railing, where the officer helped him over the side. Below
him were three boats, tied together. Two of the boats already
contained American officers. As the Tripolitan officer assisted Cowdery over the side, he felt a hand reach into his
pocket. When he arrived in the boat, he stuck his hand into
the pocket and found it empty. He had placed ten dollars
there for safekeeping.

In the boat, Cowdery found several pirates who were busy
stripping Dr. Harwood, his messmate, and Mr. Godby, the
carpenter. As Cowdery tumbled into the boat, the pirates
stood over him, sabers drawn, pistols primed and cocked, as
one of their number wrestled his surcoat from his arms.

Cowdery lay in the bottom of the boat, watching as they picked its pockets and quarreled over the contents. Seeing his chance, he quickly stood up and scrambled into the next boat in line. There, another pirate seized him, but Cowdery had had enough. The man wanted his coat, but it was too big for him, and Cowdery became angry. He grabbed the pirate, hurled him into the bottom of the boat, and leapt quickly into the last boat in line, which was full of American officers and sailors.

The pirate who guarded this boat was more civil, merely making the Americans row to shore. But two others, who had clearly not profited enough from their day's work, were unhappy. One struck Cowdery severely on the side of his head. Stunned, he fell to the deck as the men searched his pockets and took his case of surgeon's instruments as well as his notebook, handkerchief, and pencil. One of them peered through the pages of his notebook, but seeing nothing of interest, returned it. Not so with the silver pencil and handkerchief, which they eagerly kept.

Cowdery had been so busy trying to ward off the plundering corsairs that he did not realize where he was until he felt the keel of the boat scrape against the bottom. Looking up, he saw that they had landed at the foot of the Bashaw's palace, whose thick, stone walls, studded with the snouts of cannons, rose above the prisoners.

On the beach stood two rows of armed men, which the prisoners had to pass through as they were herded toward the castle. They entered a winding, narrow passage, which let out onto a paved avenue. On either side of the prisoners stood janissaries armed with a variety of hand weapons including tomahawks, muskets, and pistols. As they passed, several of the guards spat at the Americans.

The guards shoved and pushed them, chivying them toward the palace, where they were led into an ornate chamber. Before them, seated on a throne inlaid with mosaic tile and raised approximately four feet from the floor, was the Bashaw of Tripoli, Yusuf Karamanli. Cowdery thought him a good-looking man, about thirty-five years of age. He was overweight, about five feet ten inches tall, but handsome, even majestic. Sporting a black beard, his head topped by a white, beribboned turban, he wore a long silk robe embroidered in gold. Around his waist was a diamond-studded belt from which hung two gold mantle pistols and a ceremonial saber with a gold handle in its scabbard. He sat on thick, velvet cushions fringed with gold cloth. Looking around, Cowdery saw that the marble floors of the chamber were covered in rich carpets. Cowdery watched as the Bashaw looked upon the prisoners with the utmost satisfaction. The Bashaw was enjoying this day, a day on which he had dealt a mortal blow to the Americans.

On the following day, Dr. Cowdery stood on the terrace of the house that would be their prison, the former American consular house. The house featured a rooftop that commanded a view of the sea, town, castle, and palace. Cowdery stood on the terrace and watched as small boats plied back and forth from town to the stricken *Philadelphia,* bringing all articles that could be carried to shore. Cowdery also watched as small boats rowed around the frigate and men dove into the water, using ropes to bring up all the guns and weapons that had been tossed overboard.

Two days later, a fierce gale blew, ruffling the sea and turning the calm water of the harbor white with foam. Cowdery again looked out over the harbor and saw that there were many men aboard the frigate. As the gales whipped up the waves, Cowdery went indoors, to avoid getting wet.

The following morning, the American officers awoke to a shocking surprise. As they walked onto the terrace to view their ship, they saw that she was gone, no longer stuck on the rocks. Frantic eyes scanned the harbor and found her anchored beneath the guns of the castle. Later that day they learned that, during the night, the Tripolitans had used the high seas to their advantage. After caulking and plugging the holes created by the carpenter, they had used the extreme high tide caused by the storm to refloat the vessel.

Bainbridge stood on the terrace and gripped its railings, realizing that the disaster was complete. Not only had he surrendered his ship and crew without losing a man, but he had also allowed the enemy to recapture the ship. They would surely be able to restore it to fighting form. As he watched from his vantage point, he could see laborers swaying up the cannons they had retrieved from the ocean. The Bashaw now had a powerful new weapon with which to fight the Americans.

Outside the prison where the American sailors were being held, the prisoners, who had not eaten in twenty-six hours, were chivvied toward a large window that overlooked a backyard of the castle. There, before them, appeared the Bashaw; High Admiral Murad Reis, once called Peter Lisle; and several other officers. Reis approached the window, and asked the crew of the *Philadelphia* whether they thought Bainbridge was a traitor or a coward.

Neither, the men responded.

Reis replied, "Who with a frigate of 44 guns and 300 men would strike his colors to one solitary gunboat must surely be one or the other."

The crew argued that the ship was stuck fast and that because they had thrown their guns overboard, they could not defend themselves.

Reis told the Americans that they should have known that they would get off once the wind shifted, and that if they had not struck their flag, the Tripolitans would never have tried to board.

On November 24, two days out of Algiers Bay, where Preble had landed Colonel Lear and his family to begin his duties as consul to Algiers, the *Constitution* passed the southwestern tip of Sardinia on its way to Malta. A lookout shouted from the masthead that there was a sail in the distance. As they closed, the lookout declared that it was a frigate, flying the Union Jack. Preble ordered his helmsman to steer toward the vessel, and as they passed close to each other, they spoke. The *Amazon,* a thirty-eight-gun British frigate, had just come from Malta and had news for the American commodore. Preble stood on the quarterdeck and listened with shock and dismay to the words uttered by the British captain: The *Philadelphia* had been lost on the rocks at Tripoli. The British captain shouted through his speaking trumpet that the frigate had grounded after chasing a Tripolitan cruiser. After her crew and officers had surrendered, the *Philadelphia* had been refloated and taken into the harbor, where it was now anchored beneath the Bashaw's castle.

Three days later, Preble arrived in Malta, where he found a letter from Bainbridge detailing the loss of the frigate. Preble also learned from Joseph Pulis, U.S. consul to Malta, that the United States had suffered another loss as a result of the *Philadelphia* disaster. Emboldened by the seizure of the frigate, Yusuf had sent troops to oust his brother from Derna, and Hamet had fled for Alexandria, Egypt.

Preble, dismayed and shocked, took up pen and paper, and began to write a letter to the secretary of the navy, informing him of the disaster. "Would to God, that the Officers and crew of the Philadelphia, had one and all, determined to prefer death to slavery; it is possible such a determination might save them from either," he wrote.

The loss left the Americans with only one frigate, the forty-four-gun *Constitution*; two sixteen-gun brigs, the *Siren* and *Argus*; and three twelve-gun schooners, the *Enterprise, Vixen,* and *Nautilus.* Moreover, the *Philadelphia* gave the Tripolitans a powerful new weapon that was capable of tackling the best the Americans could offer. Preble no longer had the weight of arms necessary to attack Tripoli, and would have to wait for reinforcements, which he now requested. In a few short months, his diplomatic victory over Morocco had been overshadowed by this disastrous event. Whereas Morris and Dale had been ineffective, at least they had not lost a ship. Now Preble would be blamed for losing one of America's finest frigates.

Preble concluded his note with a hint of his own despair: "If it had not been for the Capture of the Philadelphia, I have no doubt, but we should have had peace with Tripoly in the Spring; but I have now no hopes of such an event."

VIII

BURNING THE *PHILADELPHIA*

Lieutenant Stephen Decatur, braced against the railing of the *Intrepid* as the vessel rolled in the light Mediterranean swell, peered through his telescope at Tripoli Harbor. In the faint light of the moon, he could just make out the jagged procession of rocks running in a line across the harbor entrance. The obstacles marked the outer limit of the Kaliusa reef on which the U.S.S. *Philadelphia* had unsuspectingly grounded herself three and a half months prior.

Decatur looked eagerly through his glass again, savoring the moment. At the age of twenty-five, he was already a lieutenant in the U.S. Navy and commander of the *Philadelphia*'s sister ship, the U.S.S. *Enterprise*. He had spent the last seventeen years at sea, descending from a naval family that spanned two continents. His grandfather had been a lieutenant in the French navy, his father a captain on one of the few ships the U.S. Navy possessed. Swinging the glass slowly over the inky black waters, Decatur found the *Philadelphia*. He knew her well—his father had once captained her; now his heart surged with a mixture of joy and sadness at the sight of an old friend. She lay at anchor, half a gunshot from the Bashaw's castle and the main battery that together contained most of Tripoli's one hundred and fifteen sea-facing guns. In the gloaming light of dusk, Decatur scanned the harbor for other dangers and saw that two enemy cruisers lay within a mere cable length of the *Philadelphia*, with several gunboats within half a gunshot of her starboard bow. These vessels might pose a problem if the Tripolitans were waiting for the American enemy.

Had they been warned? The fear gnawed at Decatur. Was
the silence of the city, cloaked in velvet darkness pinpricked
only by the bright lights of the stars, only a façade? Were he
and his men to be lulled into capture? Decatur took one last
look through his glass, then shut it, rubbing a rough hand
through his wind-tossed curly black hair. Two strokes of the
ship's bells marked the hour: seven p.m. Decatur felt the
freshening sea breeze from the northeast, and gave one last
look to seaward. He was searching for the *Siren,* a vessel that
was to have accompanied his own. But the other ship was
nowhere to be seen.

Turning to his Sicilian pilot, Salvadore Catalano, Decatur
instructed the man to take the *Intrepid* into Tripoli Harbor.
The young American glanced around the deck of his tiny
vessel to see if he could see any flaws in their disguise as a
merchantman. In reality, the ketch carried a crew of eighty-
four belowdeck, armed with cutlasses, tomahawks, and
knives, primed for action. All was in order. Satisfied, Decatur
looked beyond the line of rocks at the massive, dun-colored
walls of the battery and the towering white minarets that rose
from the ochre shore lined with date palms fluttering in the
breeze.

As Catalano threaded the boat through the rocks, washed
clean by the churning, white surf, Decatur went over his orders yet again. The plot was simple: coast in on the sea
breeze, lay the sixty-four-ton ketch up against the *Philadelphia,* then board her. Once on board, the Americans were to
dispatch the enemy, setting the ship on fire to deny her use by
the Tripolitans. If they could not board, the alternate plan
called for using the *Intrepid* as a "fire ship," sending her
crashing into the frigate, with the crew escaping in the small
boats. Both success and failure lay in getting close enough to
the *Philadelphia.* Decatur braced himself for what lay ahead,
idly watching his able pilot guide the ketch through the
treacherous rocks and into the winding channel between the
reef and the sandbars.

* * *

Decatur had first learned of the mission two weeks before, on the morning of January 31, 1804. His ship, the *Enterprise,* was lying at anchor in Syracuse Harbor, on the island of Sicily, the new U.S. base for operations against the Bashaw. A midshipman handed his young commander a message that instructed Decatur to make his way to Commodore Edward Preble's flagship. Donning his best uniform and hat, taking a last look in the mirror to ensure that the brass coat buttons shone brilliantly in the light of the early-morning sun, the young officer climbed down to the waiting barge that would take him across the harbor to the U.S.S. *Constitution.* It was a quiet morning, marred only by the grunt of his men pulling the long, wooden oars and the synchronous splash as the eight blades scythed into the blue surface, propelling the small craft toward the flagship.

Decatur wrapped himself tightly in his cloak, spying another barge headed for the *Constitution,* recognizing the stolid form of Lieutenant Charles Stewart, commander of the brig *Siren.* He knew Stewart well; they had been schoolboys together at the Protestant Episcopal Academy in Philadelphia, and in 1798 had served together aboard the frigate *United States.*

As Decatur's barge touched against the oak timbers of the flagship, he heard the familiar piping of the boatswain's call, announcing his arrival; Stewart arrived a moment later. Together they were taken belowdeck to Preble's spacious living quarters. As a marine sentry opened the door, the two men could admire the commodore's sweeping view of Syracuse's harbor and the green hills that flowed above it, all clearly seen through the stern windows of the great cabin. Preble sat at a desk, his secretary standing by his side.

The commodore went right to the point: He wanted the *Philadelphia* destroyed to deny her use by the enemy. Decatur's thin lips curved into a smile. This was the moment he had been waiting for: revenge, the payback for this black mark against the U.S. Navy's reputation. Preble shuffled through a stack of papers and pushed forward a letter from Captain Bainbridge, smuggled from the American's prison

in Tripoli. Written in code with a translation attached by
Preble's ever-efficient secretary, Decatur could read Bainbridge's audacious plan for burning his captured ship—an
unusually courageous act from a vessel's captain, consider-
ing the close emotional ties between any ship and her commander.

Bainbridge wrote that the Bashaw had sent divers to the
area where the frigate had struck the reef to recover the guns
thrown overboard during the Americans' desperate attempts
to float the vessel. Since the water was only twelve to fourteen feet deep at this point, the Tripolitans brought up all the
arms, subsequently remounting them on the frigate. The
Bashaw was making a concerted effort to ready the *Philadelphia* for sea. If he succeeded, the ship would rival any in the
American squadron, including the U.S.S. *Constitution*.

Bainbridge wrote that twenty enemy vessels lay at anchor
within hailing distance of the *Philadelphia*. These included a
polacre, a fourteen-gun brig; a ten-gun schooner ready to
be launched; five galleys with lateen sails; and twelve gunboats. The gunboats, however, had been hauled up on shore,
so they would require more time to get under way. Added to
these formidable defenses were more than one hundred and
fifteen guns inside Tripoli, their ugly black snouts pointing
from embrasures in the castles, fortresses, and walls that
overlooked the harbor. Bainbridge warned that Tripoli Harbor's currents and channel were especially treacherous and
difficult to negotiate.

But the American captain believed it was still possible for
a raiding party to burn the frigate—so long as the attempt
was made under the right conditions. The raiders would need
a land breeze, wind blowing off the ochre-colored shore of
North Africa toward the blue waters of the Mediterranean.
Land breezes typically occurred at night. Darkness would
also provide cover for the Americans, wrote Bainbridge,
concluding: "I think it very practicable with six or eight
well-manned good Boats and well and determined Officers
to destroy her. . . ."

Decatur scanned the sheets of paper, a surge of excitement

swelling in his belly as Preble instructed him to take command of the operation, using the *Intrepid* to set fire to the *Philadelphia.* The choice of this vessel was no accident. The *Intrepid* was actually a sixty-four-ton Turkish fishing smack, the *Mastico,* renamed by the Americans after Decatur captured her on December 23, 1803, off Tripoli. He had made her a prize after learning that the Turkish ship had taken part in the capture of the *Philadelphia.* She had been in the harbor when the frigate struck the reef, and had helped board more than a hundred Tripolitans to attack the helpless American vessel. Using the Turkish boat in this attack was sweet revenge; it was also the ideal vessel for the task. This type of two-masted, fore-and-aft-rigged boat was common in the Mediterranean, rigged in a fashion indigenous to the area. She would not be suspect as an American.

Decatur thought it fitting that he was to lead the attack, given his father's close connection to the *Philadelphia.* When James Decatur captained her in 1800, he sailed the vessel to the Caribbean, capturing the fourteen-gun French cruiser *Croyable.* His son knew every spar and yard of the ship.

Once back aboard the *Enterprise,* Decatur asked his first officer to pipe all hands to attention. Standing on the quarterdeck overlooking the ranks of seamen and marines, he read out the orders, asking for sixty-two volunteers to sail with him. To a man, the entire crew stepped forward.

As his lieutenants, Decatur selected James Lawrence, Joseph Bainbridge (the imprisoned captain's brother), and Jonathan Thorn. He also chose Louis Heerman as surgeon's mate and his finest midshipman, Thomas Macdonough, to accompany him; Preble had promised five additional midshipmen from the flagship. But perhaps Decatur's most important decision was to select an experienced pilot who knew the harbor and would ensure that the *Intrepid* did not meet the same fate as the *Philadelphia.* Decatur chose Salvadore Catalano; he had been in Tripoli Harbor as pilot aboard a British Maltese craft when the *Philadelphia* was captured.

Over the next two days, Decatur worked his crew at a frenzied pace, readying the *Intrepid* for her mission. Boats plied between the docks and the ketch, taking guns to the Sicilian shore, bringing back barrels of beef and hogsheads of water and biscuits, along with incendiary materials that included gunpowder, tar, and wood shavings. Other crewmembers swabbed the little ship, filthy from past use and overrun with vermin. She would be a snug fit with so many men aboard, even tighter if they had to share the vessel with an army of rats. Men flooded the hold, then pumped the bilges out until the water ran clean. Stores and weapons were packed aboard as sailors and marines performed the multitude of tasks necessary to make a ship, especially a frail one such as the *Intrepid,* ready for action.

It took three days to prepare their vessel, but by five p.m. on February 3, 1804, all was ready. They used the land breeze to take them out of Syracuse Harbor, setting sail for Tripoli. As the *Intrepid* and the *Siren* reached the open sea, propelled by fine winds, Decatur waved to Stewart, standing on the quarterdeck of the *Siren,* then cast an eye toward the south, and the open, blue-green expanse of sea that lay before them. It looked endless, but the American knew that, a mere two hundred and seventy-one nautical miles to the south, the swell that carried them now crashed against the North African shore and the rocks that guarded the entrance to Tripoli Harbor.

Stewart returned Decatur's greeting, watching the little ketch plow through the gentle seas. He was glad he was aboard his own, larger ship rather than the frail, cramped *Intrepid.* He had known Decatur since they were schoolboys together, and in 1798, when he was a midshipman aboard the frigate *United States,* where Stewart had served as a lieutenant. Now they were both twenty-five, eager, adventurous lieutenant commanders, looking to make names for themselves. Stewart tried to stifle the tinge of resentment toward his having been relegated to a supporting role in this mission. Still, better this role than none at all, he thought. There would be glory enough for both of them.

Belowdeck in his own vessel, Decatur entered the cramped

cabin he would share with three lieutenants and the surgeon's mate. Just as he was settling down to write a letter to his wife, Susan, a marine rapped on the door. The surgeon's mate, Louis Heerman, and the cook were reporting in with bad news. The cook had opened a barrel of salt beef, finding it putrid. Inspecting the beef himself, Heerman realized that all of the ship's stock was unfit for human consumption; it had been packed in poorly hooped barrels that had previously contained salted fish.

Decatur ordered the spoiled food tossed overboard, pondering the gravity of this news: They would have nothing to sustain them but biscuits and water until they returned to Syracuse. The *Siren* had only enough for her own crew, so there was no use hailing Stewart. It was a bad omen for the voyage.

The following morning dawned pleasant and cool, with a fine breeze from the west propelling the host of scudding clouds that traveled with them. As the ship's bells signaled the hour, nine o'clock, Stewart piped his crew to the deck, announcing their mission for the first time. The men cheered as they heard his words: They could finally pay back the Barbary pirates for that dastardly deed against the *Philadelphia*.

The two ships remained within sight of each other as they sailed south. Within days, Decatur noticed that the *Siren* was taking on a decidedly Mediterranean look, Stewart transforming his two-masted, square-rigged brig to look like a Turkish merchantman. By the time they reached Tripoli, four days later, Decatur saw that the *Siren*'s top gallant masts had been swayed down, replaced by a flying jib boom. The ship's guns were housed, her ports shut. Quarter clothes further improved the lie that the *Siren* was a merchant vessel rather than an American warship.

On February 7, 1804, the lookout aboard the *Intrepid* shouted "Land ho," pointing to the south. The minarets of Tripoli showed that they had arrived. As night descended, Decatur signaled to the *Siren,* now sailing far behind the *Intrepid,* that he was going to attempt to enter the harbor. The timing was perfect: It was eight p.m., getting dark, further helping to disguise their ship, allowing the *Intrepid* to get close to the frigate. But Catalano shook his head in disapproval, pointing to the foaming white breakers crashing against the harbor rocks. The weather was turning, he said, a winter squall almost upon them. As the little ketch rolled and lurched in the deepening troughs, Decatur decided that he had to try anyway. The Tripolitans may have already become suspicious at the sight of his ship. Surely they knew the Americans would attempt to take back the *Philadelphia;* this might be their only chance.

Catalano and Midshipman Charles Morris were to report on the condition of the sea at the harbor's entrance. The *Intrepid's* sailors wrapped cloth around the oars to muffle them, then lowered a small boat, bobbing and pitching, in the rough sea. Catalano braced himself in the bow as Morris rowed toward the rocks, now being swept clean by large, foaming waves.

Half an hour later, the men returned; it was all Catalano could do to grasp the rope thrown to his boat and haul himself aboard the larger vessel. After he and Morris regained the *Intrepid's* deck, the crew attempted to haul in the boat, but a particularly large wave smashed the small craft against the *Intrepid's* side, breaking it apart like a toy. Shouting against the ever-increasing wind, Catalano reported that the *Intrepid* could enter the harbor. It would be risky, but it could be done. Only it would be impossible to get out again. A dejected Decatur signaled his men to haul the anchor; much as he hated to do it, they would stand off and wait for better weather.

Aboard the *Siren,* Stewart could make out the stern lantern of the *Intrepid* bobbing and weaving as the ketch made for open water. Although Stewart had received no signal, Decatur's intentions were clear: He had decided not to press on this night but to ride out the storm. Stewart ordered his own boats, which he had readied for use, to be hauled in, the anchor raised. The clang of ships bells indicated that it was now eleven p.m. Anchored in six fathoms of water near the rocks, the *Siren* tossed about like a leaf on a river. One of her lieutenants ordered the men to the capstan bars in order to haul in the anchor, suddenly realizing it was stuck. The spinning wooden bars knocked down sailors, turning the deck slippery with a mixture of seawater and blood. The men got up over and over again, vainly attempting to raise the anchor. Finally, at four a.m., worried that the light of dawn would alert the Tripolitans to their presence, Stewart ordered the cable cut, and the *Siren* followed the *Intrepid* out to sea.

For seven days, the gale tormented the American raiders. Aboard the *Intrepid,* Decatur reefed in the sails and set his crew to man the pumps. The ketch was old; as the waves pounded the sixty-foot-long vessel, buckets of green seawater worked their way in through the seams. Decatur, who had first gone to sea as a lad of eight, had never been so concerned. He feared not only the loss of the ship, but also that of his crew.

To keep up the men's spirits, he made regular rounds, encouraging the sailors and marines to stick by their duty. But conditions were miserable. The men had been eating nothing but biscuits and water since they left Syracuse, and were growing weak. In addition, with seventy-four men aboard the tiny vessel, the crowding overwhelmed them all. The six midshipmen and pilot were wedged into a platform that was placed on top of the water casks. It was little more than a shelf on which the men could not even sit upright. On the opposite side of the ketch, eight marines slept on a similar ledge. Belowdeck, in the hold, the remaining fifty-three men remained in sloshing bilge water, tormented by vermin that had survived the earlier attempts to purge the vessel. On deck, the few men charged with keeping the *Intrepid* from broaching the waves were tied to the railings, working feverishly against the pounding waters.

The gale drove them far to the east, to the Gulf of Sidra. On February 15, the wind shifted, blowing from the north again, signaling the end of the storm. As the storm abated and the swells lessened, Decatur ordered Catalano to take them back to Tripoli. They reached Point Taguira, just east of

the harbor, at five-thirty p.m. The *Intrepid* dropped anchor,
waiting for the *Siren*. She appeared much later than expected, blown farther east during the storm. Once in view,
Stewart immediately sent over a boat of nine men to swell
the raiding party to a crew of seventy-two.

But with the treacherous seas still making the harbor dangerous, the two ships sailed away once more, agreeing to return the following evening. The plan called for the *Intrepid*
to enter Tripoli Harbor around midnight, the *Siren* awaiting
her return among the harbor rocks.

February 16 dawned bright with a fresh breeze and a clear
sky. Decatur set the sails, sweeping the horizon with his
glass; he could see no ships on the horizon. The *Siren* must
have been blown farther out to sea once again. It took all day,
but they finally regained entrance to the harbor. Decatur
asked the lookout if he could see the *Siren;* the man shook
his head "no."

Decatur mulled his two choices: wait for the *Siren* and attack later or go in now, without the other American ship. At
seven p.m. he held a council of war with his officers. Catalano said that with the wind beginning to die down, they had
to go in now. Others worried about raising enemy suspicions
if they again attempted to enter, only to depart. To a man,
they agreed: go!

Aboard the *Siren,* the lookout sighted the *Intrepid* just as
she nosed into Tripoli Harbor. Stewart pressed on, hoping he
would not miss the action. But the favorable sea breeze taking him toward shore slackened, slowing his progress. Finally, the *Siren* reached the rendezvous point, anchoring
three miles southwest of town. Stewart swept the sea with his
glass, but it was too dark to see the other American vessel.
Assuming Decatur was proceeding with their plan, he sent
two boats containing fifteen men apiece to proceed to the
eastern rocks and assist the *Intrepid* on her way out of
Tripoli.

Dressed in loose Maltese clothing, Decatur stood on his
bridge with Catalano, who was wearing similar camouflage.

Half a dozen sailors worked on the deck; any more would signal that they were more than a merchantman. Catalano steered the ketch, squinting toward the harbor, concerned about the high surf crashing against the rocks at the western entrance. He pointed a dark finger to the right; he would instead slip in through the eastern channel between the reefs and shoals. Decatur nodded, ordering him to proceed. Above them, a crescent moon began to climb into the night sky.

At eight p.m., the wind dropped and the sails flapped along with the Union Jack flying from the masthead. As Catalano carefully guided the ketch into the harbor, Decatur saw the hulking shapes of the Mandrach, the fortress that anchored the breakwater extending from town. He could also make out the angular shape of the Maltese castle and the round form of the French fort, both standing guard. A lookout from the masthead hailed his captain, pointing to the north, where the *Siren* was in the offing. All was ready; Decatur went over his plans for maybe the hundredth time to make sure he had not missed any crucial details.

The raiding party would take the spar deck first, then carry the gun deck below. Other men were assigned to the ship's boats to ensure that no vessels left the frigate or reinforced those aboard. Once they secured the ship, the Americans would place the combustibles, fire them, then rejoin the *Siren*'s boats at the mouth of the harbor. If they were unable to take the *Philadelphia*, they would set fire to the *Intrepid*, using it to burn down the frigate.

Decatur divided his men into six teams. He and fourteen other men would take the spar deck. Twelve others, led by Lieutenant William Lawrence, would capture the berth deck and forward storerooms. Lieutenant Bainbridge and ten others would secure the wardroom and steerage. Midshipman Morris and eight men would occupy the cockpit and storerooms at leeward. Midshipman Anderson and nine men would take a boat and cut off any enemy boats trying to reach the shore. Lieutenant Thorn, Surgeon's Mate Heerman, and fourteen men would remain aboard the *Intrepid* to defend her against any attack.

The *Intrepid* rode smoothly over the light swells, moving ever closer to the *Philadelphia*. All was silent save the groan of tackle, the flap of canvas, and the lapping of waves against the hull. The ship's bells clanged the hour: nine-thirty p.m. Decatur gripped the railing, watching the frigate looming ahead out of the darkness. The glimmer of lanterns on her gun deck indicated that her cannons were manned and ready, making her capture much more difficult; one well-placed shot would sink the *Intrepid*. But Decatur forced this thought out of his mind as they closed in on their prize.

His men were ready, lying concealed behind the ketch's bulwarks. So far, they had not been discovered. He could see two large pirate xebecs about a quarter mile off the starboard quarter; by the number of lights aboard, they were fully manned. Even closer, within musket shot, were two gunboats, off the starboard bow. And looming above them, half a gunshot away, was the Bashaw's castle and main battery.

As the towering wall of the frigate's port side rose above the tiny ketch, a Tripolitan naval officer hailed them from aboard the *Philadelphia*. He wanted to know the *Intrepid*'s name and where she hailed from. Catalano, the only man aboard who spoke Arabic, replied that they were the *Transfer*, from Malta. Commodore Preble had chosen this vessel deliberately after American spies reported that the Bashaw had recently purchased it and was eagerly awaiting her arrival.

But the Muslim officer aboard the *Philadelphia* was apparently unaware of his ruler's most recent acquisition; imperiously, he warned the *Intrepid* away. Catalano pleaded for his forbearance: They had lost their anchor during the storm, he said, asking the Tripolitan if they could tie up against the *Philadelphia*. At that moment, a mere twenty yards from their prize, the wind dropped and they were becalmed, directly beneath the frigate's loaded guns. Decatur silently swore at their ill luck.

The officer peered suspiciously at the small craft beneath his own. Rigged in a manner indigenous to North Africa, she deceived him for a fateful few seconds. Satisfied, he bellowed a string of orders. A moment later, a boat was lowered from the frigate, carrying a hawser. Decatur ordered his crew to carry a line from the *Intrepid* and meet the frigate's boat, watching anxiously as the two vessels converged and the lines were silently spliced. He prayed that none of his men would make the fatal mistake of uttering an oath in English, breathing a sigh of relief when his midshipman began rowing back to the *Intrepid,* the job complete. Aboard the ketch, several men began to haul on the hawser, aided by other Americans lying below the bulwark.

As the distance between the two boats closed, the ship's bells rang four times in the first watch, signaling the hour of ten p.m. Aboard the *Philadelphia,* a sailor threw over a stern line. Then Decatur heard an animated shout from this same Muslim sailor: the man pointed to the ketch's stern, his eyes locked onto the *Intrepid*'s anchor.

"Americani, Americani," he shouted.

"Board, Captain, board," Catalano yelled to Decatur.

But there was still too much sea between the ships. The American commander hesitated. His men continued to pull frantically on the lines as the alarm spread aboard the *Philadelphia*.

After what seemed like an eternity, the two boats bumped together and Decatur yelled the order they had all been waiting for: "Board! Now!"

Almost in unison, men rose from behind bulwarks armed with cutlasses, knives, pikes, and tomahawks, surging toward the *Philadelphia*. Decatur leapt onto the frigate's chain plates, swearing as he lost his footing and nearly fell into the gap between the ships. Other Americans leapt for the gun ports, with Midshipman Morris first aboard. Decatur found his footing and climbed to the deck himself. He saw the dim shape of a man before him, holding a cutlass. Raising his own sword to strike, he heard the other man's frantic whisper, "Philadelphia," the mission's password. It was Morris.

Racing across the spar deck, cutlasses out, slashing and cutting as the enemy retreated, Decatur and his fifteen-man squad rushed to the starboard side. Meanwhile, Decatur saw the dark silhouettes of the other teams making their way to

their assigned objectives. The clang of swords and cries of
the wounded echoed across the water as the enemy retreated,
leaping overboard. Decatur ordered his men to take the stern,
where the pirates did not put up much of a fight, again jumping into the sea rather than engage the Americans.

As Decatur led his party in a mad dash across the deck,
Lieutenant Lawrence along with Midshipmen Macdonough
entered the *Philadelphia* through a gun port and found the
enemy gun crews alert and ready. Initially, the Tripolitan
gunners gave ground as other American raiders joined
Lawrence's squad. But then, upon hearing the clash of steel
above them and knowing that their only escape lay in throwing themselves overboard, the Tripolitans fought hard.
Lawrence hacked at the throng of men in front of him, parry-
ing the thrust of a ramming rod and ducking the swing of a
gun swab. As the battle reached a feverish pitch, suddenly
Macdonough stumbled and fell forward, and was immediately beset upon by the enemy. Lawrence stamped his feet
and shouted at the top of his lungs for his men to renew their
attack, and they advanced, hewing and cleaving the enemy,
while one of the raiders pulled Macdonough to safety. He
was shaken, but otherwise unharmed, having tripped on a
gun tackle.

On either side now, Lawrence heard the sound of American voices, yelling and cursing. The clang of steel was accompanied by sharp cries as the Americans pressed home
their attack. Lawrence and his men attacked a group of
fierce-looking men holding crowbars and iron handspikes
who were desperately trying to swing their gun toward the
advancing Americans. The captain of the gun held a hand-
spike in one hand, a smoldering slow-match in another as his
crew heaved the gun carriage with their crowbars. Just as the
gun was in position to fire on the advancing Americans,
Bainbridge and his men surged in from the left and overwhelmed the gun crew. Lawrence stood there, panting, tired
but elated, his sword slick with blood. The battle for the gun
deck was over.

Above Lawrence on the spar deck, Decatur heard the

fighting below him taper off. The ship was almost theirs, but he was also alert for a counterattack. He looked across the inky black surface of the harbor, watching the silhouettes of men moving on the decks of Barbary gunboats. At any moment, those dangerous ships could get under way. He knew that he had enough men to burn the *Philadelphia,* but far too few to repel an attempt to retake the ship.

In the waters off the starboard side, the *Siren*'s Thomas Anderson and his crew of nine waited, the battle raging above them. Suddenly, Anderson heard the splash of a boat and the harsh guttural sound of Arabic. Scanning the side of the frigate, he could see a small boat being lowered from the stern. Rowing furiously for the shore, the pirates did not realize that Anderson's boat was blocking their path. Their officer was so intent on reaching safety, he failed to see the Americans before it was too late. The two boats touched; Anderson's crew swarmed aboard the enemy vessel, hacking and chopping until all the Arabs were dead.

Aboard the *Intrepid,* Lieutenant Thorn peered nervously toward the enemy cruisers as the sound of fighting rose from the deck of the *Philadelphia* above them. The clang of steel and the screams of those who were about to die, or those who would before the sun rose, carried across the still vastness of the harbor. Surely the enemy was now alert and would send boats to try and recapture the frigate? He clenched his cutlass tightly in his hand, and once again peered into the night, trying to discern the enemy's intentions.

There. The dark prow of a ship's boat, and another, pulling hard from the enemy frigate, appeared out of the darkness, edged by a white lining of foaming water thrown up as the frigate's bow cleaved the surface of the harbor. Thorn issued a rapid series of orders, and his men prepared themselves for boarders. The boats came closer. Suddenly, the *Intrepid* was illuminated by light. Thorn swung around and saw that lanterns had been lighted on the *Philadelphia*'s gun deck. Furthermore, the sound of fighting was absent. Thorn again peered over the starboard rail and saw the boats. But this time, they were turning around, retreating. They, too, had

seen the light, and known that the ship had been taken, and
that their hope of recapturing it was gone.

Standing on the gun deck of the *Philadelphia,* Decatur
surveyed the carnage. Twenty dead Tripolitans lay before
him. One American was wounded. The ship was theirs. He
wiped his bloody sword on a rag, a discarded headdress left
on the deck by its former owner. Catalano approached, grin-
ning; they could bring out the frigate now. Motioning to a
scrap of cloth that fluttered above them in the rigging, the Sicilian pilot indicated that there was now a strong land breeze.
Familiar as he was with the soundings, the channel, and the
current, Catalano knew exactly how it could be done. They
could save the *Philadelphia.*

But Decatur had his orders. He could almost see Preble's
words on paper: "Board the Frigate Philadelphia; burn her;
make your retreat good with the Intrepid. . . ." Preble had
been quite specific in how the frigate was to be destroyed.
"Be sure and set fire in the Gun room births, Cockpit Store
rooms forward and Births on the Birth deck. After the Ship
is well on fire, point two of the 18-pounders down the Main
Hatch and blow her bottom out. . . ." There was no latitude in
those orders. Even if Catalano had a chance at saving the
vessel, Decatur was not free to try.

In addition, the frigate had no foremast or sails, and was
anchored beneath the guns of the main battery. Sadly, the
young American commander shook his head. It was not possible.

Suddenly, the men aboard the frigate heard the roar of a
cannon from the Bashaw's castle, the ball striking the water
off the starboard bow. Other shots followed as one by one the
Bashaw's guns fired on the *Philadelphia.* There was no time
to lose. As cannon balls whizzed overhead, Decatur heard the
menacing whiz and slap of musket balls being shot at them
from the two pirate xebecs at anchor nearby.

Boxes of tar, lint, wood shavings, and gunpowder were
hurriedly carried from the *Intrepid* to the frigate. Each squad
leader carried a sperm-oil candle and a lantern slung over his
shoulder. Moving to their assigned areas—gunroom, cockpit

storeroom, and the forward berths—the squads carefully placed the combustibles as cannon balls carved huge gouts in the water. Other men rushed aboard the *Philadelphia* with pikes and small arms to defend the frigate while the combustibles were placed. In minutes, all the combustibles were ready.

Deep in the cockpit, Midshipman Morris lit a candle from the lantern, tossing it into a pile of shavings, igniting the wood in a whoosh of flame and heat. In seconds, a wall of flame, its yellow tongues licking the ceiling, blocked his retreat. Taking a lungful of air, he charged through the curtain of fire to burst onto the companionway. Reaching the deck, singed but otherwise unharmed, Morris ran for the port side as flames shot from hatches along the length of the ship.

Lieutenant Bainbridge stood belowdeck in the stern of the ship, looking out of the wardroom windows through which he could see the town coming to life. He held his lantern at the ready, a pile of shavings and a box of tar stuffed beneath the wardroom table. When he heard the signal, he gave the room one last wistful look, then touched a candle to the flickering flames of the lantern and threw it to the floor. The shavings crackled and burned; Bainbridge beat a hasty retreat as the yellow tongues of flame licked at the legs of the table.

In the forward storerooms, Lieutenant Lawrence also heard the signal and threw the lighted candle near a bail of sailcloth. The cloth was dry, and the flames spread like oil on water. Lawrence turned and ran, as all about him, the ship seemed to be on fire. Fire shot from the galley as he ran by it, and found a hatchway. As he clambered up, smoke billowed out, and flames crackled and shot from every seam and opening. The ship was as dry as tinder.

On deck it appeared to Lawrence as though he was playing a part in Dante's Inferno. Flame shot out of hatchways and climbed the rigging, illuminating the dark silhouettes of the American raiders who had just set the ship on fire and were running for their lives, only steps ahead of the enveloping flames.

Decatur watched as the conflagration advanced, and waited

until he saw that all of his men had appeared on deck. Satisfied that they had all made it, he leapt for the deck of the *Intrepid* but got caught in the rigging once more. Scrabbling for a handhold, the commander tumbled down the ratlines toward the inky surface of the harbor, catching hold of a rope at the last minute. He swung himself onto the ketch, Morris jumping after him, both landing safely.

The *Philadelphia* was bone-dry, and burned like a tinderbox. Since the land breeze was quite faint and would not allow the *Intrepid* to sail out of the harbor, Anderson's boat would tow the ship out. Decatur ordered a midshipman, ax at the ready, to sever the bowline attaching the frigate and the ketch. But before the man could do so, the line burned away. They were clear.

Yet the *Intrepid* still did not move. Lying in the lee of the ship, she was a mere two feet from the blazing *Philadelphia*. Steaming tar poured onto the ketch, threatening the ship. The burning frigate illuminated tarpaulin-covered barrels on the small vessel's deck, containing additional combustibles in case they had to turn the *Intrepid* into a fire ship. If they didn't get away soon, the *Intrepid* would go up like a rocket.

The ketch didn't budge. Decatur saw that the *Intrepid*'s long lateen boom was caught on the frigate's stern so that fire was now singing *Intrepid*'s sails. He ordered a squad of men to free the boom, and the *Intrepid* began to respond to the sweeps. But it still seemed anchored in some way. Then Decatur remembered the stern line; they were still tied to the *Philadelphia*. Seeing the midshipman with the ax, he shouted an order and the young man raced to the stern.

Moments later, the *Intrepid* surged away from the incredible inferno. As his ship gathered headway, Decatur finally caught his breath. It was only now that he realized he had dropped the Tripolitan ensign, his souvenir for Preble.

Flames continued to shoot out of the *Philadelphia*'s gun ports and scupper holes, climbing the rigging, igniting the tar-covered ropes, burning like a mighty torch. The fire lit up the night sky, illuminating the domes of the mosques, the turrets of the castles, and the minarets of the town. Flaming spars and rigging fell, hissing into the water.

Suddenly, the roar of a cannon was accompanied by a great tearing sound as one of the Bashaw's cannon balls shot through the *Intrepid*'s topgallant sail. Sailors swarmed over the rigging to repair the rent canvas. A bit closer and they would have gone up like the frigate.

Just then, the fire reached the *Philadelphia*'s guns, her portside cannons popping off one after the other in a ragged broadside. Shot screamed overhead and tore gashes in the dark water, sending great plumes of white spray into the night sky. Decatur watched awestruck as the fire reached the touchholes of the frigate's starboard guns. His crew cheered as cannon after cannon fired, emptying the entire broadside into the Bashaw's fortress. From across the water, Decatur could still hear the clang of iron balls against stone.

Inside the Bashaw's prison, lying at the base of the Muslim ruler's castle, the thundering crash of cannon fire woke the American prisoners. One crept to a window, from which he could see a reddish glow light the night sky. Hearing the panicked shouts of the guards and the clattering footsteps of men running to the battlements, the *Philadelphia*'s sailors knew at once that something was happening—but what? They prayed it meant an American raid to set them free.

Dr. Cowdery was awakened by the most hideous yelling and screaming from one end of the town to the other. Getting out of bed, he heard the firing of cannon from the castle. He stood and made his way to the window, which overlooked the harbor. There, he saw the *Philadelphia* in flames.

As her oarsmen pulled and strained, the *Intrepid* moved slowly toward the rocks and safety. As the ketch approached the rocky barrier separating Tripoli Harbor from the open sea, the ship's bells rang the hour of eleven p.m. Decatur could still see the *Philadelphia* as the great ship's tops fell with a great hiss into the dark waters. Beyond the blazing frigate, the fire continued to illuminate Tripoli itself. Decatur swung his telescope toward the sea, spying the lights of the

Siren waiting for them. The breeze freshened, helping to fill the sails that blew them gently out of the harbor.

Suddenly, by the harbor rocks, a lookout spied the dark silhouette of boats filled with sailors. Were they to be captured after all, becoming Barbary prisoners as the thanks they'd have for almost losing their lives aboard the *Philadelphia*? But then a man in the nearest boat called out: "*Siren*'s boats, sir. Have you a line?" Decatur breathed a sigh of relief. They were safe.

At one a.m., the *Siren* took them in tow. The burning frigate continued to cast a reddish glow over the night sky as Decatur gratefully took a cup of coffee. He sipped the steaming dark liquid as he watched the thin, dark shoreline of North Africa recede in the distance. Stewart offered his own cabin to guarantee a well-earned night's rest but Decatur refused. Wrapping his cloak tight around his shoulders to ward off the chill of the morning air, he remained on deck, standing there until the ship's bells marked six a.m. and the sun began to climb into the dawn sky. Faraway to the south, he could still make out the reddish glow of the burning frigate. Decatur smiled; the Barbary pirates would no longer take the Americans' war lightly.

On March 9, a boat touched at Boston and the captain handed a packet of official dispatches, wrapped in oilskin and sealed with wax, to a courier with instructions to deliver them to Secretary of the Navy Robert Smith.

Ten days later, after a wearisome journey, the courier arrived in Washington. Robert Smith opened the dispatch cases and read Preble's letter with dismay. The *Philadelphia* had been lost; America had suffered her greatest naval disaster since the Revolutionary War. After the disappointment of Morris, Smith had hoped that Preble would turn the tide of the war in their favor. True, he had pacified Morocco, but the loss of his second most powerful vessel was a signal disaster. Smith continued to read and saw that Preble was asking for at least two more ships to replace the *Philadelphia,* as well as gunboats, to bring the war to a conclusion.

Across town, Eaton fumed over the lack of action. He had arrived in Washington in January, hoping Jefferson and Madison would embrace his call for more forceful action against Tripoli. Although Jefferson had cashiered Morris, Eaton had still not been invited to the White House, and whenever he spoke with Madison, the secretary avoided discussing Eaton's plan to install Hamet Karamanli on the throne.

Eaton glanced at the newspaper, announcing the loss of the *Philadelphia*. Would this change Jefferson's approach to the war?

As if in answer to his question, several days later, Jefferson invited Eaton to the White House. Seated in the Cabinet Room, Jefferson came straight to the point, telling Eaton that in light of the troubling news about the *Philadelphia*, he had decided to apply additional pressure on Tripoli and would be grateful for Eaton's assistance. Jefferson told Eaton that he had learned from intelligence reports that Hamet was in Derna, where he had become governor and had defeated Yusuf's forces in battle. Furthermore, Jefferson said, he would now agree to Eaton's request to help Hamet, and promised artillery, a thousand stands of arms, and $40,000 to cover the costs of the campaign. Eaton was heartened as he listened to the president's words; Jefferson's promise was a first, tentative step toward usurping Yusuf.

As he finished his coffee, Eaton doubted that the task could be accomplished with the limited funds Jefferson had offered. He knew that without the backing of the U.S. Navy and Marine Corps, the enterprise would fail. However, Eaton knew that if he were to succeed, he would need to continue his efforts to persuade the new commodore to support his plan.

Eaton received more good news in April, when Jefferson announced that he was appointing Eaton as naval agent to the Barbary States. Eaton learned that he would report to Lear, but would, in his capacity, provide assistance to Hamet. Eaton began readying for departure. He instructed Eli Danielson to travel to New York and ask Morton Jones Martin, one of the city's most respected sword smiths, to fashion him a scimitar of Toledo steel. He also asked Danielson to purchase tents, saddles, cooking equipment, and other gear required for a campaign on Tripoli.

May arrived and with it bad news from North Africa. Hamet had been forced to retreat for lack of supplies. Eaton was summoned to the White House, where he learned that Jefferson had withdrawn his offer of armaments and money for Hamet. After the meeting, Eaton returned to his lodgings, sat down at his writing desk, and poured out his thoughts on Jefferson's change of heart: "discouragement supercedes resolution with our Executive, and economy supplants good faith and honesty," he wrote. Eaton sat back and passed a hand over his forehead. Would Jefferson ever take the actions required to win the war?

Meanwhile, on May 14, hundreds of miles to the west, Captain William Clark finished loading all of the expedition's provisions and equipment aboard three boats, which bobbed in the current of the Missouri River: a twenty-two-oar boat, a seventy-one-oar pirogue, and a smaller six-oar pirogue. All of the boats were also equipped with sails. At four p.m., they set off up the river, heading for the French village of St. Charles, seven leagues upriver, where they would meet Meriwether Lewis, who was traveling overland from St. Louis. The Lewis and Clark expedition had begun.

On May 26, Thomas Jefferson held a cabinet meeting. The past two months had been disturbing: first the news of the *Philadelphia* disaster, then, from April 3 to April 13, a court of inquiry had formed at Stella's Hotel to look into Commodore Morris's conduct. The court had determined that Morris's sluggish approach to the war permitted the navy to court-martial him. However, Secretary of the Navy Robert Smith persuaded Jefferson that enough evidence had already been gathered to forgo a formal court-martial and to merely dismiss Morris from the navy. Jefferson was angered by the man's conduct and handling of the war, and agreed with Smith's recommendation. On May 16, Smith revoked Morris's captaincy in the U.S. Navy.

The cabinet members gathered to discuss the situation in the Mediterranean, specifically to determine what instructions the president should provide to the new commodore. The war with the Barbary States had occupied Jefferson's thoughts for the past three years, and the struggle against them, inseparable from the struggles of a young nation to find its footing in the world, had occupied his thoughts for almost twenty years. On one hand, the war had achieved its purpose: instead of paying annuities to the pirates, Jefferson had built a navy. He had also, up until the loss of the *Philadelphia,* achieved his secondary goal of improving America's stature among the European nations. But the war had become a drain on America. Meanwhile, Jefferson had increasingly begun to look toward the west. The Louisiana Purchase had doubled the size of the new nation, and the land west of the Mississippi, the domain of British fur trappers, was ripe for exploration.

Yet the war persisted, and so he had asked the cabinet members to meet to discuss how best to conclude the war. Jefferson was sending four new frigates to the Mediterranean. If these ships, along with the ships already on station, could not beat Tripoli, then he would authorize Tobias Lear to pay up to $20,000 to make peace, along with the promise of an $8,000 to $10,000 annuity and $500 ransom for each prisoner. The cabinet assented and the meeting ended.

As the members filed out, Jefferson missed one of the familiar faces whose company he had enjoyed not only as a cabinet member but also as a tenant of the White House. Meriwether Lewis had gone west, to lead an expedition with Captain William Clark to explore the western reaches of the continent. Jefferson ran over the objectives of the expedition, which he had outlined in a letter to Lewis:

The Object of your mission is to explore the Missouri river & such principal stream of it as by its course and communication with the waters of the Pacific ocean, whether the Columbia, Oregon, Colorado or any other river may offer the most direct &

practicable water communication across this continent for the purpose of commerce.

In June, Eaton finally got his wish; he was ordered to return to the Barbary Coast and install Hamet on the throne of Tripoli. As he stowed his trunks in the cabin assigned to him aboard the *John Adams,* he opened one of the trunks and admired the beautifully crafted scimitar that had cost him the staggering sum of $85. He picked up the blade and turned it over in his hands. It was a magnificent weapon, perfectly balanced, with steel so hard it would hold an edge through weeks of hard campaigning. Eaton returned the sword to its place. Once his remaining gear was stowed, Eaton clambered on deck and admired the fleet Jefferson had assembled. Finally Jefferson was backing up words with action. Prompted by the loss of the *Philadelphia,* the president was sending fresh ships to the Mediterranean to defeat Tripoli. Eaton spied the *Congress, Essex,* and *Constellation* readying to make sail. Four new frigates would compensate for the loss of the *Philadelphia* and allow Preble to hit Yusuf hard.

Eaton had also been given the nod to proceed with his plan to help Hamet overthrow Yusuf. Hamet was somewhere in Egypt. Eaton would have to find him before building an army to defeat Yusuf. Still, Eaton was troubled, and later that night, as the ships rocked in the ocean swell, on a course for Gibraltar, Eaton sat down and wrote a letter by the light of an oil lamp to his friend Colonel Thomas Dwight of Springfield, Massachusetts.

On my arrival in Washington I remonstrated with Mr. Madison. He evaded the subject. I waited on the President and the Attorney General. One was civil, the other grave; but neither disposed to give me the satisfaction I demanded and which common honesty should have induced them voluntarily to render. It was very easy for me to perceive that changes had been adopted in our system of intercourse with the Regency I had left, which rendered my news nugatory; and that though all acknowledged my zeal and decision agreeably to instructions, all seemed indifferent about the sacrifice thence resulting to myself and careful to conceal from me what those changes were. Notwithstanding which I endeavoured to enforce conviction on the mind of the Attorney General of the necessity of meeting the aggressions of Barbary by retaliation.

He waived the subject: and amazed me with predictions of a political millennium which was about to happen in the United States. It was to usher in upon us as the irresistible consequence of the goodness of heart, integrity of mind and correctness of disposition of Mr. Jefferson. All nations, even pirates and savages were moved by the influence of his persuasive virtue and masterly skill in diplomacy. . . .

. . . The Secretary of War believes we had better pay tribute (he said this to me in his own office); Gallatin, like a coward, shrinks behind the counter; Mr. Madison leaves everything to the Secretary of the Navy. . . . Lest this expedition should fail and my intuitions consequently be distorted into a mere matter of speculation, I have resolved not to accept any compensation for my services, except a sufficiency to cover my actual expenses.

I can therefore say, as a Spartan Ambassador to the King of Persia's lieutenant, when asked whether he came with a public commission or on his own account—If successful for the public, if unsuccessful for myself.

Preble paced the quarterdeck of the *Constitution* as it rocked gently at anchor some six miles northwest of Tripoli. It was August 7. These past two months, Preble had pressed his attack on Tripoli, acquiring gunboats from Naples and bringing his entire fleet to Tripoli, where he had sunk a number of gunboats and repeatedly bombarded the town. But he also realized that despite the number of shots fired, and the number of Tripolitan sailors and soldiers killed and wounded, the Bashaw had not sued for peace. Nor would he; the Bashaw could stand to lose a few ships and men, but he understood that Preble didn't have enough men or ships to defeat him. And thus, the American fleet sortied out each day and bombarded Tripoli's batteries, and the Tripolitans fired back. It was a stalemate.

Just then the lookout hailed the deck, announcing that a

strange sail that had appeared on the horizon was no stranger at all: It was the frigate *John Adams*. At last, the reinforcements he had asked for had arrived. Preble returned to his cabin and told his executive officer to signal her captain to come aboard with dispatches.

Later that evening, three cheers from the crew announced the *John Adams*'s arrival. A little while later, a knock on the cabin door announced the arrival of her captain, Master Commandant Isaac Chauncey, who saluted, then handed over a sealed oilskinned package containing dispatches from Washington. Preble bade Chauncey sit and opened the package, finding three letters from Secretary of the Navy Robert Smith. He scanned the lines of the first one and saw that his request had been granted: The president had ordered "a force which would be able, beyond the possibility of a doubt, to coerce the enemy to a peace upon terms compatible with our honor and our interest." Chauncey told Preble that indeed, four frigates were on their way: the *President,* commanded by Samuel Barron; the *Congress,* commanded by John Rodgers; the *Essex,* commanded by James Barron, Samuel's brother; and the *Constellation,* commanded by Hugh G. Campbell.

Preble took this in without a murmur, but realized the implications of what Chauncey had told him. Two of the officers, Rodgers and Samuel Barron, outranked him. That meant only one thing: He was being relieved. Preble wondered if it was a result of losing the *Philadelphia,* or if the decision to replace him had been made prior to that. It mattered little. Preble took up Smith's letter and confirmed his suspicions:

Be assured, Sir, that no want of confidence in you has been mingled with the considerations which have imposed upon us the necessity of this measure. You have fulfilled our highest expectations, and the President has given it in an especial charge to me to declare that he has the highest confidence in your activity, judgment and valor. Through me, he desires to convey to you his thanks for the very important services which you have rendered to your country.

I repeat to you the assurance that your whole conduct has received the unqualified approbation of the President of the United States and that his confidence in you remains unabated.

On September 9, Preble stood up from his writing desk and made his way to the quarterdeck, where he took up his glass and swung it to the southeast; Tripoli lay some fifteen miles away. Swinging the glass over the rough blue-green ocean, he found the *Argus,* keeping station to the east, and then, searching the western horizon, he found the *Vixen.* They were both far off, yet within signal range. But more important, the blockade held.

Suddenly, a lookout from the maintop cried out and the signal officer repeated his message. The *Argus* had signaled, "discovering strange ships northeast." The sky was hazy; Preble could make out little except waves and mist beyond the *Argus.* He ordered the *Constitution* to give chase.

It was Sunday afternoon and Preble had his regular dinner as a guest of the wardroom. Toward the end of the dinner, he excused himself and went back on deck. They were sailing into the wind, tacking to reach the strange ships. Ahead he could see the *Argus* signaling to the two ships that were now much closer. Signal flags fluttered atop the *Argus;* the signal officer reported that the strange sails were no strangers at all: The *President* and *Constellation* had arrived. A little while later, as the *Constitution* came upon them, Preble ordered his broad pennant struck and then clambered over the side and into a waiting boat to call on the new commodore.

On September 15, Commodore Samuel Barron invited Eaton and Isaac Hull aboard the *President.* Barron was not feeling well. His doctor wished him to sail for Syracuse and spend the winter resting ashore. They would head north soon, but in the meantime, the *President* cut through the ocean swell off Tripoli, maintaining the blockade along with the *Argus.*

Barron invited both men to sit. He was impressed with both of them; Hull for his actions under Preble, Eaton for his service to the country and his plan to mount an invasion of Tripoli from land. Barron knew the fleet would be less active in the coming months since the weather would hamper their operations. He also knew that Jefferson and Secretary of the Navy Smith favored Eaton's plan, while Tobias Lear was firmly against it. Barron understood that Lear was against it because he did not like Eaton and was opposed to overthrowing a sovereign government. And Barron could not help but confess that he would like to see the navy finish the job. But he was also practical, and realized that Eaton's plan would be instrumental in assisting the navy, and for that reason, among a host of other, smaller reasons, Barron wished to support Eaton as much as possible. Certainly he could not place his entire fleet at Eaton's disposal, but sending him off in the *Argus* was an entirely feasible experiment.

After his guests had seated themselves, Barron thanked them for coming and then handed Isaac Hull a packet and addressed him:

"Sir, the written orders, I here hand you, to proceed to the port of Alexandria or Smyrna for the purpose of convoying to Malta any vessel you may find there, are intended to disguise the real object of your expedition, which is to proceed with Mr. Eaton to Alexandria in search of Hamet Bashaw, the rival brother and legitimate sovereign of the reigning Bashaw of Tripoli, and to convoy him and his suite to Derna or such other place on the coast as may be determined the most proper for cooperating with the naval force under my command against the common enemy, or, if more agreeable to him, to bring him to me before Tripoli.

"Should Hamet Bashaw not be found in Alexandria, you have the discretion to proceed to any other place for him where the safety of your ship can be, in your opinion, relied upon.

"The Bashaw may be assured of the support of my squadron at Benghazi or Derna, where you are at liberty to put in, if required, and if it can be done without too great risk. And you may assure him also that I will take the most effectual measures with the forces under my command for cooperating with him against the usurper, his brother, and for reestablishing him in the regency of Tripoli. Arrangements to this effect with him are confided to the discretion with which Mr. Eaton is vested by the Government."

Inwardly Eaton smiled. At last he had the orders and the backing of the navy to pursue his plan. He now had one objective: find Hamet and bring him to Derna.

IX

SEARCHING FOR HAMET

On November 25, 1804, William Eaton stood beside Master Commandant Isaac Hull aboard the brig *Argus* as they lay off Alexandria, Egypt. As the boat carrying their pilot approached, Eaton examined the fabled port city named after Alexander the Great and built on one of the many tributaries of the Nile as it splintered and divided on its way to the Mediterranean. Eaton scanned the harbor and saw a forest of lateen-rigged vessels in various states of loading and unloading along wharves that jutted out into the sea. A long mole, anchored by a battery, protected Alexandria from the ocean swell. Behind the wharves, Eaton spied ochre-colored buildings crowned by minarets and the domes of mosques.

Alexandria was a bustling seaport. Eaton also knew that it was under siege in a country that had fallen into anarchy. Egypt was a province of the Turkish Empire, but the war between the British and French had undone the ties to the Sultan and created a power vacuum. After the French had invaded in July 1798 to secure Egypt and begin a march on British India, where Tippoo Sahib had been induced to revolt against British rule, Nelson had soundly defeated the French fleet at the battle of Aboukir in August 1798. Undaunted, Napoléon had marched on Cairo and established French rule. He then began his long march to India, and made it as far as Syria, where he was defeated at Acre in May 1799. General Abercromby had finished the job, defeating the remaining French forces in Egypt in 1801 and establishing British rule, which ended in 1803. The Turks had reestab-

lished nominal control of the country. And somewhere out
there was Hamet, waiting for him.

At half past one, the pilot came aboard and skillfully navigated the brig into the old port. At anchor was a Turkish ship
of the line accompanied by six frigates. An admiral's broad
pennant fluttered from the masthead of the Turkish warship.
Hull ordered the *Argus* to salute the admiral, and moments
later, the air was torn by the muffled thunder of a seventeen-
gun salute. The admiral returned the greeting, firing seventeen guns in reply as the *Argus* dropped her anchor and
awaited the British consul.

A little while later, Eaton, Hull, and the British consul,
Samuel Briggs, sat down in Hull's cabin and Eaton handed
Briggs his letters of introduction from the British governor
of Malta, Sir Alexander Ball. Briggs read the letters, and
then, over refreshments, proceeded to give Hull and Eaton an
understanding of the political situation so that Eaton might
begin his mission with a better than even chance of succeed-
ing.

Briggs told Eaton and Hull that after the end of British
rule in 1803, the Turks had tried to reestablish their rule, but
had run into difficulties. The Turkish viceroy, Muhammed
Khurshid, held power in the cities, such as Cairo, Rosetta,
and Alexandria. However, two warring camps of Mameluke
Beys, the slave generals of the Turks, were fighting against
Turkish rule and effectively governed the rest of Egypt. The
army of one Mameluke Bey was headquartered in Minyeh, a
town above Cairo in Upper Egypt, while the other operated
from Damanhur in the Nile delta. Thrown into the fray were
bands of Albanian mercenaries, called Arnauts, who had de-
serted from the Turks, and who now roamed the countryside
and were at war with both the Turks and the Mamelukes.

Briggs told Eaton that Hamet Karamanli had allied himself with the Mameluke Bey in Minyeh. Eaton stated his intention to proceed directly to Cairo. Briggs, however,
strongly recommended against making so perilous a journey.
Not only would he have to make his way up the Nile through
lawless country, but there was no longer a British resident in

Cairo. Major Misset, the former resident, had evacuated to
Rosetta because Cairo had become so unsafe. Briggs also
warned Eaton that the French still held some influence in
Egypt in the personage of Monsieur Drovetti, who was the
French consul in Cairo. Drovetti would view any American
activity with suspicion, especially if he was able to establish
that the British had helped Eaton. Drovetti's mind-set was to
thwart any British action in Egypt. By arriving armed with
letters of introduction from Governor Ball and meeting with
Briggs, Eaton had made himself a target. He would have to
be wary of Drovetti, Briggs warned.

Indeed, Eaton had already noticed that the French were
decidedly anti-American in Egypt. When they had arrived,
he had seen the flags of several nations fluttering along the
consular row, indicating those consuls who wished to pay a
visit to the ship. Eaton had seen no French or Spanish flags.

Eaton thanked Briggs for his briefing and then made his
decision. He would travel to Rosetta and thence down the
Nile to Cairo, a distance of some one hundred and thirty
miles. Hull listened to the conversation and stepped in with
an offer of a strong escort. Briggs promised to assist in any
way he could, and the meeting was concluded.

After Briggs made his departure, Eaton ruminated on his
mission. For four long years he had waited for this day. Now,
somewhere to the south, Hamet and his followers were en-
camped. Eaton had to find him, raise an army, and bring him
back to Alexandria, where they would board the *Argus* and
sail for Derna. But first he would have to get to Cairo.

On November 30, Eaton and his party boarded barges and
sailed for Rosetta, which lay east along the coast. Accompanying him was his stepson Eli Danielson, a midshipman
aboard the *Argus*; Lieutenant Blake from the *Argus*; marine
lieutenant Presley O'Bannon; Midshipman George W.
Mann; Seid Selim, a janissary; Alli, a dragoman; marine private David Thomas; and six servants. Eaton was especially
impressed with O'Bannon, who was a tough, twenty-nine-
year-old Irish American who hailed from the Blue Ridge

foothills. He had served in the Mediterranean since 1802 and
knew the ways of the Barbary.

The following day they arrived in Rosetta and Eaton met
Major Misset. The major was an old soldier, and the two got
along well. Eaton told him that he wished to travel to Cairo
in order to find Hamet and bring him to Derna. Misset, unlike Briggs, did not try to dissuade him. Instead, he helped
Eaton procure boats for the expedition. They would take two
marche, Misset told Eaton, a type of schooner displacing
forty tons that was used on the river.

While preparations were being made, Eaton ran into his
old friend Dr. Francesco Mendrici, who had lived in Tunis
and had been the Bey's physician while Eaton was consul.
Eaton had lost touch with the man, who was now the physician for Khurshid Pasha as well as the British. Eaton invited
Mendrici to join them and he accepted. That evening, they
joined Major Misset for dinner. The dinner was delicious,
but Misset, in true British fashion, apologized that he could
offer them neither Porter nor Madeira.

While the boats were being readied, Eaton decided to visit
the nearby Bay of Aboukir, where Abercromby had defeated
the French general Menou's army almost four years ago.
Eaton strode through the old battleground, amazed to find it
still covered with skeletons, monuments to Napoléon's failed
policy in Egypt. After touring the battlefield, Blake made his
departure, returning to Alexandria with dispatches from
Eaton, requesting Hull to bring the *Argus* to the Bay of
Aboukir and to wait for him there. Eaton told Hull that he
hoped to return in ten days' time.

On the morning of December 4, Eaton sat down at a desk,
took out a sheet of paper, dipped his pen into the inkpot, and
began to write. Before leaving, he would send a secret message to Hamet, to let him know that he was on his way and
was looking for him. He would send the letter down the river
by a messenger, who was instructed to take it to Minyeh and
not divulge its contents to anyone. He hoped that the messenger would make good time and that Hamet would join
them in Cairo when they arrived. Eaton wrote the following:

Excellency, I am the American Consul who made an agreement with your Excellency previously to your leaving Tunis for Malta; and am sent forward by the United States to carry that agreement into effect. I desire to be informed of the channel of communication with your Excellency in such a manner as not to embroil my government with any of the Chiefs of this country—

America is at peace with all the world, except your brother, Jussuf. With him we will never be at peace; for he is unjust towards all men—But when God shall have established the rightful sovereign upon the throne of Tripoli we will seek peace with that kingdom

I am your Excellency's sincere friend.

At three p.m. the expedition set off down the Nile in two schooners. One boat, commanded by Eaton and his party, flew the American flag, the other the British ensign. Aboard Eaton's boat was his party, armed with some of the one thousand rifles Eaton had brought from the United States for use by Hamet's army. A friend of Major Misset, Captain Vincents, commanded the other boat, which flew the British ensign. Dr. Mendrici and four servants filled out the crew. The British boat was also well armed, mounting two swivel guns, and the crew was armed with muskets, pistols, and sabers.

Eaton hoped the American and British flags would ease their passage down the Nile, for Misset had warned him that the countryside between Rosetta and Cairo was hostile. Marauding bands of Arabs roamed the banks of the Nile. They might also encounter Arnauts, Albanian mercenaries who had quit the Turkish army and were living off the land. It would be a dangerous journey.

They made good progress, and on the following day Eaton ordered the boats to tie up beside a village named Fuor. They dined in a garden and after drawing the cloth, Eaton decided that it would not harm the expedition if word spread that they were armed with the most modern rifles. To get the word out, Eaton organized target practice. This would alert anyone with hostile intentions as well as allow Eaton to determine the level of expertise among the party. Eaton used an orange to demonstrate the effectiveness of his new rifles. Pacing

thirty-two yards from the fruit, he aimed as a group of villagers stood by and watched. Eaton carefully sighted down
the barrel and pulled the trigger—and the orange split in
two. Eaton replaced the orange, and missed. Then, firing
again, split it in half. Eaton was satisfied; word would now
spread about the Americans, and Eaton wanted the words to
be ones of respect.

Two days later, Eaton's party arrived at Sabour, a village
that had been decimated by Arnauts. According to locals, a
group of five hundred Arnaut deserters from the viceroy's
army had recently plundered the town and stripped it bare.
They had left, but a party of Arab raiders was camped about
four miles upriver, and the villagers urged Eaton to be careful; the Arabs were attacking passing boats. However, the
following day they passed the Arab encampment without in-
cident, and on December 8 arrived at Bulac, the gateway to
Cairo, and sent word to the viceroy that they had arrived and
wished to pay their respects.

The following morning a party of Turks arrived, bringing
with them horses to carry Eaton and his party to Cairo, along
with attendants to ensure that they arrived unmolested.
Eaton climbed onto a waiting horse, scimitar strapped to his
side, and a short time later they entered the narrow, winding
streets of the city, where throngs of people lined their path,
coming to see what an American looked like, for word had
spread that they were American naval and military officers
visiting Cairo during the winter suspension of operations
against Tripoli.

Their escort conveyed them to the British ministerial
house, where Eaton and his men were given several apartments. Later in the day the viceroy's interpreter arrived to
welcome them and inform them that the viceroy would receive them at nine o'clock the following evening. He explained that this hour was required because the feast of
Ramadan had begun, and devout Muslims could only eat and
enjoy refreshments after sunset.

Eaton put the intervening hours to good use. He had heard
nothing so far from his messenger, so on the following day,

December 10, Eaton hired men to determine if Hamet, or any of his entourage, were in Cairo. Later that day they came back with Hamet's former secretary of state and two ex-governors. Eaton pressed them for information about Hamet, and confirmed what he had heard in Alexandria, that Hamet commanded a troop of Tripolitans fighting with Elfi Bey. They were stationed in the village of Minyeh on the upper Nile.

Hamet's alliance with a Mameluke Bey was a problem. The Mamelukes were fighting the Turks. By association, therefore, Hamet was also an enemy of the Turks. Eaton realized that this made a rendezvous difficult. Hamet would need the viceroy's guarantee, a firman, in order to travel unmolested to Cairo. Eaton would have to take up the point with the viceroy, realizing that the best course of action would be to show the viceroy that by allowing Hamet to leave Egypt, Eaton would be removing a friend of his enemy. Eaton hoped the viceroy would be amenable to the argument, for without his approval, Hamet was indeed in exile, and beyond his reach. And without Hamet, the plan to overthrow Yusuf was merely a mirage.

At eight o'clock on the evening of December 10, six richly caparisoned Arabian horses and a Turkish escort appeared in the courtyard below Eaton's apartment. Eaton took a last look at himself in the looking glass, seeing that his dark blue naval uniform was in order, and descended to the courtyard, where Captain Vincents and Dr. Mendrici, resplendent in the rich red uniform of the British army, awaited him. They mounted their horses and were led to the palace. On the way, Eaton saw that the streets ahead were lined with spectators and that their way was lighted with torches and flambeaux for a mile and a half up to the gates of the Citadel. The crowds had come to see the Americans, who hailed from the New World.

At the gates, guards let them into the Citadel courtyard, where the viceroy greeted them with a parade of his troops. Once this formal greeting was over, attendants helped them off their horses. They entered the Citadel and climbed a

flight of stairs flanked by well-armed and superbly dressed
Turkish officers. As they reached the top, they found themselves in a grand salon, and walked into a magnificent hall.
Eaton was awed; he had never seen anything to rival it. Before them sat the viceroy, Khurshid Pasha, seated on a purple
sofa of damask cushions. As they arrived, he stood and extended his hand in greeting, beckoning Eaton to sit beside
him. Mendrici and Vincents took seats on either side.

Attendants arrived and offered coffee, water pipes, and
bowls of sherbet. The conversation began with pleasantries.
The viceroy asked for news of the war between the French
and British. He then proceeded to ask Eaton about the
United States. How big was the new nation? Who was she at
war with? What were her chief products? Eaton sipped coffee and regaled the viceroy with tales of America. Finally,
the viceroy signaled to his courtiers, who retired and left the
viceroy alone with his interpreter. The actual business of the
meeting would now take place.

The viceroy, speaking through his interpreter, asked Eaton
why he took this opportunity to visit Egypt. It would seem,
he remarked, that Eaton was here for another reason apart
from satisfying his curiosity. Eaton took his cue and spoke in
French, which the viceroy understood, and began by telling
the viceroy how Yusuf Karamanli had declared war on the
United States, and how the United States had responded.
Eaton told the viceroy that he was here in search of the true
sovereign of Tripoli, Hamet Karamanli. Once found, Eaton
said, he intended to transport him back to Tripoli and install
him on the throne. The United States would do this not to
conquer Tripoli, but to assert the United States' rights to free
trade and show the world that the United States would stand
up for her rights. This course, Eaton told Khurshid Pasha,
was a just course, and the one that would result in the least
bloodshed.

The viceroy listened and when Eaton finished, told him
that he knew Hamet and had provided him with provisions,
although he did not know where he was at present. He also
told Eaton that he would help in any way he could in order to

take the humane approach to ending the war that Eaton had outlined. The viceroy paused for a moment to reflect, then stated that if, however, Hamet had joined the Mamelukes, that would change the viceroy's disposition toward him. Instead, he would consider Hamet an enemy.

Eaton responded carefully. He told the viceroy that Hamet was in distress, and a magnanimous ruler such as the viceroy would never have resentment toward a fallen sovereign such as Hamet. Eaton continued, noting that God would pardon, not punish, an enemy who repented. The viceroy inclined his head toward Eaton, signifying that he agreed. He then promised Eaton that he would send couriers to find Hamet, and bring him to Cairo. Eaton thanked the viceroy and the conference ended.

Eaton reflected upon the challenge now faced by Hamet. He had the assurance of the viceroy that the Turks would not harm him, nor would they impede his departure from the country. But how would Hamet make his departure from the Mamelukes without being labeled a traitor? Elfi Bey, if he learned of the viceroy's decision, could very well put Hamet to death.

Eaton spent the next few days writing to Secretary of the Navy Robert Smith and Governor Sir Alexander John Ball, describing his adventures thus far and his progress in finding Hamet. He also dashed off letters to Hamet, sending them out with the couriers instructed by the viceroy to find Hamet and bring him to Cairo. Eaton sent out notes with each of the viceroy's couriers, inducing Hamet to come to Alexandria without delay:

> Excellency, From Alexandria and Rosetta I sent your Excellency some letters which will be delivered to you accompanied by a letter from one of your subjects who might be very useful to us. I pray your Excellency to retire to Rosetta without delay and place yourself under the protection of the British Minister, who is there at present, and that you will have the kindness to send me certain information as to when I shall be able to meet your Excellency in that town. I shall wait here ten days for your reply.

If your Excellency has troops attached to you, I venture to suggest that you send them to Alexandria in order to await your orders there.

I am very respectfully your Excellency's most faithful friend.

Eaton hoped that one of the letters would reach Hamet, but he knew that it would be difficult for him to leave Minyeh. Three thousand Mameluke soldiers were ensconced in Minyeh, surrounded by a force of eight thousand Albanian mercenaries and Levant Turks. There had been a battle, but since the Mamelukes had not retreated and the Turks had not been defeated, although they had run away, the forces were in a stalemate. The Mamelukes were inside the walls and the Turkish forces were camped around them. A courier would have to make his way through the lines, and somehow Hamet would have to escape.

Eaton heard nothing and waited, until troubling news galvanized him into action. Several days later, word reached Eaton that the French consul in Alexandria, Monsieur Drovetti, had spread word that Eaton and his party were British spies wearing American masks. Furthermore, he insinuated that Eaton's desire to find Hamet was merely a ruse by which the British would be able to open a dialogue with the Mamelukes, and then join with them to fight the Turks.

The rumors were troubling, and Eaton was angered. Not only would Drovetti's accusation make finding Hamet more difficult, but spies were put to death. Of course the British had helped him, but he was not assisting them in opening an alliance with the Mamelukes. Eaton's only recourse was to again ask for an interview with the viceroy. He would blunt Drovetti's words directly, before the viceroy withdrew his support.

At the meeting, he managed to secure a letter of amnesty and passport of safe conduct from the viceroy. Money exchanged hands and removed the difficulties Eaton had faced. Drovetti's move had been thwarted, momentarily, but Eaton would have to be wary of the Frenchman. On December 15, Eaton wrote again to Hamet:

Excellency, God ordained that you should see trouble. We believe he hath ordained also that your troubles shall now have an
end—

Your Excellency will rejoice when I tell you that His Highness, Ahamet Hourshet Bashaw, with a greatness of mind worthy
of a Prince, and a goodness of heart resembling Heaven, forgetting actual situations, and remembering only what you were, orders that your Excellency may pass, unmolested, through any
part of his country, and embark with me at any port you please—

If the generals with whom you are, moved by equal goodness,
will consent that your Excellency may profit of this occasion
once more to see your subjects and embrace your family, certainly you will lose no time in repairing, with your suite, to
Rosetta, and meeting me at the English Consul's, where the Minister, Major Misset now resides—

I pray the Almighty may grant Your Excellency his protection
and favor—

Eaton made four copies of the letter, and sent each letter
with a separate messenger in the hope that one of the letters
would get through the Turkish lines to Hamet.

One of the men he entrusted to carry the letter was a man
he had met in Cairo, Colonel Jean Eugene Lietensdorfer. He
handed him a copy of the letter and instructed him to find
Hamet and bring him to Cairo. Lietensdorfer understood the
importance of finding Hamet; he was now Eaton's chief of
staff and was helping the general raise an army.

Lietensdorfer set off later that evening with one attendant,
riding camels through the dark streets of Cairo to avoid detection. He knew that while there were enemies in the countryside, there were also spies within Cairo who, if they knew
he was traveling to Minyeh with a letter for Hamet, would
see to it that he never left.

Lietensdorfer's real name was Gervasso Prodasio Santuari
and he was thirty-three years old. He was an Italian, hailing
from a village near Trent in the Tyrol. His parents would have
been aghast if they had known where he was now. They had
wanted him to become a priest, but this was the life he chose,
which he began when he quit school at the age of seventeen,

got married, and then joined the Austrian army in its campaign against the Turks. He fought at Belgrade from 1789 to 1790, and continued serving in the Austrian army during the siege of Mantua. Then, in 1797, the Austrian army collapsed, surrendering to Napoléon.

Santuari did not wish to remain with the losers, so he changed his name to Carlo Hossondo and joined the French army. Here, he was accused of being a spy and was thrown into a French jail. He escaped by poisoning his guards and changed his name again, this time to Jean Eugene Leitensdorfer. He rejoined the French army and had been part of the force that invaded Egypt, but had switched sides later on and joined the British. Since then, he had wandered. After trying to live a quiet life as the proprietor of a coffee shop for British officers in Alexandria, he had married a Coptic maiden, his second wife. But when the British withdrew, he left as well, leaving behind his wife and making his way to Messina, where he tried the life his parents had set out for him by entering a Capuchin monastery as a novice friar.

That life did not suit him, so he left, and made his way to Constantinople, where he became a dervish and a Muslim. He went by the name Murat Aga, wandering through the Middle East, eventually making his way to Mecca and Jedda. Finally, he took up as an interpreter to Lord Gordon, a Scottish gentleman, accompanying him on a tour of Abyssinia, and returned to Egypt, where he had met Eaton.

Leitensdorfer and his servant rode through the night, and all through the next day, never resting apart from a nap in the saddle as the camel's rolling gait put them to sleep. Several days later, they reached the Mameluke camp in Minyeh and after enjoying coffee with the sheik, were allowed to see Hamet.

Leitensdorfer handed Hamet the letter he carried from Eaton and waited for him to read its contents. Hamet, however, was at a loss for how to leave the camp. Leitensdorfer had spent the past few days during his long ride thinking this over. He told Hamet that he should take his men out on a night reconnaissance. The Mamelukes would allow that, certainly. Then, once outside the camp, Hamet could make his way south, the wind hiding the tracks of his party from any Mamelukes who were foolish enough to pursue him. In that way, Hamet could flee. Armed with the letter of amnesty and passage of safe conduct, Hamet could make his way to Cairo. Hamet agreed. It was January 3; they would try that night.

While waiting for Hamet's reply, Eaton began to assemble the core group of officers his army would need to take to Tripoli. He calculated that three hundred to five hundred men would be needed, along with men to lead them. He would also need money, which he borrowed from Briggs Brothers, to begin recruiting and purchasing provisions. Eaton also wrote to Hull, telling him he would wait until the courier returned, and hoped to bring Hamet with him to Alexandria. In the meantime, he instructed Hull to prepare for the arrival of Hamet's army and take on provisions enough to feed them on a short cruise to Derna.

Eaton also sought out Tripolitans who had emigrated to Egypt in order to learn more about the situation in Tripoli. He found one, an Arnaut Turk, who had served Yusuf during the previous summer's blockade. Eaton pressed the man for news about the effects of the blockade. The man was wary until Eaton told him he was an Englishman, interested in the war between America and Tripoli. Unguarded and unreserved, the man opened up to Eaton, and told him that Tripoli had suffered during the blockade. Many men had died, the town had been damaged, and people were so fearful of the shelling that most people slept outside the city and conducted business elsewhere.

The man was quite obviously sympathetic to Yusuf, for when pressed about Hamet, he told Eaton that Yusuf would never submit to the Americans until they had been humbled and had paid for the damage they had caused. But what about Hamet, Eaton asked? The man responded: Yusuf had taken care of him. Yusuf had sent out paid assassins to poison his brother, and one of them had succeeded.

Eaton pondered this as he thanked the man for his time.

He had recently heard a report that Hamet was dead, but had not put much faith in it. Still, Yusuf was cunning and his agents were ruthless. What if Hamet had choked on a poisonous meal prepared by one of the assassins? It was possible, Eaton realized, and prayed for word from Hamet to discredit the report.

Hull sat in his cabin aboard the *Argus,* which rocked at anchor in the Bay of Aboukir, and read Eaton's dispatches with interest and some trepidation. Eaton had proposed raising an army to take Derna, and had requested Hull's assistance in transporting it by sea. But Hull did not have the ships available to put Eaton's plan in motion. He also had no money, and was already seeking credit from Briggs Brothers for provisions and stores.

Hull wished to assist Eaton, but Eaton's plan was risky. Instead, Hull decided it would be better to carry Hamet and his escort to Syracuse, where they could raise an army of between eight hundred and a thousand, which Hull believed was the number required to mount a successful assault, and then proceed to Derna. This made sense, since the *Argus* was only one small ship at anchor in a country at war, fought over by the Turks and Mamelukes, and a battleground for British and French intrigue. It would be far better to mount a proper expedition from Syracuse. Hull wrote all of this in a letter to Eaton, which he would send by the next available packet boat. He hoped that in Eaton's next correspondence there would be some word of Hamet, for he could not wait forever; he wished to conclude this business and return to Syracuse. Their provisions and supplies were running low and they would have to borrow even more money from the Briggs Brothers if they did not soon leave this place.

Eaton read Hull's response to his letter and realized that he would have to modify his plans. What Hull suggested— taking the nucleus of an army to Syracuse and then raising an army to attack Derna—was not feasible. The offensive would have to be mounted in the spring. If he took Hamet to

Syracuse they would undoubtedly lose another season of fighting. Eaton made up his mind and began to write orders to Richard Farquhar, who he would send on the next packet boat to Alexandria, to begin recruiting an army for the march across the desert, a distance of more than five hundred miles.

December drifted into January and still Eaton waited for word from Hamet. He had now been in Cairo for almost a month and was beginning to feel restless. He knew that if Hamet would not come to him, he would have to decamp and make his way to Minyeh, to personally bring Hamet back to Alexandria. Yet the dangers were grave: Even accompanied by Lieutenant O'Bannon and his marine escort, they could be robbed or they could fall in among the Arnauts. And if they found that Eaton was working with the viceroy, they would certainly execute him. Even if they managed not to be robbed, and to avoid the Arnauts, they could still end up being taken by the Mamelukes and executed as spies. Still, Eaton knew that he had to reach the objective he had set for himself many long months ago: to establish contact with Hamet and capture Derna. That was the objective, and if it necessitated risk, he accepted it. The alternative, release of American prisoners after paying ransom, and annual tribute as a condition for peace, was too disgraceful to imagine. And time was running out. He had heard that Benghazi and Derna had been reinforced with troops and that a gunboat now defended each town. He would like to strike before either place was further reinforced.

Finally, on January 8, a messenger arrived at the apartment Eaton was using in the British ministerial house, bearing a letter. The messenger had come from Minyeh. Eaton thanked him and, opening the envelope, scanned the words written in Arabic. The letter was dated January 3, 1805. Eaton read the lines and smiled: "On this date I am leaving for Behara in order to go to the house of the Sheik el Arrrab called Abdelgaviv el Bekouchi, where I suggest that you go also." Eaton read further, seeing that Hamet agreed to his plan and was ready. "Thus you must assist from the sea and

I from the land, and God will aid us in establishing peace and tranquility."

Eaton hoped, instead, that Hamet would follow his instructions, set out in his messages, and rendezvous at the English house in Rosetta. Meanwhile, he and his entourage packed their bags and descended the Nile, heading for Rosetta where, hopefully, he would find Hamet.

Several days later, when Eaton arrived, he found, to his disappointment, that Hamet was making his way to Fiaume, which was just south of Alexandria, where he would await Eaton's arrival. Again, Eaton and his men packed their gear, thanked Major Misset and Captain Vincents for their assistance, and made their way back to Alexandria.

On January 22, Eaton, accompanied by Lieutenant Blake, Midshipman Mann, and an escort of twenty-three men, left Alexandria, passing through the Turkish lines at the Cutt, the narrow passageway between the Bay of Aboukir and Lake Mareotis. They had headed southwest toward their rendezvous with Hamet. Now, some seventy-five miles from Alexandria, they had reached a town called Damanhur. As they entered the town, Eaton saw the Turkish flag fluttering and spied troops. Several of them walked toward the Americans and ordered them to halt and climb down from their horses. Eaton did as he was told and was taken to the commander. He was led into a tent, where he was introduced to the Kerchief of Damanhur. The man glanced up from his writing desk and told Eaton he would not let him pass through his lines.

Eaton explained that he was trying to rendezvous with Hamet Karamanli, the rightful Bashaw of Tripoli. He also told the man that he had met with the viceroy, who had approved of this meeting and had assisted him in finding Hamet. Eaton showed him the viceroy's letter. The Kerchief scanned it briefly, then handed it back. He stood and shouted at Eaton, telling him that Hamet was an enemy of the Turks, and had, until recently, been with the Mamelukes in Minyeh. Furthermore, he told Eaton, the French had denounced the

Americans as spies of the British, hostile to Turkish interests. Eaton began to speak, but the Kerchief was unmoved, and ordered his men to take Eaton away.

Eaton found himself in a small, filthy cell inside a Turkish prison. The stench was terrible, and he saw vermin and rodents in the darkness, scurrying among the debris that cluttered the floor of his cell. Eaton called out to the guards, in Arabic, and asked that they take him back to the Kerchief.

Hours later, Eaton was taken from the cell and brought back to the Kerchief's tent. Eaton was shown to a seat. The general was a fierce man, as Eaton had already witnessed. He was also arrogant and proud, and naturally suspicious of twenty-six armed Americans. Eaton decided to take a different approach. He complimented the man on the correctness of his vigilance and conduct. He certainly would have conducted himself in the same manner if an armed party of Turks were roaming through the United States. But Eaton then told the Kerchief that his mission was not against the Turks, but was humane and in the Turks' best interest. He related his meeting with the viceroy, again displayed the letter he had received from him, and told the Kerchief that he was removing an enemy of the Turks, who had only become one, briefly, because he had been driven from his throne and was now destitute.

The Kerchief listened and ordered a meal brought to the tent. The two men ate and Eaton told the Turk that of course he was charged with tendering the man a small sum in recognition of his assistance in their cause, and added that in case he had reservations about letting Eaton and his men pass, perhaps a messenger could be sent to Fiaume to bring Hamet to Damanhur. The Turk eyed the English pistols that hung from Eaton's belt. Eaton divined the general's wishes, unbuckled the pistols, and handed them to him.

The general was moved, and called out to the guards, who returned a little while later with an Arab dressed in a flowing robe. The man was the chief of a tribe who, the man explained, had been driven from Tripoli since Yusuf took the throne. The Kerchief told the man what Eaton had related to him, and asked if he could provide an account of Hamet.

The young man smiled and said he knew everything. Eaton asked him to explain and the man said that twenty thousand men were ready to march with Hamet to recover his country and his inheritance, and that he would personally find Hamet and bring him here within a fortnight. The Kerchief agreed, and instructed the man to take one of his men, find Hamet, and bring him to Damanhur.

The next morning, the man set off. Meanwhile, Eaton dispatched most of his men back to Alexandria, to show the Kerchief that he did not need an armed escort, and that he trusted the Turks. Lieutenant Blake and Midshipman Mann, however, along with their servants, would remain. The Turks were cordial, but Eaton saw that while he no longer occupied a cell, he was not free to leave. The Arab chief may have dispelled some of the Turk's reservations, but the Kerchief was a military man, and would only free Eaton upon proof that his intentions were not hostile to Turkish interests. The Frenchman, Drovetti, would answer for this. First, he had shown contempt for the American flag when the *Argus* arrived in Alexandria. Then he had engaged in criminally hostile acts, by denouncing them as British spies. Eaton could not wait to meet the little Monsieur and call him out.

The Turks provided the American with a house in the village. The following day, the Turks erected a tent upon the terrace of the adjacent house. Eaton asked the Kerchief its purpose, and he explained that a contingent of guards was to be posted there. Armed guards also entered the house, and remained there, to prevent intruders, assured the chief of the Turkish contingent assigned to protect Eaton. And whenever Eaton walked from his house, guards accompanied him. To Eaton, it seemed ridiculous, but the Kerchief was now polite and civil, and Eaton would put up with a close watch on himself and his men so long as the ultimate goal, meeting Hamet, was realized. His servant, Selim, was given more freedom and returned one afternoon and told Eaton that two Frenchmen, dressed as Arabs, were in the Kerchief's suite. The French, it seemed, were everywhere.

The next day, a messenger arrived from Alexandria, bearing a letter from Hull. Eaton opened it and scanned the contents, feeling the anger rise as he read the lines. The French were attempting to thwart his every move. Hull wrote that the governor of Alexandria had sent for Mr. Briggs and told him that he had received a firman from the viceroy forbidding the Americans from recruiting in Alexandria. The French must have had a hand in this. Clearly the French and the governor of Alexandria were allied, for Eaton had received nothing but offense and trouble from that quarter. The viceroy had assisted him and aided him, but no doubt words had been twisted so that the viceroy had issued a firman forbidding recruitment. Hull had written that as a result, they had been compelled to give up the rendezvous house. Nevertheless, Eaton knew that Lietensdorfer and Farquhar would outfox the French. They would recruit, through third parties, and assemble an army, the French be damned. But he would have to be careful, for Hull wrote that there was alarm over the American actions. Clearly the Turks were nervous, and the French had made them even more so.

One evening, Eaton spied a small boy standing on the porch of the house. He gazed in, looking sad. Eaton asked him if he would like to come in. The boy refused. Eaton asked him what troubled him. The boy responded that this had been his father's house, and that he had been a rich man, one of the richest in the village. Four months ago, the Kerchief had cut off his father's head and taken the house and all of their property. Eaton was shocked to learn that he, his mother, and his four siblings lived a few houses away and had no bread, nor anything to eat. Eaton searched his pockets and gave the boy all the money he could find. The child began to cry. He took Eaton's hand and kissed it, then left. Eaton thanked God his children were American.

A thousand or so miles to the west, Captain William Bainbridge sat at his writing desk in the American consular house in Tripoli and began yet another letter to Tobias Lear. He had not heard from Lear since August and was desperate for news. He wrote some pleasantries and asked after the health of two of their mutual acquaintances, Monsieur Thainville and Consul Bille, then set down the pen and took up another one. This time, instead of an inkpot, he dipped the nib into a bowl of lemon juice and quickly wrote the substance of his message, in invisible ink, only discernible when held up to a strong light.

"I believe the Bashaw is desirous of peace, and was a negotiation attempted I think it probably would succeed, for the Bashaw apprehends a very severe attack; and the apprehension perhaps would have as great an effect as the attack itself."

Bainbridge tried to guess how much the Bashaw would demand for freeing him and his men. "I believe he would take at this moment much less than what he demanded of Com. Preble last August."

Bainbridge finished and sealed the letter, hoping that the Danish consul would safely deliver the message and that he would soon hear a reply from Lear. They had been prisoners now for more than a year. Peace through ransom was their only hope.

Four days after his escort had left for Alexandria, Eaton received word that Hamet and his entourage had arrived. Eaton stepped outside and saw a swirl of dust, which marked the arrival of the rightful Bashaw, and then watched as the dark, beetlelike figures on the horizon took shape. He waited expectantly as Hamet and his retinue of some forty men, accompanied by a twenty-man honor guard supplied by the Kerchief, entered the village, and made their way toward the pavilion where Eaton waited for them.

Hamet climbed down from his horse and Eaton made the customary greeting. He felt relief that after two and a half months, and years of planning, the objective of his mission had been met. Hamet was here, and he was ready to lead the army to Derna.

While Hamet's entourage and the Turkish officers enjoyed refreshments, a messenger arrived, bearing a letter for Eaton from the viceroy. Eaton read the letter, which contained word that the viceroy, unlike the governor of Alexandria, supported his plan and would allow him to take any Christians he recruited in Alexandria with him to Derna. It was now a matter of getting Hamet aboard the *Argus.* They had lost much time, but still, the weather was good, and based on fresh reports from Hull, neither Derna nor Benghazi had been reinforced as had previously been thought.

After the official welcome, Eaton sat down with Hamet and discussed their plan. Eaton wanted to bring Hamet to Alexandria, take him and his men aboard the *Argus,* and transport them to Derna. Hamet, however, was hesitant. If he were to embark on the *Argus,* he would have to leave many of his men behind to make their own way overland to Derna. Whether they did or not would trouble him, for he believed that many would give up hope and remain in Egypt. Eaton argued that Hamet should at least come to Alexandria to meet with Hull, and to this, Hamet agreed. He knew the French and the governor of Alexandria were in collusion and against him, viewing him as an enemy. But he had the viceroy's firman and pass of safe conduct, so on February 6, they set off for Alexandria, arriving at the English Cutt the following day.

As they approached the Turkish guards, Eaton handed over his papers. The guard examined them, then those of Hamet, which included the passage of safe conduct. The guard then handed them back and told Eaton and Hamet that the jurisdiction of the viceroy did not extend beyond the low-water mark, and placed them under arrest. They were also told that Hamet was forbidden to enter the city or embark from it.

Eaton fumed. Clearly the French consul had paid off these men, and was in league with the governor, who appeared ambitious and interested in promoting his own authority over that of the viceroy in Cairo. Eaton wasted no time in paying the required sums, the lubricant of all business in these parts, and gaining their freedom.

Afterward, Eaton made his way to the ship while Hamet returned to camp. The arrest had cemented Hamet's decision to attack by land. He had always felt that this approach was the wisest, since if he embarked many of his men would lose patience and abandon his standard. So Eaton went to tell Hull, and to bring the men they had surreptitiously recruited, while Hamet and his entourage journeyed to a place called Arab's tower, thirty miles west of the city, to wait for Eaton.

On board, Hull invited Eaton to his cabin, where Eaton told him of their arrest and release, then told Hull the news he had been waiting for since late November: He could depart. The army would march from Arab's tower in a fortnight. Eaton would lead the army across the desert to Bomba, a bay two days' march to the east of Derna, where they would rendezvous with the *Argus,* and then, replenished, attack Derna.

Eaton asked Hull to meet him in Bomba with supplies and provisions, including one hundred stand of arms and cartridges, two brass fieldpieces with train and sufficient ammunition, and one hundred marines. Eaton also requested two smaller vessels as well as a bomb ketch. Hull told Eaton he would relay his request to Barron, whom he planned on seeing at the United States' naval base in Syracuse when he replenished his ship.

Eaton spent several days aboard ship, preparing for the march. He saw to the final recruitment of the army, and wrote letters to the secretary of the navy and Commodore Barron. On February 12, a ketch arrived in harbor, and Eaton spied the flag of Tripoli flying at her masthead. Later on he learned from his spy, the secretary of the governor, that the ship had been sent by Yusuf with the sole purpose of prevailing on the governor and admiral to stop Hamet from leaving Egypt. The secretary told Eaton that Yusuf was confident he could repel the U.S. Navy with his batteries, but if Hamet was allowed to return, Yusuf feared he would have to leave the kingdom since his people would desert him; they were tired of war and would flock to Hamet's banner. Eaton was pleased to hear this, realizing that his plan, all along treated with disdain by the navy, was what Yusuf feared most. They were close to actually executing the plan and beginning the march; Eaton realized they would have to be careful until they left; the French consul and governor were trying to stop them at every turn.

Meanwhile, a firman finally arrived from Cairo allowing Hamet to enter the city. Instead, he sent his secretary of state, Mahumed, who would travel with Hull to Syracuse as Hamet's representative.

On February 20, at the head of a column of men, Eaton, flanked by Lieutenant O'Bannon, seven marines, and Midshipman Pascal Paoli Peck, spied the fluttering flags of the army and the dull, ochre-colored walls of Burj el Arab, or Arab's tower.

The tower was actually an old Roman or Ptolemaic fortress some three hundred feet square with walls thirty feet high and five feet thick. It served as an outpost and market center for the Western Desert Arabs. It was also the rallying point for Hamet's army. As the men entered the camp, Eaton saw that Hamet had been busy; the men were starting to take on the appearance of an army. Tents were set up in neat rows and the camp bustled with military efficiency. All was in readiness, and they would start as soon as one last, important piece of business was concluded.

On February 23, 1805, Eaton and Hamet signed a fourteen-article convention between Tripoli and the United States witnessed by Lieutenant O'Bannon, Dr. Francesco Mendrici, and Midshipman Peck. There was also a secret clause that outlined the real purpose of the mission, which Eaton reread before signing:

His Highness Hamet Bashaw will use his utmost exertions to cause to surrender to the Commander in chief of the American Forces in the Mediterranean, the Usurper Joseph Bashaw along with his family and Chief Admiral called Mamad [Murad] Rais, alias Peter Lisle, to be held by the Government of the United

States as hostages, and as a guarantee of the faithful observance of the stipulations entered into by convention 23rd February, 1805 . . .

It was now up to Eaton and Hamet to lead their men across five hundred miles of desert and storm Derna, and bring to an end the rule of Yusuf.

X

ACROSS THE DESERT

Eaton sat on his horse, scimitar strapped to his side, a cocked hat securely on his head to ward off the harsh rays of the sun. It was March 6, 1805. From this vantage point, Eaton surveyed his army. Arrayed on the dusty ground before him were the fruits of three months of labor: a small, mobile army that would march five hundred miles across the Western Desert and storm the pirate fortress of Derna, then take Benghazi, and ultimately, Tripoli, more than a thousand miles distant from this sandy patch of earth.

The men standing at attention before him were the nucleus of the force that would gather to the banner of Hamet Karamanli as they marched west. Among their party were many sheiks of the Western Desert who promised that their tribes would join Hamet en route. The men, some on foot, others on horseback, were strangely quiet apart from the clink of weapons, the creak of saddles, or the neigh of horses. They were waiting for his orders.

Eaton examined the force arrayed before him. Standing beside him was his chief of staff, Colonel Jean Eugene Lietensdorfer, and Hamet Karamanli and his staff. Before them, standing ramrod straight, was his headquarters guard: Lieutenant O'Bannon, Midshipman Peck, a marine sergeant, and six marines. Ten Americans, including himself, would lead the force. Eaton cast an eye toward O'Bannon and was glad to have him on his side. The man was steady, fearless, and loyal. He would not let him down.

Next, Eaton viewed the company of Greeks he had recruited in Alexandria. The forty well-trained soldiers were led by Captain Luco Ulovix and Lieutenant Constantine. There was also a company of cannoniers, commanded by Selim Comb, his janissary and translator, and Lieutenants Connant and Rocco. They had one field gun, and numbered twenty-five men.

Then there was Hamet's personal escort, about ninety men, followed by a troop of sixty Arab cavalry commanded by Sheik Mahomet and Sheik il Taiib. Finally, there were approximately four hundred Arab foot soldiers. A transport group containing one hundred and ninety camels as well as some horses and donkeys, along with their handlers, would carry provisions for the long march.

The army was a seasoned force. Most of the men were veterans of European wars. Many were mercenaries, guns for hire. But all, Eaton found, had joined because they were seeking adventure. And he aimed to see that they got it, for there were easier ways to make a living than marching across five hundred miles of forsaken desert to attack a small town in the backwaters of North Africa. Yet Eaton knew that what drove men like Connant and Ulovix, Leitensdorfer and Comb, was the craving to do something no man had done before, and to do so in the company of men like themselves. And if they succeeded, history would one day reflect their contribution, long after their footsteps in the sand had been obscured by the wind.

Eaton glanced to the west, where Derna lay somewhere beyond the scrub, sand, rocks, and desert. There was, after all, no map, no guide, apart from Eaton's knowledge that Derna was there, over the horizon, and the local knowledge of the men in the army who hailed from this desert. Eaton reflected, momentarily, on what they had had to go through to get to this place. He had searched for Hamet for two and a half months and then, just as they were ready to leave, their departure was delayed after learning that the quartermaster had embezzled the money Eaton had entrusted to him to purchase provisions. Eaton had summarily discharged him and had scrambled to find money to purchase food and provisions for the long march to Derna.

They had also been delayed because Eaton had had to negotiate the use of the camels, which were vital to transport
the army's provisions and equipment. Sheik il Taiib had
agreed to a sum of $11 per camel for the entire journey, from
Burj el Arab to Derna, but after settling on this price, continued to raise fresh demands for more money. The sheik had
threatened to delay the march, but Eaton had overcome his
objections. How true was Hamet's first letter, in which he
had written at the start of this adventure: "Friend, you must
have courage; do not think about money because the occasion demands heavy expenditure. It is a matter of making
war, and war calls for money and men." Eaton knew that, but
increasingly he had come to understand that for Hamet it was
mostly about money. Eaton would have to watch the pack of
them.

With a signal from Eaton, the army began to move, a bray-
ing, creaking crowd of men and animals stirring up a dust
cloud that could be seen for miles. Eaton intended to follow
the coast, where possible, but cut across peninsulas and out-
crops and journey inland when they were able to shorten
their route. They would first march for Bomba, a bay two
days' march east of Derna, where they would meet up with
supply ships that would replenish their provisions and offload the artillery needed to take Derna. Eaton hoped the
ships would also carry the one hundred additional marines
he had requested of Barron.

With each step the sun climbed higher into the sky, baking
the land. The army made good progress, and by evening,
Midshipman Peck estimated that they had traveled some
forty miles. That night they camped near a well. As the
camels were unloaded and tents set up, Peck looked into the
well and saw that it appeared to be dry. And in the last six
hours, no water had been available. Eaton ordered men to
clear the well, but many were too tired or too thirsty to comply. Peck was exhausted, unused to marching after so many
months at sea. And he had also failed to bring a skin of water,
though he was thankful that he had at least brought some oranges to slacken his thirst. As the sun set, Peck laid down and

tried to sleep, but, almost dead from lack of water, he lay there and thought how if he was rich he would give a vast sum of money for a gill of water. Dreaming of water, he fell into a deep, bone-tired sleep.

Meanwhile, in his tent, Eaton read a packet of letters sent by express from Briggs Brothers in Alexandria. How could he ever hope to repay the kindness of these gentlemen? He read their letter, in which they wrote that Dr. Mendrici had proposed hiring a small vessel to be sent to Bomba loaded with provisions. The vessel would be used to resupply the army before its final push on Derna, and also to gather intelligence. Briggs wrote that since food was scarce in Alexandria, the boat would sail for Syracuse, then on to Bomba. Briggs would supply the money necessary to purchase the ship and the supplies.

Eaton also learned that the French consul was watching Eaton's movements and sending word to Yusuf that Eaton, at the head of an army of five hundred, had marched for Derna. Eaton smiled. He would have to thank Drovetti. The information he sent would trouble the Bashaw since it was coming from a credible source and would let Yusuf know that a coalition of his enemies had entered his dominion. Once word got out, it would cause problems for Yusuf, and the people of Tripoli would grow agitated. Let the Frenchman report on his army, Eaton thought. In this instance, it served America's purpose. Eaton wrote back to Briggs, indicating his approval of Mendrici's proposal, and adding a list of food and provisions to bring to Bomba. Then, putting away paper and pen, he, too, fell asleep.

The next morning, Eaton examined the well, which they had cleared the night before, and saw to his happiness that it contained water. There was a small amount now for each man. Peck was too thirsty to worry about the stench of the water, which smelled worse than bilge water. He took a hearty sip; the liquid was more delicious than any cordial he had ever sipped.

Over the next few days, the army made halting progress, less than Eaton wished, but progress nevertheless. On Sun-

day, March 10, however, as the army began the march, Eaton
saw that the camel drivers and footmen who brought up the
rear were standing still. Eaton asked why they were not
marching and found that Sheik il Taiib had told them that if
they were not paid in advance by the Christians they would
be taken advantage of. Eaton turned to Hamet for assistance,
but he was irresolute and despondent. Money, thought
Eaton, was the only thing these Arabs cared for. As the sun
climbed into the sky and the day wore on, Eaton tried to reason with the sheik, stating that he had paid $11 per head for
the camels and that there was no more money.

The sheik was unmoved, so finally, Eaton ordered the
Christian half of the force to march. He told Hamet and the
sheik that they would march alone, if need be, and abandon
the Arabs to their fate. Eaton turned his back on them and set
off. A little while later he looked back, and saw the camel
drivers and Arabs moving forward, following them. The
mutiny had been suppressed.

Over the course of the next three days, the army passed
through low, sandy valleys and rocky plains. On Wednesday,
March 13, at two p.m., Eaton saw a lone horseman riding
toward them. When he came within hailing distance, he asked
for Hamet Karamanli and handed him a dispatch. Hamet
read the message, then told Eaton and his men that word of
their march was spreading and Yusuf's regime was crum-
bling; the province containing Derna was ready to receive
him, and the governor was now shut up in his castle.

Upon receiving this news, Hamet's entourage began to
shoot their guns into the air in celebration, while some raced
their horses back and forth. Eaton watched in amusement.
Suddenly, Eaton heard gunfire to the rear, among the Arab
footmen who were with the baggage and pack animals.
Eaton turned in his saddle and saw that the Arabs were attacking the Christians among the baggage. What was going
on? Why had a celebration among Hamet's men turned into
a battle between Christians and Muslims?

Eaton sent riders to investigate and soon learned what had
happened: The Arab footmen had thought the Christians in

the caravan were being attacked by a desert raiding party, so they had attacked the Christians nearest them. No one had been hurt, since one of the more prominent Arabs who was with the footmen had stopped the firing until the reason for the gunshot had been made clear. This was alarming news to Eaton, and indicated the fragile nature of the alliance, which rested, it appeared, on loyalty to Hamet and money, although Eaton feared the latter held these men together more than the former. He would have to be careful; they were now seventeen days from Burj el Arab and the small party of Christians could only count on themselves for defense.

On March 18 they reached a castle called Massouah, which was situated on a flat plain surrounded on three sides by stony desert and on one side by massive white sand dunes. A roughly hewn eleven-foot-high wall, cut with loopholes, surrounded the castle, which was approximately one hundred feet square. As the army made its way toward the fort, Eaton spied the vestiges of former civilizations: gardens, the foundations of houses, and other buildings. The castle, it appeared, was a trading center, like Arab's tower. As the army settled down for the evening, Eaton learned that produce was brought here from outlying regions. He desperately wanted to buy some of the cattle, sheep, goats, fowls, butter, dates, and milk offered for sale, but learned that the prices were high and, furthermore, he had little remaining cash. Instead, Eaton settled down to a meal of rice and bread. He would have to husband the cash for emergencies, one of which might very soon be lack of provisions, since the army's progress had been slower than anticipated. Eaton reckoned they were only about a third of the way to Derna and already they were reduced to rice and bread.

Suddenly, Eaton heard a commotion outside. A moment later, the tent flap opened and Lietensdorfer stepped inside. There was trouble in the Arab camp, he told him. Eaton strapped on his scimitar, secured his hat firmly on his head, and strode over to Hamet's tent, where he found Sheik il Taiib speaking with Hamet. Eaton saw that the men were engaged in a heated discussion, and soon learned why: Many

of the camels carrying the army's provisions had only been
partially unloaded and some not at all. Eaton asked Hamet
and Sheik il Taiib why they were not settling down for the
night. The sheik told Eaton that Hamet had only paid him to
take the army to this place. If they wished to continue farther, Eaton would have to pay more. Eaton was incredulous.
He had paid to freight the camels to Derna; now the sheik
told him that he had merely paid for a third of the journey.

Eaton tried to persuade them to continue. Many of the
men, the sheik told Eaton, were worried about their families
in Behara and wished to return. Eaton promised them that if
they marched two more days, then they could return home.
In two days, Eaton expected to find Arab tribes and hire another caravan. Sheik il Taiib agreed, provided they were paid.
Eaton fumed and rode off, taking up a collection from his
men and presenting the results to Hamet, some $673. He had
to borrow $140 from his men to supplement what was in his
treasury, but they had found the money to continue onward
for two more days. Eaton was angry but had little recourse.
He understood what had happened: Hamet had skimmed off
funds that were due the sheik. But Eaton could not call him
out. Eaton went to sleep believing he had bought himself two
days' respite.

The following morning, Eaton awoke and found that all
but forty of the camel drivers had left for Egypt the previous
evening. Eaton was enraged, and Hamet was apologetic and
proposed leaving the expedition's gear and remaining provisions in the castle, and marching two days to the camp of
Arabs, where Eaton expected to find a new caravan. Eaton
shook his head; that was too risky he told Hamet. The army
could not separate from its provisions. To do so might cause
their downfall. But what other option did they have? The
forty remaining drivers would not move, and without them,
neither could the army.

As the day drifted toward evening, Eaton struggled to deal
with the crisis. As night fell, Hamet and the Arab chiefs repaired to their tent. Eaton was not invited. Instead, he waited
until late at night, when a messenger arrived at his tent and

asked him to come to Hamet's tent. Eaton strode over, with his aides, and entered the tent, where he found Hamet and his chiefs. They told him that Hamet had received a report from a Moroccan pilgrim on his way to Mecca who had passed through Benghazi and Derna. The pilgrim had seen an army leaving Tripoli bound for Derna. He estimated that it contained at least eight hundred cavalry and many footmen. The sheiks and Hamet told Eaton they would go no farther until they had assurances from him that the American ships had arrived at Bomba. Only then would they march.

Eaton tried to persuade them that reports of an army marching on Derna should suggest to them an acceleration of the march rather than delay. Eaton was asked to leave the tent while they debated among themselves. Standing outside, the stars bright overhead, the dusty smell of the desert mingled with the salty tang of sea air, he wondered if all his planning would end here.

A short while later, the tent flap opened and he was beckoned inside, where he learned that they had agreed to remain here while a runner journeyed to Bomba. Only when he returned with news that the American vessels had arrived would they continue the march. Eaton was furious and told them that their rations were stopped until they marched, then stormed out of the tent. It was midnight; Eaton thought about taking the Christians and securing themselves in the fortress against attack from the Arabs should they try and take their rations by force, but soon abandoned the idea. Eaton was frustrated; they had journeyed two hundred miles, less than half the distance to Derna. Tomorrow would determine the fate of the expedition.

Eaton awoke on the morning of March 20 expecting the worst. He quickly dressed and walked to the Arab encampment. To his surprise, he saw at least fifty camels being readied for a march. They must have been prevailed upon to return during the night. By eleven a.m. they set off. The expedition would live another day. However, the wrangling and dissension had cost them two precious days.

* * *

Commodore Barron read through the dispatches brought to him by Isaac Hull. He cursed the infirmity that kept him ashore, in this house he had rented in Malta. However, he read with particular interest Eaton's letters describing how he had finally succeeded in finding Hamet, and his last letter, requesting additional ships, marines, and provisions to take Derna. Barron admired Eaton's energy and perseverance, and wished to assist in any way possible. He could provide Eaton with money and stores, and had directed Captain Hull to provide both. Hull would sail in the *Argus,* accompanied by the sloop *Hornet,* commanded by Lieutenant Samuel Evans. However, he could not spare the one hundred marines Eaton had requested. The squadron was already short of hands. Eaton would have to simply make do with the men he had.

While happy with Eaton's progress, Barron was alarmed by his promise to install Hamet on the throne. Eaton had no right to make such an agreement. While the United States might cooperate with the exiled Bashaw, that did not imply that he would be reinstated as regent. It was a means to an end; didn't Eaton realize that? His entire mission was just that. And it had worked: Tobias Lear was receiving messages from Captain Bainbridge, indicating that Yusuf had heard reports of the army's march on Derna. Through his minister, Sidi Mahomet Dghies, Yusuf was sending out peace feelers, indicating that the price of peace was somewhat lower than he had previously demanded. Eaton's march had already served its purpose in getting Yusuf to the peace table. If the price was right, didn't Eaton know that Jefferson would take it? And in doing so, he would withdraw his support for Hamet Karamanli. America had made her point, had fought the pirates and burnished American honor while training the officers of a growing navy and Marine Corps. But then, Eaton wouldn't understand that. The man was an idealist. Well, let him march. It served America's purpose, and if he could take Derna, so much the better.

Captain Bainbridge wondered why the Tripolitans were now interested in peace. Only six days ago, the Bashaw's

minister had sent for him and told him in confidence that the
Bashaw was eager to negotiate a peace treaty, and that he had
written to Commodore Barron requesting peace negotiations. The minister also asked Bainbridge to write a letter in
invisible ink to make the same request. Bainbridge gladly
took on the role of messenger and wrote the following to
Commodore Barron: "I have no doubt that if a Person was to
come here to negotiate before an attack was made that Peace
could be effected for one hundred & twenty thousand dollars."

Bainbridge knew that the Bashaw was worried. Dr. Cowdery had told him that the Bashaw's son-in-law had been sent
to recruit an army to protect Tripoli but had failed. No one
wished to fight for him since he had stripped the surrounding
countryside of money to fight the war. Then news arrived
that ten thousand men loyal to the Bashaw would muster on
the beach, where the Bashaw would deliver a speech. Days
passed, but the men never appeared. The Bashaw needed to
end the war before he was overthrown.

At three o'clock in the afternoon of March 22, Eaton
crested a rise and saw before him an extensive inclined plain
along the seashore; in the distance were the Arab encamp-
ments they had been marching toward these past two days. It
was there that Eaton hoped to hire camels to continue their
march. As they approached, he saw herds of camels, horses,
and cattle and flocks of sheep and goats. The Arabs watched
them intently as they approached; they were the first Christians to visit this place.

After Eaton had set up his tent, he wrote a letter to Captain
Hull and handed it to a messenger, who was instructed to return with word of the squadron's arrival. As the courier rode
off in a cloud of dust and a clatter of hooves, Eaton hoped
that Hull was there, waiting for him with cash and supplies.
If the messenger did not return with word of Hull's arrival,
he doubted he could keep the army together; the expedition
would certainly fail.

They remained in camp the next day, destitute of cash and

only able to buy a five-day supply of dates. Other items were offered—ostrich and young gazelles—but Eaton no longer possessed the funds to buy anything but subsistence rations. All they had was hard bread, rice, and dates. Fortunately, the camp was well watered, so the horses fed on grass. Eaton knew that until he received new funds, the expedition was in jeopardy. But there was some luck still left. While they had lost many of the baggage animals, the army's ranks began to swell with the arrival of fighters who professed their loyalty to Hamet. One day, eighty mounted Arabs arrived in their camp. When Hamet asked them to join him, however, they requested payment, and Eaton had to shake his head. No money was available. Eaton realized how naive he had been; he had thought Hamet and his vanguard would march for honor. But instead he learned that while Arabs made a great display of their religion, their true deity was cash.

Fortunately the Arabs here were desperate for money, and agreed to hire ninety camels for $11 per head to take the army to Bomba. And some of them, too, were induced to join the army. Forty-seven tents of Arabs—men, women, children, and one hundred and fifty warriors—joined the army. They joined for Hamet, and for plunder. Eaton accepted them, and began to feel that perhaps the expedition would reach Derna after all.

On the following morning, as the army was preparing to march, a messenger rode into camp. The courier found Hamet and told him that he had ridden from Derna, where five hundred of Yusuf's cavalry, along with many footmen, were a few days' march from that place. They had been sent to reinforce the town against attack. As the news brought by the messenger spread, Eaton saw fear and alarm grip the Arabs. He noticed that Hamet seemed to waver in his resolve, while once again the camel drivers, led by Sheik il Taiib, saddled up their beasts in readiness to march back to Egypt. Eaton realized that he had to do something to stop this insurrection and ordered all rations for the departing Arabs stopped unless they marched west, toward Derna.

Hamet called a council with his sheiks while Eaton

waited. Finally, at eleven a.m., he heard that Sheik il Taiib had once again resolved to go no farther until he received proof that American vessels were at Bomba. Eaton was furious and confronted the sheik, telling him that he lacked both courage and fidelity. All along, he had made promises, but had not fulfilled them. Furthermore, Eaton told him, he would be glad if the sheik finally left for good. It would put an end to the threats, provided that he took himself and his men, and did not try to get the other sheiks to go with him. The sheik was enraged, and told Eaton that he would leave that instant, and that he was finished with the expedition. He swore revenge against Hamet and his Christian sovereigns.

As he strode off, his robes flowing behind him like the wake of a ship, Eaton hoped that this time the troublesome sheik would carry his plans to conclusion. The man had been trouble since the first day. Eaton would rather have a small, loyal army than a larger army that, upon every vicissitude, threatened to halt and wait for money, or the certainty of American ships waiting at Bomba.

As the sheik and his men moved off, stirring a cloud of dust as they headed east, a messenger arrived with a note from Hamet. Eaton tore open the letter and read the contents: Hamet asked Eaton to send an officer to the sheik and, in his name, request his return. He also wrote that he feared that if Eaton did not do so, the sheik would use his influence against them. Eaton took up pen and paper and scribbled a note to Hamet, folded it, and placed it in the hands of the courier.

He had written that he would never ask the sheik for something that he considered a right. He had paid for the sheik's services, and the sheik had pledged to fulfill them. Eaton would not ask him to return; he demanded it. He would be damned if the sheik dictated terms and measures by threats and countermarches. Eaton preferred an open enemy to a treacherous friend, and if the sheik chose to ally himself against Eaton, then Eaton had a rifle and saber that he would use to punish the sheik.

The following morning, Eaton again ordered the army to

march, and this time they were under way by seven-thirty, the first march in four days. Two and a half hours later, a messenger appeared from the east, bearing news from the sheik. The message stated that he and his men had begun their march to Behara. Eaton sent a note back to the sheik, stating that if he had chosen to return to Egypt, Eaton would be forced to take measures to recover the property and cash the sheik had taken from the army. The army continued forward as the messenger left to deliver Eaton's reply.

Two hours later, the messenger returned with another note from the sheik. Eaton tore open the envelope and read the lines: "The Sheik il Taiib will join if the camp halt seasonably." Eaton asked Hamet if he wished to halt and Hamet agreed, so by half past noon, after gaining only five miles, the army halted. An hour and a half later, the sheik and his entourage arrived and the sheik appeared at Eaton's tent. "You see the influence I have among these people!" he shouted. Eaton responded that he did, and also saw the disgraceful use he made of it.

As Eaton had feared, the return of the sheik was no blessing. On the following morning, as the army prepared to march, the poisonous influence of the sheik was evident. Eaton saw that Hamet was again reluctant to continue and proved this by asking for the horses he had lent Eaton's officers. Eaton instructed the men to ready for march, and as they waited for the order to advance, Hamet stood off to one side with his men. Eaton strode toward him and asked him if he would march. Hamet wavered, and Eaton ordered the army forward, with the baggage in the lead. As they moved out, Hamet and his men remained.

Two hours later, as they moved across rocky plains toward Bomba, Hamet and his men appeared and joined the march. However, when they camped that night, having gained only twelve and a half miles, Eaton found that the Arabs who had joined them on the twenty-fifth had left, discouraged and dissuaded by the sheik. Hamet sent an officer, Hamet Gurgies, and several men to try and persuade them to return.

That night the army camped beside another ruined castle

and remained there the following day, waiting for Hamet
Gurgies to return. The castle was of similar dimensions to
the one at Massouah, with rough stone walls ten feet high. It
was a castle, but also, like the castles he had seen along the
way, a trading station between tribes from the interior and
those from the coast. Cattle, sheep, butter, eggs, fowl, and
dates were available, but all Eaton and his men had to pay for
these goods was rice, which they bartered for some of the
produce.

As Eaton waited, he surveyed the landscape, a vast plain
on which stood the castle surrounded by several small, en-
closed gardens containing figs and palm trees. It would be a
productive place were it not for war, which had ravaged the
area. Eaton spied an Arab horseman leave the castle and approach him. The man asked if he would like to see the inside
of the castle, a mark of distinction, Eaton realized, from the
sheik who lived there. Eaton gratefully accepted and as he
entered, all the people of the tribe stood and watched. Once
inside, they examined the lace of his hat, and his epaulettes,
buttons, spurs, and weapons. They thought all of this was either gold or silver and told Eaton's interpreter that they could
not believe that God would provide such riches to a man who
followed the religion of the devil.

After finishing his visit, Eaton spied a cloud of dust to the
east, which turned out to be Hamet Gurgies at the head of
the column of Arabs. Eaton decided that when they marched
the following morning, he would place the baggage in the
caravan with the Christians to prevent the sheik from recall-
ing the camel caravan. An additional reason for this precau-
tion was that the camels carried the army's provisions, and
Eaton had made it plain that any Arab who wished to march
for Egypt would receive no rations. Only those men who accompanied the army would be fed.

They set off at six a.m. It was now March 30, and they had
been marching for three and a half weeks. They desperately
needed to reach Bomba and replenish their supplies, but the
Arabs were so irresolute in their allegiance that every step of
the way was made begrudgingly and only with persuasion

and the threat of stopped rations. As the Christians and baggage moved off, Eaton saw that Sheik Mahomet and Sheik il Taiib were arguing while the Arabs stood still, awaiting the outcome. Eaton ordered the army forward; he could not wait any longer for these men. The Christians and the baggage made good progress, and by two p.m. Eaton estimated that they had traveled fifteen miles when Hamet and twelve horsemen appeared.

Hamet told Eaton that he had given Sheik il Taiib $1,500 to distribute evenly between the two men, but the sheik had only given Sheik Mahomet part of the money. Mahomet and his men had left for Egypt; Hamet had sent Hamet Gurgies to bring them back. Hamet told Eaton that the expedition could not hope to succeed without those two sheiks, who held influence over the tribes near Derna. He asked Eaton to wait. Eaton agreed. However, since the nearest water was three miles behind them, Eaton ordered a countermarch and reached the water hole at five p.m. While the army set up camp, Hamet, an escort of twelve men, and Eaton's interpreter, returned to the castle to try and bring the sheiks back into the fold.

Sitting in his tent, Eaton was furious. The journey from Alexandria had been a series of continual problems. The Arabs had stolen from the Christians; they had made promises and not kept them; and they had threatened to leave numerous times. Eaton had expected that patriotism and honor would guide them, but instead, only money, avarice, and threats to cut off rations kept the army moving forward.

Early the next morning, Sheik il Taiib and five sheiks came to Eaton's tent. Hamet Gurgies had still not returned. Sheik il Taiib climbed down from his horse, strode up to Eaton, flanked by the sheiks, and demanded that Eaton increase the rations. Eaton refused and the sheik grew angry. Eaton told him that he was the cause of all of their delays. They had been marching for almost four weeks, and had only come half the distance. Originally the sheik had promised to bring Eaton to Bomba in fourteen days. Instead, he had thwarted their progress at every step of the way.

The sheik cautioned Eaton again on the subject of rations, telling him there would be a mutiny if they were not increased. He shouted that he could not live only on rice; he required bread as well.

Eaton stood firmly before the six men and asked the sheik if he intended to compel the measure.

The sheik replied, "Remember, you are in a desert, and a country not your own. I am a greater man here than either you or the Bashaw."

"I have found you at the head of every commotion that has happened since we left Alexandria," replied Eaton. "You are the instigator of the present among the chiefs. Leave my tent! But mark, if I find a mutiny in camp during the absence of the Bashaw, I will put you to instant death as the fomenter of it."

While the sheik rode off, Eaton asked Hamet's Hasnadar, or treasurer, to come to his tent and told him of the sheik's demand. Eaton asked him to keep the other sheiks in line, at least until Hamet's return.

Morning passed with no word of Hamet. Eaton watched the eastern horizon, hoping for a telltale dust plume that would announce his arrival. Instead, at two p.m., the sheik returned and entered the tent of Eaton's officers. After he had left, Midshipman Peck reported on their conversation. The sheik had told him and Mr. Farquhar, the former quartermaster's younger brother, that he regretted that he had lost Eaton's confidence and believed it was because his enemies had altered Eaton's opinion of him. He told Midshipman Peck and Mr. Farquhar that he was devoted to Eaton and would follow Eaton even over Hamet, and asked them to assist with a reconciliation.

At five o'clock, the sheik returned to Eaton's tent, and his tone was one of apology. He wished to reconcile their differences and told Eaton he supported him, and hoped there would be some opportunity to show Eaton that he was a man.

Eaton told the sheik that if he did not cause any more trouble, and swore an oath of fidelity to Hamet, that was enough.

The sheik agreed, swearing an oath and offering Eaton his hand.

The next day, the army continued on, a fragile peace holding them together. And even while disputes raged, the army increased in size. Eaton estimated that he now had between six hundred and seven hundred fighting men, and twelve hundred in all, including women and children. If only they could reach Bomba and the resupply vessels were there as promised, Eaton was confident he could take Derna. But the real difficulty lay in reaching Bomba. It was now April 5. Rations were low, and they were camped beside another ancient castle. As they pitched their tents, Eaton examined the site. The one-hundred-and-eighty-foot-square castle was made of stone with walls five feet thick and eighteen feet high. The surrounding landscape was barren desert, sprinkled with ruins. To the west Eaton spied a high mountain that extended southeast as far as the eye could see. The guides estimated that they were now a hundred and fifty miles from Derna. If they made good time, the rations might just hold.

The following day their route took them over the mountain and down its western slope. Water was hard to find, and so on the morning of the eighth, after marching three hours, Eaton called for a halt beside a cistern excavated in the rock at the bottom of a deep ravine. The cistern was brimming with pure rainwater and was the first good water the army had found in many days.

While each soldier took his turn at the basin, Eaton took a small party off on a reconnaissance of the coast, which lay a short distance away. A little while later, he returned and saw that tents had been pitched and the camels unloaded. Eaton strode toward Hamet's tent and demanded to know who had ordered the army to make camp. Hamet replied that he had; his army was tired and they needed a day of rest.

Eaton spied a man readying a horse and asked Hamet why, if they were camping, was he getting ready to ride? He responded that the man was a courier that he was sending to Bomba, to learn if the American vessels had arrived. Eaton understood immediately; Hamet, as a result of the conniving

Sheik il Taiib, had ordered the army to remain here until the messenger returned with news from Bomba.

Eaton was enraged and demanded to know if this was why Hamet had ordered a halt. The Bashaw murmured his assent. Eaton replied that the army had six days' ration of rice, no bread or meat or other rations. The circumstances urged speed, not repose. If Hamet preferred famine to fatigue, Eaton told him, then he was ordering their rations stopped. With that, Eaton returned to the Christian encampment.

Morning passed into afternoon; finally, at three p.m., Hamet ordered the tents struck and the baggage animals loaded, and Eaton learned that he had ordered the army to return to Fiaume. Eaton watched without emotion as the baggage animals set off for the west. As the Arab fighters formed up, however, Eaton sensed that something was wrong. Several of the Arabs carried weapons at the ready, and others were forming up not for a march but for an attack. Sensing that disaster was imminent, Eaton commanded to arms and the Christians formed a line in front of the magazine tent. If the Arabs wished to take the rations and weapons, they would have to use force.

For an hour, the Arabs and Christians faced off. Hamet called out to his men to withdraw and had them unpack and pitch his tent. Eaton breathed a sigh of relief, but decided not to disband until the threat was removed. Instead, he ordered his men to conduct their arms exercises, which they did every day. The Arabs grew alarmed and leapt back on their horses as one of them cried out: "The Christians are preparing to fire on us!"

The Arab horsemen, about two hundred in number, with Hamet at the head, suddenly charged toward the thin line of Christians. As the horses thundered toward them, Eaton was grateful that his men remained motionless and did not flee. Lieutenant O'Bannon and his marines stood with calm indifference as the Arabs swept toward them. Beside Eaton, Midshipman Peck and Mr. Farquhar stood their ground, and along the line, Selim Aga, captain of the cannoniers, and with his lieutenants and the Greek officers, did not waver. Only the doctor ran off.

At the very last moment, the Arabs pulled up and retired a small distance from the Christians. Several pointed toward Eaton and his officers and then Eaton heard the word he dreaded: "Fire."

"For God's sake, do not fire," shouted several of Hamet's officers. "The Christians are our friends."

One of the Arabs snapped a pistol and pointed it toward Mr. Farquhar. The gun misfired and Farquhar stood his ground, unmoved.

Eaton stepped forward, into the bare ground between the Christians and Arabs, and walked slowly, deliberately toward Hamet, who held his horse steady while his men fingered their muskets and scimitars. Eaton approached Hamet and cautioned him against pursuing this desperate act. The Arab soldiers leveled their muskets at Eaton's breast. They began to shout and Hamet turned away, distracted by a commotion in the ranks. Eaton shouted to be heard; the situation would soon become unmanageable unless he reasserted command immediately.

Eaton waved his hand for attention and as he did so, some of Hamet's officers and several of the sheiks rode between Eaton and the Arabs and drove back the mutinous troops. Eaton turned to Hamet and reproached him. His Casnadar turned to him and asked if he was in his right mind. Hamet struck the man with his saber and Eaton sensed that a fight might yet break out; everyone's nerves were so taut, the least slight might spark a battle. Quickly, Eaton grabbed Hamet by his arm, led him away from the crowd, and asked him if he knew who his friends were and where his interests lay.

Hamet relaxed, calling Eaton his friend, and asked Eaton to follow him to his tent while he ordered his men to disperse. As they walked, Hamet told Eaton that if he would issue a ration of rice, the mutineers would quiet down. Eaton told him that he would do so under one condition: The next morning, at the beating of reveille, Hamet's men would march. Hamet agreed and Eaton ordered the ration distributed. The crisis was over.

The following morning, Hamet gave the order for his men to march and they did so, covering ten miles and camping at a cistern where they found two dead men floating in the water. They were most likely pilgrims murdered by Arabs. Since the cistern was the only available water, the men had no choice but to drink it.

The following day the army marched another ten miles, and at noon they camped in a valley between the two ranges of desert mountains. The basin contained good feed for the horses, and there was a water hole. Still, the men grumbled over half rations of rice and water. Eaton was growing worried; by this time they should have received word from Bomba. Had Hull been somehow detained? Had the war taken a different turn that had forced Barron to abandon him?

Eaton walked to Hamet's tent. Hamet asked him to take a seat and asked him if his aim was only to use him to extract a peace treaty from his brother. Christians had twice deceived him, he told Eaton, and the British had deceived Elfi Bey. Eaton told him that his intention was to install him on the throne as the rightful Bashaw. He had not wavered, and yet Hamet had at each turn. Eaton tried to convince him that their interests were aligned, but he could not make promises for Barron. He only knew that his own intentions were honorable: The defeat of Yusuf Bashaw and the return of Hamet were his goals. He had signed a charter stating this and, more important, he had given his word.

Hamet, however, still wavered. Eaton called a general council of war and learned that the sheiks and Hamet were concerned that without news of the arrival of the American ships, their men would mutiny or desert. Eaton realized that in spite of having only three days' rations, he could not push these men again by refusing them rations. The rations would run out soon enough, compelling them to move. Instead, he agreed with Hamet and the sheiks, stating that they would march two more days, then halt and wait for intelligence. To this the Arabs agreed; Eaton had bought some time, but was it enough and would it matter? If Hull had not arrived, the army was doomed.

Eaton retired to his tent. At seven p.m. an officer told him that his cannoniers were about to mutiny; they were forming up to march on his tent and ask for full rations. Eaton told his officer to suppress the mutiny gently, but if that did not work, to tell the mutineers that if they did not disband, they would be executed.

The officer left and Eaton waited. Would persuasion work or would the cannoniers come to take their rations? It hardly mattered; there was no more food to issue. They were at the end of their rope.

Half an hour later, Eaton heard the sound of horses' hooves; opening the flap to his tent, he spied a rider approaching from the west. It was the courier he had sent to Bomba. As the messenger entered camp, the Arabs began to shout, and amid the din Eaton learned that the courier had reached Bomba and had seen ships flying the Stars and Stripes. Eaton breathed a sigh of relief. They had survived.

XI

THE ASSAULT ON DERNA

The army arrived at Bomba on the afternoon of April 15. They had barely made it. Even propelled by the promise of supplies, the men had been so hungry and tired that they had struggled forward, and spent a good part of each day in search of wild roots and vegetables since they had run out of food. Some of the men found wild fennel and sorrel, which helped ease the burden of hunger, but most of the army had not eaten in three days. In the past twenty-five days they had not tasted meat; in the past fifteen days they had not eaten bread or rice.

As the bay came into view, Eaton saw only blue, shimmering water surrounded by dry, barren hills. There were no settlements, no water, and, more important, no ships. How could this be? Earlier in the day, Eaton had spoken to three Arabs who had seen two vessels several days ago. He had questioned them and determined that by their description, one of the vessels was the *Argus*. Had Hull given up on Eaton? After all, Eaton had told him they would arrive in two weeks. It was now the fortieth day of the march. But surely Hull would have sent runners into the desert to learn the fate of the army before leaving?

Upon sighting the empty bay, Hamet and the Arabs fell into despair, which was followed by angry murmurings. Eaton knew that if the ships had truly left them to their fate, the Arabs would surely turn on the Christians. As Eaton pitched his tent, he heard the shouts of "infidel" and "imposter." That night, the Arabs kept to themselves, and Eaton felt the army's discipline, which had kept it together for forty days, cracking. Hamet told Eaton that the Arabs would separate from the Christians on the morrow. Eaton replied that the best course of action would be to make for Derna, but Hamet thought it impossible. The army was dying of hunger, and did not possess the cannons needed to bombard the town and stiffen the Arabs' resolve.

As the two camps, Christian and Arab, settled down to a troubled night of sleep with empty stomachs and hearts full of angst, Eaton put his men on alert in case some of the Arabs tried something rash. He also lit a bonfire atop a high mountain to the rear of the camp and kept it going all night. If the *Argus* was out there, surely she would see the signal fire and return. Eaton prayed she would arrive in time.

But on the following morning, as the camps were being taken apart and the baggage packed, Eaton scanned the ocean and saw nothing, neither a ship nor a mast. They wearily packed their gear as the Arabs did likewise. And it was clear, this time, that the Arabs intended to leave the Christians to their fate. All unity of purpose was gone, and Eaton worried that the Arabs might attack them.

Suddenly, Eaton heard shouting from the rear and saw a man running down from the mountain. Fearing that an attack was already under way, Eaton braced himself for troubling news. A few minutes later Hamet's Casnadar stumbled into camp and told Eaton that he had hiked up to the lookout one last time and had seen a sail. Eaton took out his glass, fixed it on the blue ocean, and saw a puff of white towering above the familiar, trim lines of the *Argus*. Hull had not abandoned them after all.

For the next six days, the army rested and replenished itself. Stores and provisions were brought to shore from the *Argus* and the *Hornet*. Midshipman Peck was happy to rejoin his messmates aboard the *Argus,* recounting his adventure across the sands of Egypt. After dinner, standing against the rail of the ship as it rocked at anchor, he could hardly believe they had succeeded. They had marched through a desert where no Christians had ever set foot, where Arab thieves would shoot a man for his buttons, and where Christians were sworn enemies. There had been no houses or trees, and only one permanent settlement. Many times they had marched for twenty-four hours without water, and once for forty-seven hours. Their horses had fared worse, going three days without feed and with nothing for the past twenty days but the occasional green shoot or blade of grass. And yet somehow they had made it. It had been an extraordinary adventure.

Eaton, too, enjoyed a dinner aboard ship with Hull, and remained there the first night. The only troubling news he received was that the *Congress* had not yet arrived with field guns, which Eaton would need to take Derna. He had heard from travelers who had come from Derna that the town was occupied, and was defended by a battery and at least five hundred men. Eaton knew that field artillery could very well decide the outcome of the approaching battle. With a cannon he could neutralize the opposing battery, demoralize the enemy, and boost the morale of his own men. Given the troubles he had encountered thus far, he doubted the Arabs would attack without the backing of artillery. They needed every stiffening element he could find; the fieldpieces were essential.

Eaton discussed his concerns with Hull and requested that if the *Congress* did not arrive in time, could he instead rely on two brass fieldpieces from the *Argus*? Hull agreed and also arranged to use all of his ships, which also included the *Nautilus,* now sailing off Cape Razatin, to support Eaton's assault from the sea.

Eaton enjoyed his time aboard ship. He felt better now, rested and recovered from the ordeal in the desert. But it was time to finish the business and he decided that the army would march on the morrow. Before he left, Eaton wished to handle a personal matter. He told Hull that he was leaving several items onboard, in case he did not return, and would Hull kindly distribute them if that was the case? He left his cloak and small sword to Hull. In his chest, Hull would find the Damascus saber, which Hull should give to Commodore Barron. The chest also contained his gold watch and chain, which Eaton requested Hull give to Eli Danielson. Eaton asked Hull to deliver everything else to Charles Wadsworth, his executor. The two men shook hands, and Eaton clambered down the side of the ship into the waiting jolly boat, ready to take Derna.

For two days the army marched, refreshed and replenished. They picked their way over mountainous and broken ground across Cape Razatin, which lay between Bomba and Derna. The mountains were well watered, and covered with red cedars, the first forest Eaton had seen on this march. That night they camped in a green valley, cultivated with fields of barley. His scouts reported that they were a five-mile march from Derna.

As they approached the outskirts of the city, scouts reported disturbing news: The governor of Derna had fortified the town and was ready to defend it. Furthermore, Yusuf's army, led by Hassan Aga, which he had dispatched from Tripoli to reinforce Derna, was a day's forced march to the west and would probably arrive before them, especially since the *Argus, Nautilus,* and *Hornet* had been blown out to sea during the gales that had buffeted them these past two days.

Eaton watched as the sheiks and Hamet gathered in the Bashaw's tent. He was not invited. Would they push forward or use this news as an excuse to retreat? Eaton went to sleep. He would find out in the morning what Hamet intended to do.

At six in the morning, Eaton beat general quarters and gave the order to march. He watched carefully for any signs of dissent, and saw that while most of the Arabs were packing and making ready to march, the Bedouins refused to leave. Eaton also saw that Sheik il Taiib and Sheik Mahomet were at the head of the cavalry and were moving east, back toward Bomba. They were mutinying.

Eaton found Hamet and reproached him, but then offered a carrot. If the sheiks would continue and attack the town, Eaton would provide them with $2,000, which they could share among themselves. As usual, money boosted their confidence, and the mutiny was suppressed. The army moved forward, winding its way steadily uphill toward the summit of Jebel Akdar, which rose above Derna, driven now not by honor but by greed and desire. By two o'clock that afternoon, the army crested a rise, and before them lay the object of a march that had taken them across five hundred miles of desert in fifty-two days: The pirate fortress of Derna, easternmost outpost of Tripoli.

Eaton ordered the army to halt. As the men erected tents, he took out his telescope and surveyed the city. Derna was set back a mile from the sea on a bay. The city was well watered by the Wadi Derna, which rushed down the flanks of the mountain and through the town. Eaton squinted through the glass and saw a town of narrow, winding streets and lush gardens and orchards. Derna was the center of a coastal oasis; all around the town were fields that produced melons, grapes, figs, bananas, oranges, and groves of date palms.

Derna was pretty, but Eaton had his eye on capturing it, and turned from admiring the town to analyzing its defenses and how best to capture it. Eaton saw that the Wadi Derna divided the town. To the northwest were three districts: El Gebila, which was closest to the sea; El Bilad, where the governor's castle was located; and Mesreat. To the southeast was the Bu Mansur district.

Eaton closely examined the town and saw that to the northwest, the governor's defenses consisted of a line of temporary breastworks and the walls of old buildings, pierced by loopholes. To the southeast, the terraces and walls of the houses of Bu Mansur had been turned into a defensive position; loopholes showed the position of the governor's army. Eaton swept his glass over the governor's palace, which spies had informed him had a ten-inch howitzer mounted on the terrace.

He swept his glass toward the sea and saw the town's main defensive position. On the promontory of Raz el Matariz there stood a fortress guarding the seaward approaches to Derna. The stronghold housed eight nine-pound guns. These were relatively small guns against naval ships, but if the defenders could turn them on his small force, they would be both deadly and decisive.

Finally, he swept his glass across the flat blue-green of the Mediterranean looking for a mast or sail. But nothing was out there. Hull must have been blown well offshore by the recent gale. Eaton could not attack without him.

He closed the glass and began to plan the attack. Speed and assistance from the navy would be the deciding factors. If Hull could pin down as many of the defenders as possible with accurate naval fire, Eaton's men could move quickly and breach the first line of defense. If they did not pause and allow the defenders to regroup, they just might succeed in reaching the fortress before the guns could be turned on them. But could he count on Hamet and his men? Eaton would soon find out.

Later that evening, a number of sheiks came from the town to meet with Hamet. They assured Hamet of their loyalty toward him and promised that two of the city's three departments would follow his standard. However, the department that would side with the governor, Bu Mansur, was the most heavily defended, and contained his palace and the battery. They also cautioned Hamet, telling him that the governor had at least eight hundred men who would fight to defend the town. Furthermore, Hassan Aga's army was near at hand, which would strengthen the resolve of the governor, along with the fact that he had fortified the town against attack from both land and sea.

Eaton watched as the confidence drained from Hamet's face. The rightful Bashaw looked as though he wished he were back in Fiaume. Whatever task he was given in the fight, Eaton knew it would have to be one that was not critical to the success of the overall operations. He could not count on a man who had run so many times in the past two months. Eaton knew that if he succeeded, Hamet would follow. But he knew Hamet would not lead.

That night, Eaton sat in his tent and wrote a note to the governor of Derna, giving him one last chance to surrender the town.

Sir, I want no territory. With me is advancing the legitimate Sovereign of your country—Give us a passage through your city; and for the supplies of which we shall have need you shall receive fair compensation—Let no differences of religion induce us to shed the blood of harmless men who think little & know nothing.—If you are a man of liberal mind you will not balance on the propositions I offer.—Hamet Bashaw pledges himself to me that you shall be established in your government.—I shall see you tomorrow in a way of your choice.—

On the following morning, Eaton sent a party of men under a flag of truce to deliver his message to the governor. As the horses rode off, Eaton had men light a signal fire on the mountain; he wished to speak with Hull. He needed field artillery for the attack, which would begin tomorrow if the governor refused his offer.

As the bonfire crackled and smoke rose high into the sky, the riders returned from their meeting in town. The courier handed Eaton a note. He tore it open and saw that it was the same message he had sent to the governor. However, at the bottom, the governor had scrawled his reply: "My head or yours. Mustifa."

Eaton had not expected the governor to give up without a fight, especially since Hassan Aga's army was near at hand. Yet Mustifa's note decided it; they would have to attack tomorrow, before reinforcements arrived. Eaton walked back to his tent, stuffing the note into his pocket. There was much to be done in preparation for the attack.

Fortunately, Eaton's luck still held. At two p.m. an officer came to his tent and told him that a ship had appeared on the horizon. Four hours later, the ship, now close enough for Eaton to read her signals, indicated that she was the *Nautilus* and was carrying his fieldpieces. Furthermore, she signaled that the *Argus* and *Hornet* were in position and ready for Eaton's orders. The attack would commence on the morrow.

The morning of April 27 dawned bright and clear, with a favorable land breeze that would allow the ships to approach

Derna and support Eaton's attack. At five-thirty a lookout
spied the *Argus* and *Hornet* making their way toward the bay.
Seeing that all was ready, Eaton beat to quarters and ordered
the army to advance toward the city. To the staccato banging
of the drums, the men moved out. Eaton could not help
thinking of the Compte de Volney, a traveler and writer who
had described the camps of the Egyptian Beys as a rabble
rather than an army. At least the army was now a signifi-
cantly larger horde than had departed Egypt almost two
months earlier. Hamet now had two thousand Arabs marching with him.

Eaton turned his attention to the Christian contingent and
the small party of Arab foot soldiers who would assist them.
They were the core of the army, the group that would not falter, the men who he and O'Bannon would lead into battle.
Eaton watched as the eight marines, with O'Bannon at their
head, marched out, followed by Ulovic and Constantine at
the head of their company of Greeks, forty in all. Finally,
there were the twenty-eight cannoniers and their small fieldpiece, led by Selim Comb, Connant, and Rocco. These were
the men Eaton was counting on to take the town.

Eaton's plan was simple: offload the field artillery from
the *Nautilus* and use it to support the Christians' attack
against the governor's stronghold of Bu Mansur in the southeastern quarter of the town. The defense of this district was
being led by Muhammed el Layyas, a stanch loyalist. Eaton
would rely on the *Argus* and *Hornet* to suppress the battery
at Raz el Matariz and support their attack. Meanwhile,
Hamet and his men would sweep to the left, encircle the
town, and attack the two quarters that had sworn fealty to
him while also preventing Hassan Aga's army from reaching
the city. If they could prevent reinforcements and ensure that
the two departments switched sides, they would have accomplished their goal.

The army surged forward, past Eaton, and, as it flowed
down the flanks of the mountain, split into two groups, the
Arabs heading west, the Christians heading northeast. A
short time later, the Christians reached the coast just east of

town, and found that there was no safe or easy place to land
field artillery. Instead, the coast was rocky, with cliffs lining
the shore. Eaton peered out at the ocean and saw the *Nautilus*
riding at anchor, and her small boat pulling toward shore.

As her crew shipped their oars, the boat cut through the
surf and grounded on the beach. Eaton saw that it contained
one of the promised fieldpieces as well as a great deal of
powder and ammunition. Eaton and his men assisted the seamen in offloading the cannon, but the chief difficulty was in
moving the weapon off the beach. A rock cliff some twenty
feet high hemmed in the sandy crescent. After several hours
of work, they were finally able to get their equipment off the
beach by rigging a line up the cliff and hauling the gun and
ammunition up the precipice. Eaton watched as the sun
climbed higher into the sky. It had taken hours to offload one
gun. They could not afford to wait for the other. Eaton
thanked the naval officer and his men, and told him that he
would have to attack with just the one piece.

He also sent a note to Hull instructing him to anchor in position to fire on the battery and support his attack on the
southeastern quarter of town. Eaton watched as the officer
clambered back into the boat and the seamen pulled through
the surf heading out to sea, toward the waiting squadron.

As the boat departed, men hurriedly hauled the gun into
position to support their fire on the town, while others carried the ammunition, 200 bags of musket balls for use as
grape, 150 round shot, and 9 barrels of powder, as well as additional musket balls and lead. There was little time to spare.

Isaac Hull stood on the *Argus*'s quarterdeck and peered
through his telescope at the battery on Raz el Matariz that
guarded Derna's harbor. He counted eight embrasures, and
Eaton's spies had told him that the fortress mounted nine-
pound guns. They were approximately half a mile from shore
now; any minute, the fortress would open up on them. Hull
swept his glass to the left and saw the rest of the squadron,
moving in line abreast toward the shore. Closest to him was
the *Hornet,* commanded by Lieutenant Evans, while the

Nautilus, commanded by Lieutenant Dent, anchored the left end of the line.

As he watched, he saw the *Nautilus*'s anchors drop into the water, followed by those of the *Hornet.* Aboard the *Argus,* the sound of the anchor chain rattling through the hawsehole indicated that the *Argus,* too, was on station. Belowdeck, Hull heard the sharp orders of his gun captains followed by the screech of gun carriages as the cannons were run out. He peered over the railing down onto the main deck and saw his men prepare for action. The gun captains ordered their crews to load the guns. The powder boys distributed flannel bags containing powder to each of the spongers, who took the bags and rammed them down the muzzles. Using a priming iron thrust through the priming hole, the captain of the gun felt for the flannel bag. The cry of "home" echoed in rapid succession through the gun deck. Next, the sponger rammed a twenty-four-pound shot into the muzzle, followed by a wad, to keep the ball in place. Finished loading, each gun crew now hauled on the tackles, heaving to run out the gun. Meanwhile, the gun captain pricked the bag of powder with the priming iron, and then poured gunpowder from his powder horn into the firing pan. The guns were elevated using crowbars and handspikes to fire at the embrasures. And now they waited, the smell of slow matches burning in their tubs beside each gun, water used to swab the guns rocking gently in the buckets, mimicking the rolling swell of the harbor. The gun crews were ready, the gunner waiting for command to fire.

For a moment, the ship was still, almost quiet, and then the *Nautilus* began to fire into the town, followed by the *Hornet.* Suddenly there was a loud bang and the timbers of the *Argus* shuddered as her guns fired in rapid succession. Hull watched as the balls struck the fortress, sending stones and dust flying into the air. He also saw that his gunners were firing into the town, to keep the enemy pinned down to allow Eaton to advance.

Suddenly, Hull heard the whistle of shot and then saw great furrows carved into the waters nearby as the fortress returned fire. He marked the flash of the gun and then the whistle and fall of the shot as the three American warships dueled with the Tripolitan gunners. But the enemy only had eight guns, while he could bring almost three times that number to bear. The *Nautilus*'s broadside of five six-pound guns rippled and flashed, and the balls flew straight and true into the town, where troops were massing in defense of Eaton's advance. Meanwhile, Evans ordered a broadside of six guns to fire on the fortress, and stones and dust marked their impact. But it was the *Argus*'s twenty-four-pounders that had a damaging effect, as Hull watched them smash in embrasures and destroy the enemy battlements.

As the fire of cannons crackled and boomed across the bay, the army hurried forward and gained a height along the shore overlooking the town and the ravine carved by the Wadi Derna. Eaton peered through his telescope and saw that the defenders had thrown up a temporary parapet on the far side of the ravine. As the gun was moved into place on the height, Eaton ordered his men forward down the slope, across the ravine, and toward the parapet. They would have to move quickly, under cover of their single fieldpiece.

The men moved downhill as musket fire flashed from the parapet. From his position, Eaton could also see Hamet's progress. His cavalry had swung around to the south and seized an old castle that overlooked the town on the south-southwest. He could see riders fanning out to the south and west, tightening the ring around the town. If Hassan Aga's army arrived, they would now have to fight their way into town.

It had taken longer than expected to get the gun in place; it was now two p.m. and the fire on all sides was intense. Eaton and his men fired on the Arabs behind the parapet as the defenders fired back. Meanwhile, the fieldpiece boomed and balls struck the parapet, ripping apart the breastworks and flinging men backward like dolls.

* * *

Hull watched as one by one the guns of the battery fell silent. He could see the gunners leaving the fortress, running through the gardens behind the castle and into the town. Hull ordered his men to redirect their fire to support Eaton. Hull swung his glass over the battlefield and saw that although the American gunners were firing their single fieldpiece at the parapets that had been thrown up by the defenders, the Americans and their Christian allies were pinned down. The one gun was not providing enough covering fire, and the enemy at the parapets had just grown in number as the gunners from the fort swelled their ranks.

Suddenly, Hull saw Eaton's field gun fire and saw the rammer fly high into the sky. After that, the gun fell silent, useless without a means of ramming the cannon ball and powder down the barrel. Hull ordered his gunners to sweep the beach of enemy soldiers and aim for the parapets in the hope that he could pin down the Arabs long enough for Eaton to make his assault.

As the gunners from the fort swelled the enemy's ranks in front of them, the fire increased in intensity. All around him, Eaton saw that his men were close to panicking. Some of them were not disciplined soldiers, and try as their officers might, they kept glancing to the rear, where their fieldpiece had become silent. Any moment now, they would flee. If they did, the battle was lost, and the squadron could not continue its supporting fire much longer. Amid the crackle of muskets and the whistle of balls, Eaton conferred with O'Bannon.

After a brief council, both men realized that there was only one thing to do: charge. It was a last, desperate act, but it was their only choice. Eaton ordered the bugler to sound the charge, and as the thin, wailing notes mingled with the whistle and crack of musket balls, Eaton and O'Bannon led their men forward against a force more than ten times their number. Struggling through a hail of withering fire, some men stumbled and fell. Eaton and O'Bannon urged them on; moments later, they reached the ramparts. The defenders managed to fire one final volley, then broke and ran. As the marines and Christians surged through town, the enemy retreated, firing from behind low walls or palm trees, anything that afforded cover. But still Eaton and his men rushed forward. Suddenly, Eaton felt a blow. He dropped his rifle and saw blood welling from a hole in his left wrist.

Ahead of him, Eaton saw O'Bannon and his marines, accompanied by Midshipman Mann, the Greeks, and the cannoniers, now firing their own fieldpiece, surge forward through a shower of musket balls aimed from the loopholed walls of houses where the enemy kept up a stiff resistance. But O'Bannon and his men did not falter; they surged forward and entered the fortress.

Hull watched all of this and then smiled as the enemy flag was lowered, followed by the unfurling of an American flag on the wall of the battery. The fortress had been taken. Hull noted the time, three-thirty p.m., and ordered the small boats to shore to take ammunition to the fort and bring off any wounded.

Meanwhile, in the fortress, O'Bannon saw that the gunners had fled after loading and priming their guns. He quickly ordered his men to turn the guns on the town. From his vantage point, he saw that Hamet and his men had taken the other two departments, and that the remains of the governor's army were caught between Hamet's forces and the Christians. As soon as the guns were shifted into place, the cannoniers began to fire on the remaining loyalists, who were now caught between two fires. This was too much for the defenders. Fired on by the battery and the American warships, and pursued by Hamet's two thousand Arabs, they surrendered half an hour later. Derna was the Americans'.

After making arrangements to guard the town and ensuring that all was in order in the fort, Eaton finally came aboard the *Argus*. It was half past five when he entered the surgery to have his own wound dressed and to see his men, who had fought so valiantly. He asked the surgeon for the butcher's bill. One dead, he replied, and one mortally wounded. Who?

asked Eaton. The surgeon pointed to the corpse of marine private John Wilton, covered by a blanket. The still form of another marine by the name of David Thomas was lying nearby in a hammock. He had been gravely wounded during the assault on the fortress. The surgeon shook his head, indicating that the wound was mortal. Other wounded men, including another marine, lay recovering in their hammocks. In all, half of O'Bannon's small contingent had been wounded, as well as seven Greeks and a Maltese soldier, Angelo Fermoso. One killed and thirteen wounded was a steep price, but one Eaton was willing to pay for possession of Derna.

There was, however, still work to be done. The governor had fled to a mosque and then to a Hiram, a sacred sanctuary, where he was now holed up. Meanwhile, riders had intercepted communications from Hassan Aga's army; they were fourteen hours' march from Derna. Eaton would have to see to the defenses as soon as his wound had been bandaged.

Later that evening, Eaton stood on the quarterdeck with Hull and looked out over the now dark, silent town. Above them, the canvas flapped in the breeze, the ship creaking and groaning as it rolled in the gentle swell. In the dim light of dusk, Eaton saw the Stars and Stripes fluttering above the battery and saw the cooking fires of the men camped along the beach. After a march of fifty-two days across five hundred miles of wasteland, and fighting not only the desert but his purported allies, Eaton had won a signal victory for the United States.

Now they would have to press on and take Benghazi, some two hundred and twenty-five miles to the west. Once they had secured that town, they would make their final assault on Tripoli. But the most difficult part of the campaign was over. With a victory behind them, the Arabs would follow Hamet, and the rightful Bashaw, Eaton hoped, would no longer falter.

His wrist ached, a dull, painful ache, but it was a small price to pay for this moment.

XII

BETRAYED

Eaton busied himself with preparations for defending the town against the approach of Hassan Aga's army. Guns, powder, and stores were brought ashore. Work details were sent to position the battery's guns so they could fire on the town and the surrounding hills. Eaton also ordered the construction of a fortification above the Wadi Derna from which Hamet had attacked El Mogar and El Bilad. The fort, which was built using the remains of a much older fort, was built on a bluff that overlooked the entire town. Each day, work parties rowed ashore from the *Argus* to build the stronghold, moving rocks, digging trenches, and erecting walls.

On May 8, Eaton awoke to find the heights from which he had attacked the town occupied by Hassan Aga's army. The alarm among his people was palpable, and Eaton realized that their hard-won victory was now in the balance. Added to this worry was the continued presence of Mustafa Bey, the former governor, who was holed up in a Hiram in town and was inciting revolt among the people. His presence was a poison, and could easily incite a rebellion among those still loyal to Yusuf.

Eaton had spoken with the sheik of Mesreat, who was in charge of one of the departments of town still loyal to Hamet and who was providing refuge for Mustafa. He had tried persuasion, bribery, and menace but nothing had moved the old sheik. Now that the enemy was on the heights, preparing for an attack, Eaton had to deal with Mustafa once and for all.

Eaton set off from the battery with a troop of Christians and headed for the Hiram. When he arrived, he spoke to the sheik and told him that if he did not release Mustafa into his custody—he was rightfully a prisoner of war—Eaton would order the *Argus* to cannonade his department.

The sheik refused to yield. He told Eaton that whatever the weakness of Arabs, there had never been an instance of one of them giving up someone who had sought their protection and hospitality. It was a sacred principle that he could not break. If he did so, God would take vengeance upon him. Eaton was angry but he realized that to take Mustafa by force was folly and would incite a rebellion. So instead, Eaton marched back to the fortress and waited for events to unfold.

For four days, Hassan Aga fortified his position above the town and sent spies into the city to try and bring over Derna without a fight. From his sanctuary in the Hiram, Mustafa Bey assisted Hassan Aga while Eaton grew more and more enraged. The Bey was an active enemy and was not entitled, as the sheik had insisted, to privileges of hospitality. He was assisting the enemy and would have to be stopped.

Finally, Eaton decided that Mustafa had to be removed, either by force or the threat of it. So, on May 12, he outfitted fifty Christians with muskets and bayonets and marched on the Hiram. Eaton watched as the men and women of Mesreat panicked at the approach of his force and heard the alarm spread throughout the streets: "The Christians no longer respect the customs of our fathers and our laws of hospitality."

Eaton found the sheik and told him that he had come to take Mustafa from his sanctuary by force. Eaton told the sheik that the man was an outlaw and had forfeited his protection by rejecting the terms of peace Eaton had offered him prior to the assault on the town. Furthermore, stated Eaton, he had been beaten and was now in a conquered town, which made him by the laws of war an American prisoner. And now, continued Eaton, he was carrying on the war from his sanctuary. Eaton told the sheik that he intended to take Mustafa dead or alive, but one way or another, Mustafa would be removed from the Hiram.

All around them, Eaton could see the effects of his action

as the people of Mesreat prepared to defend their department. The sheik stood his ground and refused to hand over
Mustafa. Hamet arrived with his entourage and told Eaton
that he was stirring up an insurrection; he begged him to take
his men out of Mesreat and give him a day to speak with the
sheik. Eaton assented. He had never seriously entertained an
assault, merely threatening one to force the sheik's hand; if
Hamet could remove Mustafa by negotiation, so much the
better. Eaton ordered his soldiers to march back to the
fortress.

Meanwhile, above the town, on the slopes of Jebel Akdar,
Hassan Aga's army continued to ready itself for an assault.
They had now been there for eight days, mustering support
within town, and appeared to be readying for battle, but
when, Eaton wondered?

Eaton only had to wait until five o'clock the next morning
to find out. He rose from his cot to cries of alarm. Peering
through his glass at the flanks of Jebel Akdar, he saw Hassan
Aga's army massed for attack. Five standards, one for each of
the Beys in the enemy camp, fluttered in the early-morning
breeze. Eaton knew that a troop of Hamet's cavalry was stationed below Hassan Aga's force, about a mile from town,
and was guarding the approach.

Meanwhile, Eaton watched as Hassan Aga sent scouts out
to reconnoiter their position and prepare for an assault. More
troubling still was news that reached Eaton from Mesreat.
Mustafa, along with fifteen or sixteen of his followers, had
escaped during the night. He was now with Hassan Aga and
had detailed information about the number of Eaton's Christian soldiers as well as their defenses. It was probably this information, Eaton believed, that had given Hassan Aga the
confidence to now attack the town.

Eaton turned his glass toward the sea and saw that both
Hull and Dent were readying their respective vessels to repel
an assault. The *Argus* and *Nautilus* were anchored just offshore, and Eaton saw that the guns had been run out and that
both ships were ready.

Just then, the mass of Hassan Aga's army began to surge

forward. Eaton noted the time: half past nine. They appeared
to be heading directly for the Bashaw's palace. From his vantage point in the battery, Eaton watched as the enemy fell on
Hamet's cavalry and forced them back toward town. They
put up a brave fight as the sound of musket fire crackling in
the distance attested, but there were simply too many enemy
soldiers before them, and they yielded.

As the enemy entered the town, the *Argus* and *Nautilus*
began to fire on them. Meanwhile, Eaton ordered the battery's guns as well as the Greeks' fieldpieces to fire on Hassan Aga's army, but they continued to pursue Hamet's forces
into town. As they entered the narrow streets of Derna, the
sound of muskets and the flash of gunfire erupted anew as
Hamet's force used the previous occupants' defenses to make
a stand.

Eaton wanted to send a detachment of Christians to aid
Hamet, but if he did so, he would leave the battery dreadfully
exposed. Their position was simply too weak to offer assistance; Hamet would have to repel Hassan Aga with his own
forces, but as Eaton watched, he feared that the battle was already lost. He could now hear only the scattered fire of mus-
ketry, as if the defenses had already been broken. Eaton
decided, as a last resort, to turn his guns on the town, believing that Hassan Aga had already taken it.

Meanwhile, Hamet watched as his men were routed by
Hassan's superior force. They had pushed his cavalry from
the slopes of the mountain, pursued them into town, and now
entered the courtyard of the palace. A small piece of good
fortune was that soldiers loyal to the sheik of Mesreat had
bolstered his forces. But even his men were not enough, it
appeared, to tip the balance.

Hamet heard the sound of cannon fire shift from the slopes
of the mountain and into town. Eaton must have thought the
day was lost or he would never have fired on Derna. Was
the day lost? Should he continue to fight, or should he flee to
the sanctuary recently offered to Mustafa that he knew
would protect him as well? Where was Eaton? As the sound

of cannon balls striking stone added to the din of musket fire, Hamet hoped Hassan Aga's army would retreat.

Suddenly, two enemy horsemen in the courtyard were bowled over by a cannon ball, killed instantly. The strike of the cannon ball, as if by an invisible iron hand, turned the day. Immediately, the enemy, which had been poised to take the palace, panicked and sounded the retreat. Hamet watched as they fled the courtyard and retreated from the town in headlong flight. Hamet ordered his men to pursue them as cannon fire from the *Argus* and *Nautilus* shifted and peppered the fleeing enemy. As the enemy troops made their way back up the mountain, they left behind clumps of dead men and dead horses near ground grooved by the strike of shot.

By eleven o'clock, the battle was over. Hamet returned to the palace, where the sheik of Mesreat greeted him, kissed his hand, and seated himself before him.

"I have this day given you, I trust, an unequivocal demonstration of my personal attachment and fidelity," said the sheik, who sat before him as a supplicant. "I ought to say to you that you have not merited it. You would have yielded to the instances of the Christian General in violating the hospitality of my house, and of degrading the honor of my name. You should have recollected that, not quite two years ago, you were saved in this same asylum, and secured in your escape by the same hospitality, from the vengeance of this very same Bey. Had the fortune of this day gone against you I should have suppressed these sentiments of reproach: as it is I have acquitted myself to God and my conscience."

That night, an Italian slave escaped from Hassan Aga's army, made his way to the American camp, and confirmed that the fortune of the day had indeed gone the way of Hamet and Eaton. The man reported that Hassan Aga had lost twenty-eight men killed and double that wounded, eleven of whom subsequently died. Hamet had lost only fourteen killed and wounded.

The following day, however, the enemy was still there, occupying the heights Eaton had stood on three weeks ago. Spies brought intelligence that they were preparing for another assault and that they possessed a secret weapon: camels. They were scouring the countryside for drome- daries, which they would use as mobile breastworks to se- cure their flanks and front. Let them, thought Eaton; his army would need those camels for its march on Benghazi.

Eaton watched and waited for the assault, but still the enemy did not sally forth. Instead, deserters and spies told the story of an army divided. The Beys and Tripolitan troops were urging another assault, but the Arabs recruited on the march were against it. They would not go against the Ameri- can cannons, nor would they risk their camels. Spies told Eaton that Hassan Aga had less than one thousand men: three hundred and fifty mounted Tripolitan troops, between two hundred and three hundred mounted Arabs, and three hundred Bedouins, who were on foot. Of the total, spies in- formed him, two hundred of them had fled the town after the defeat of Mustafa's forces on the twenty-seventh. The dis- sension told by the spies mirrored the problems Eaton had faced on his long journey to Derna. He hoped that Hassan Aga's problems were as intractable as his had been.

Eaton had hoped the enemy would simply leave, but instead they stayed, building breastworks and loose stone walls. That was in one sense a good sign, signifying that Hassan Aga had gone on the defensive. But it also meant that he planned on staying. Indeed, Eaton heard fresh reports that the enemy troops had been sent to plunder corn and forage from the sur- rounding countryside.

Eaton knew they were vulnerable and could be defeated, and suggested as much to Hamet. A coup de main at night would destroy Hassan Aga's army and break the stalemate, but Hamet refused. Arabs did not fight at night, he told Eaton. Eaton fumed. He had too few men to assault the enemy with Christians alone, and Hull and Dent couldn't provide additional men, who were needed aboard ship. If Hamet would not attack, their only hope lay in Hassan Aga leaving, which he would not do. They were at a stalemate.

That night, Eaton heard the crackle of musket fire at the

base of the mountain. The fire was brief, and then died down. Probably a raiding party, intent on plunder. Would the enemy try a night assault? Not if the Arabs had a say in it; they, like their brethren who fought for Hamet, would not fight at night.

Eaton sat at his desk in the battery, now named Fort Enterprise, and penned a letter to Captain Samuel Barron. It was May 17, and the *Nautilus* would sail this evening with dispatches. He told Barron all that had passed since the *Hornet* had left with dispatches on May 1, and begged him to send supplies. Hassan Aga had cut off all sources of food from the countryside, and the town was desperate for bread, rice, coffee, and sugar if it could be had, and above all, ammunition.

Captain Barron sat at his desk, pen in hand. He was too debilitated and ill to sit at a desk for long periods of time, but his declining state of health and his duty to the U.S. Navy made it a necessity. Beside him lay Eaton's dispatches of May 1, which the *Hornet* had just delivered after laboring for sixteen days against heavy winds and heavy gales on its passage from Derna.

The dispatches troubled him, specifically Eaton's description of the character of Hamet Karamanli. Months ago, Barron had been filled with the hope that cooperation with Hamet would bring an end to the war. But based on Hamet's want of energy and military talent, as well as lack of resources, Barron felt his faith in Eaton's plan diminish.

The commodore was writing a letter to Tobias Lear in which he intended to inform him of his resignation as the commodore of the squadron and provide him with instructions for ending the war.

I am of the opinion that if the Ex Bashaw, having received the first impulse from our strength and being put in possession of Derna, the province where his interest is supposed to be the strongest has not in himself sufficient energy address and courage, and cannot command sufficient means to move on with firm steps toward the usurper's residence whilst we second his operations by sea. He must be considered as no longer a fit subject for our support and cooperation.

Barron paused. He knew, however, that while he no longer trusted Hamet to carry the day, the taking of Derna had had a powerful effect on Yusuf, and would assist Lear at the negotiating table.

These facts and considerations Sir for the due appreciation of which you are fitted by your talents and the length and particular line of your experience seem to point out the present as auspicious beyond any former occasion, and indeed as the very moment for attempting a negotiation especially when we combine with these reflections the certainty that our force respectable as it is yet greatly exaggerated at Tripoli and consider the effect which such a view of his enemy added to the movements of his brother must have on the mind of Yusuf Bashaw strongly persuaded that your conclusions upon these points have anticipated my own, I am induced to state to you my earnest wish that you may deem it expedient to meet the overture lately made by his excellency through the Spanish Consul so far as to found on it the commencement of negotiations.

Barron set down his pen. Peace was now their only hope to end a war that had dragged on for five long years.

At two bells in the afternoon watch, Master Commandant Isaac Hull heard his crew piping Mr. Eaton and Hamet Karamanli aboard and greeted them in his cabin, whose windows provided a fine view of the open sea. The weather was pleasant, with winds from the north, and the boat rocked gently at anchor as the men took seats and helped themselves to refreshments.

Hull waited for Hamet to state the nature of his visit, and found its purpose all too familiar: money. Hamet had none, and desperately needed $300 to pay the Arab sheiks who had recently fought with him. They were threatening to join the enemy unless they were paid.

Hull told Hamet that he did not have that much cash

aboard the *Argus* and that they would have to wait for a vessel from Malta to bring new funds. He told Hamet he must have patience for a few more days.

Hamet's spirits sank. He told Hull that he did not feel safe in his own home if he didn't have the funds required to satisfy the sheiks.

Hull told Hamet that if the Arabs were not faithful he would turn the guns of the *Argus* and the battery on the town and destroy all of the houses. Tell them that, and they would be more than satisfied, he said.

But Hamet was not. Hull offered them dinner, but Hamet refused. He had no appetite. Instead, he told Hull he wished to return to the shore, and stood, taking his leave with Eaton. As he was departing, Hull told Hamet that he would send ashore some of the prize goods he had aboard ship, which Hamet could use to satisfy the sheiks. He would send them to Eaton.

The following day, as launches plied the waters between the *Argus* and the fort, taking work parties to shore to build a wharf and dig a ditch around the fort, the wind began to strengthen and blow from the desert. It was a hot, dry wind that increased steadily in strength. Hull signaled for the launch and by half past three, the vessel was back aboard and all hands prepared for the rough seas that Hull felt were soon to follow.

Hull stood on deck and gazed at the town. Suddenly, he saw a wall of sand rising above Derna, extending three to four miles from north to south with every appearance of a whirlwind. It was moving toward them. Hull issued a rapid series of orders to secure the ship and clear the cables and moments later the cloud of sand descended upon the *Argus*.

The sea grew heavy and the ship pitched violently as the sandstorm blasted the vessel. Only with difficulty could Hull peer to windward, but doing so was painful, as the sand and dust stung his eyes. The ship strained against her cables, and it appeared that at any moment the line would part and the *Argus* would be cast adrift. The rigging and spars were cov-

ered in sand and fine dust, and the sky darkened as the sandstorm consumed them.

As the *Argus* rode like a bucking horse against a single anchor, Hull ordered the topsails and fore topmast staysail
ready to be loosened instantly in case the cable parted. If the
cable were to break and the ship had no sails ready, he would
be unable to keep her pointed into the wind and the oncom-
ing swell. If she turned sideways, she might broach, and if
that happened, not only would he lose the ship and his crew,
but Eaton would be on his own.

All that night they rode out the storm, the ship rolling and
pulling at her anchor. Hull wanted to know how Eaton was
faring but the seas were too high to permit him to send a boat
ashore, nor could he see any signals from either the fort or
the enemy on the mountain. All was obscured. He could only
hope that the enemy was as occupied as he was and would
not mount an assault under cover of the storm. If they did,
no guns from either the ship or the battery could be brought
to bear.

Ashore, Eaton fumed as the sirocco overcame the town.
Reports from spies, as well as from an Arab chief who had
been put in chains in the enemy camp to ensure the fidelity of
his men, told the story of how an enemy could be beaten
without firing another shot if only he had the cash to buy the
loyalty of the Arabs. Eaton understood now the true nature of
war in North Africa. Victory went to the army with the most
money. Hassan Bey was offering $6,000 for Eaton's head
and double that for him alive. The price for Christians was
$30 each. Let Hassan Bey come and take his head, thought
Eaton as the winds shrieked and the sand blasted Fort Enterprise.

Eaton peered out the window and saw a column of heated
dust and sand, which looked like the smoke from a fire and
turned the sun into a melted copper disk. Everything was
filled with fine, hot sand that made breathing difficult and
caused him to perspire from every pore in his body. He retreated from the window and tried to protect himself from

the flying debris, but there was no letup. All through the night, the wind blew, covering everything with fine powder.

The next day, the sirocco continued to blow, causing the pine boards of the camp tables and the book covers to warp. The heated dust coated everything, impregnating his clothes, and making his wound feel like it was burning. Seated at his desk, Eaton reached for a cool glass of water he had just poured and found it hot to the touch.

One thousand miles to the west, Dr. Cowdery was called to the Bashaw's apartments, where he found the Bashaw in an extreme state of agitation. It was May 24, and news had just reached Tripoli of the loss of Derna. The Bashaw declared that if it was in his power to make peace and give up the American prisoners, he would gladly do so without consideration of money. The Bashaw was worried, and repented not accepting the original terms of peace.

The Bashaw did not have to repent for long. Two days later, three frigates stood in for Tripoli. At eleven a.m. the smallest of the three approached, and Cowdery saw that she was the *Essex,* and was flying the white flag at the foremast, a sign of peace, and a Spanish flag at the mizzen, indicating that she requested the Spanish consul, Don Joseph de Souza, to come aboard. Cowdery watched and waited. Would the Bashaw raise the white flag as well? A little while later, a white flag was unfurled and sent up the castle's flagpole. The Bashaw would treat, but would he finally come to terms, wondered Cowdery?

The *Hornet* arrived in Derna on June 1 carrying Barron's letter to Eaton. Eaton sat at his desk in Fort Enterprise and reread the letter, which damned all of his efforts and indicated that Barron was contemplating a withdrawal from Derna.

The commodore had written that the Bashaw of Tripoli, through the Spanish consul, had made overtures of peace. Of course he had, fumed Eaton, and that was why they had marched on Derna. But now was not the time to treat. They

first needed to seal the victory and begin the march on Benghazi, meanwhile putting American naval forces into action
against Tripoli. Then they could discuss terms. They had
fought for too long to treat now, especially with the Spanish
consul, who had been in Tunis during Eaton's tenure there.
Cathcart had told Eaton that de Souza had advised the
Bashaw to begin the war in the first place, and Eaton remembered hearing de Souza making the following statement in
December 1801: "The Americans miscalculated if they
thought of forcing a peace without paying for it." How could
Barron and Lear countenance dealing with the man, who
was said to be the confidant of Yusuf? He was no better than
Beaussier, the French chargé d'affaires Preble had worked
with.

Eaton took up his pen and wrote a long reply, hoping that
the words flowing from the tip of his pen would somehow
reach the commodore and save the situation. He told Barron
he would wait for additional instructions, and then wrote
from his heart:

> You would weep, Sir, were you on the spot, to witness the un-
> bounded confidence placed in the American character here, and
> to reflect that this confidence must shortly sink into contempt
> and immortal hatred; you would feel that this confidence at any
> price, should be carried through the Barbary regencies, at least
> to Tripoli, by the same means that it has been inspired here—
> But if no further aids come to our assistance and we are com-
> pelled to leave the place under its actual circumstances, humanity
> itself must weep: The whole city of Derna, together with numer-
> ous families of Arabs who attached themselves to Hamet Bashaw
> and who resisted Joseph's troops in expectation of succor from
> us, must be abandoned to their fate—havoc & slaughter will be
> the inevitable consequence.

Eaton finished the letter and set down his pen. All he
needed was cash and supplies to complete the victory. If
Hassan Aga was vanquished, nothing could stop them, and
then Lear could sail for Tripoli and receive the American
prisoners without paying one Spanish dollar in ransom.

* * *

The sound of twenty-one guns firing from the Bashaw's castle echoed off the stone walls of the town, and was followed immediately by an answering salute from the American frigates. The twenty-one-gun salute announced the end of the war. A peace treaty had been signed. The date was June 3, 1805. Dr. Cowdery, now a free man, walked to the Danish consul's house, where Colonel Lear arrived a short time later. That night, they celebrated, and the American officers and Colonel Lear remained guests of Mr. Nissen. Their nineteen-month imprisonment was over.

Colonel Lear was satisfied; he had secured the release of the American prisoners for $60,000 as part of a prisoner exchange in which the Americans handed over one hundred and twenty Tripolitans, and the Bashaw returned the three hundred or so crewmembers of the *Philadelphia*. Eaton and Hamet would also have to give up Derna. But considering that Yusuf had once demanded an annual tribute of $160,000, this was a small price to pay since there would be no annual payment.

There was, however, one issue that remained, and that was the return of Hamet's wife and children. In the treaty that had been signed, this exchange would occur after Hamet departed Derna. The Bashaw, however, was worried that without any hostages, Hamet might incite the people against him. Therefore, Lear, at Mr. Nissan's instance, had included a secret article to the peace treaty in which he had written that Yusuf would have four years in which to give up Hamet's wife and children. Lear had delivered this article to Mr. Nissan; it would not appear in the official treaty ratified by the U.S. Congress, nor would Eaton or Hamet learn of it. Lear was not troubled by it; it was a necessary evil to pay for peace.

At dinner that evening, Lear also learned from Captain Bainbridge that Beaussier was demanding the wages of three sailors who had been aboard the *Philadelphia* and who had been imprisoned with the rest of the crew. Beaussier claimed they were Frenchmen. To Lear, this was an example of the

French perfidy that he had learned all too well in dispatches from Eaton related to the French consul in Alexandria, and Preble's experience with Beaussier the previous year. The man was simply asking to be paid for his part in the negotiations and was using this false claim as justification. If they had truly been French, why had he not demanded their release nineteen months ago? Why had he let them languish in the Bashaw's prison? He would write the man on the morrow and explain it to him, but for now, Lear enjoyed the evening in the company of the newly liberated American officers.

Master Commander Isaac Hull saw the familiar sails standing in for Derna from the West. It was the *Constellation,* probably bringing dispatches from Tripoli. A short time later, Captain Hugh Campbell requested that Hull come aboard and told him the news: The United States and Tripoli were at peace. The war was over. Campbell sent a jollyboat to Fort Enterprise to apprise Eaton. They would withdraw posthaste.

Eaton received the dispatches handed to him by Lieutenant Wederstrandt and knew before opening them what they contained. The war was over; the United States had sold out Hamet and the people of Derna. Eaton was incensed. He would take this crime before the president, before Congress. He would not let this betrayal stand. But there was nothing he could do at the moment save implement the secret evacuation plan he had worked out.

On the following night, June 12, Eaton, O'Bannon, and Hamet, along with as many of their followers as they could take, rowed out to the waiting frigate. As the oars dipped into the water and the boat surged forward, Eaton was angry. Not only had they abandoned those they left behind to certain slaughter, but they had also done a grave injustice to the American flag. They had struck their flag in the presence of an enemy who did not merit the victory. They were retreating when victory had been a certainty. Only two days ago they had defeated another attempt to take the town, causing such loss among the enemy that Eaton knew they would never be

able to mount another assault. Yet instead, they left under
cover of darkness, sending the wrong message to the Barbary tyrants and putting a black mark against the Americans'
national character.

The *Constellation* got under way the following morning.
From his cabin, Eaton glanced out the window and saw the
shores of Tripoli, and the green oasis of Derna receding into
the distance. He paused for a moment to take in what would
in all probability be his last look at this place, then dipped
the pen into the inkpot and continued his letter to the new
commodore:

> In a few minutes more we shall loose sight of this devoted city,
> which has experienced as strange a reverse in so short a time
> as ever was recorded in the disasters of war; thrown from
> proud success and elated prospects into an abyss of hopeless
> wretchedness—Six hours ago the enemy were seeking safety
> from them by flight—this moment we drop them from ours into
> the hands of this enemy for no other crime but too much confi-
> dence in us! The man whose fortune we have accompanied thus
> far experiences a reverse as striking—He falls from the most
> flattering prospects of a Kingdom to beggary!
>
> Our peace with Tripoli is certainly more favorable—and, sep-
> arately considered, more honorable than any peace obtained by
> any Christian nation with a Barbary regency at any period within
> a hundred years; but it might have been more favorable and more
> honorable.

EPILOGUE

On November 14, 1805, the prow of the *Congress* cut a white trough through the ruffled waters of Hampton Roads. As the anchor settled into the muddy depths of the Chesapeake, Eaton wasted no time getting ashore. Long weeks confined aboard ship had honed his sense of injustice over Lear's betrayal. He intended to travel to Washington immediately to stop ratification of the Lear peace treaty and press Congress to appoint a commission to inquire into the matter. Eaton also hoped to settle his remaining accounts and request money for Hamet and his men, whom America had betrayed.

Three days later he arrived in Washington, D.C., and realized how much his life had changed since he had left almost a year and a half ago. In the towns and villages along the way, people greeted him as the hero of Derna. In Washington, he made his way to a hotel and glanced at a copy of the *National Intelligencer,* which had an article about his arrival:

On Monday arrived in this city, our gallant and distinguished countryman, GENERAL EATON in good health. His achievements merit, and we entertain no doubt will receive, the respectful attention of his fellow citizens in every part of the union.

Eaton was also heartened to read an open letter written by Edward Preble that appeared in the newspaper:

The arduous and dangerous services you have performed have justly immortalized your name, and astonished not only your

country but the world. If pecuniary resources and naval strength
had been at our command, what would you not have done. . . .
You have acquired immortal honours and established the fame of
your country in the East.

At least, thought Eaton, the public knew that taking Derna
had compelled the Bashaw to sign a peace treaty. And if the
navy had supported him and Lear hadn't meddled, Eaton
would have installed Hamet on the throne.

Eaton spent his days visiting congressmen, making his
case against Barron and Lear. The administration treated
Eaton respectfully, inviting him to parties and dinners in his
honor. But Jefferson, Eaton knew, had given Lear his instructions, and Eaton harbored a grudge against the administration and would not allow numerous parties and dinners to
smooth over the issue. At one dinner, Eaton sat back in his
chair after enjoying yet another meal in his honor. Around
the table were eleven senators, some congressmen, and four
cabinet members. Eaton listened as yet another flowery
speech was given, extolling his actions in North Africa.

Eaton abruptly cut off the speaker. "I don't want your kind
words of welcome, your rich food and your fine wines. I demand justice! Let there be an inquiry into the sorry state of
this nation!" The senators and congressmen were aghast.
Later that month, those same members of Congress debated
a motion to present Eaton with a Congressional Medal and
decided against doing so.

In January 1806, however, Eaton got his wish. A Commission of Enquiry was formed to look into the peace treaty.
Eaton waited anxiously for the commission to reach its conclusion, which it published in a 473-page report released to
the public in April. Eaton read the report with satisfaction; it
vindicated him and damned Lear and Barron. The conclusion summed up his own feelings about the role Lear had
played in the war:

However unpleasant the task, the Committee are impelled by
obligation of truth and duty to state further that Mr. Lear . . . ap-

pears to have gained complete ascendancy over the Commodore, to have dictated every measure, to have paralyzed every military operation by sea and land; and finally, without displaying the fleet or squadron before Tripoli, without even consulting the safety of the ex-Bashaw or his army, against the opinion of all the officers of the fleet . . . and of Commodore Rodgers, to have entered into a convention with the reigning Bashaw, by which contrary to his instructions, he stipulated to pay him sixty thousand dollars. . . . The Committee forebear to make any comment on the impropriety of the order issued to General Eaton to evacuate Derna . . . nor will the Committee condescend to enter into consideration of pretended reasons assigned by Mr. Lear to palliate the management of the affairs of the negotiation. . . . They appear to the Committee to have no foundation in fact, and are used rather as a veil to cover an inglorious deed, than solid reason to justify the negotiator's conduct.

Eaton sat back. He had won a singular victory. He also learned that he had won compensation for the men who had fought with him at Derna; Hamet was provided with an appropriation of $2,400 and a pension of $200 a month for life, which would lessen the sting of betrayal.

Later that spring, Eaton traveled to Washington, where he again tried to settle his accounts. He calculated that he had spent $29,108 of his own money in assisting Hamet, and asked Congress to reimburse the funds. Instead they put off paying Eaton until one year later, when they finally agreed to pay him $12,636.60.

Eaton longed for something to do, and hinted to Secretary of State Smith that he would be honored to accept the position of brigadier general in the army. Meanwhile, in the spring of 1807, Eaton was pleased to learn that the citizens of Brimfield had voted him to a seat in the Massachusetts legislature. Eaton accepted, but before taking his seat, he had urgent business to attend to in Richmond, Virginia, where he had been subpoenaed to appear as a witness in the trial of Aaron Burr for treason.

Eaton arrived in early June, wearing the gold medal Congress had finally agreed to present him. Eaton, however, was

unhappy. He was not a politician, and longed for a position
in the military, even as military attaché. To drown his frustra-
tions, Eaton began to drink more and more. During the four-
and-a-half-month trial, he enjoyed his favorite drink, called
flip, which was a mixture of sherry and rum. Bored with the
proceedings, Eaton also gambled and entertained women
guests in his lodgings. As the trial wore on, Eaton noticed a
change in people's attitude toward him. Although people
continued to treat him with respect, he began to sense that
his star had faded.

After the trial, Eaton returned to Massachusetts, but he
knew in his heart that although he had served as a diplomat,
he was not a politician. He was not surprised, therefore,
when he was not asked to seek reelection in the spring of
1808.

Eaton continued to make inquiries to Secretary of State
Smith about the possibility of serving as a brigadier general,
but learned that all of the available positions were filled.
Eaton asked Smith again about becoming a military attaché,
but learned that these posts were reserved for the rank of
lieutenant colonel or lower.

Eaton returned to Brimfield, bored and sullen. He drank
even more, and then in August, a messenger arrived with a
letter. Eaton tore open the envelope and collapsed into a
chair. Eli Danielson had been killed in a duel with another
naval officer in New York. Danielson had been like a son to
him; he was heartbroken.

Eaton kept pursuing positions with the government, but
gradually lost his ardor. In 1809 he began to suffer from
rheumatism and gout, which continued into the next year.

On January 15, 1810, Eaton wrote a letter to his friend
Humbert in Tunis.

Fortune has reversed her tables. I am no more Eaton. I live, or
rather stay, in obscurity and uselessness. The wound I received
on the coast of Tripoli, and others more early, have deprived me
of an arm to use, and the use of a leg. Want of economy, which I
never learned, want of judgment in the speculative concerns of

private life, which I never studied; and what is more, privation of
the consideration of a government which I served, have un-
manned me. . . . A fellow first fed on horse chestnuts and then on
charity now bestrides the world and fattens on gore. We Americans venerate.him . . . but our wars are on paper. Free presses, no
heavy metal.

   . . . I am glad you are well; when I am so, I will write more.
Death has laid himself alongside and thrown his grappling hooks
upon my quarter and forecastle, but I keep him off amidships
yet.

Eaton only managed to keep death at bay for a year and a
half. He died on June 1, 1811. He was forty-eight years old.

On June 28, 1815, Stephen Decatur stood on the quarterdeck of the forty-four-gun frigate *Guerrière* and eyed the familiar harbor of Algiers. He savored the moment and the
changing fortunes of Algiers and the United States. Fifteen
years ago, William Bainbridge had entered this harbor as
captain of the *George Washington,* a converted merchantman, and had been beguiled into anchoring beneath the Dey's
guns. At the Dey's mercy, he was forced to carry the despot's
presents and ambassador to Constantinople.

Furthermore, Algiers had sided with Britain during the
War of 1812 and had snatched up American ships and forced
the U.S. consul, Tobias Lear, to flee for Gibraltar. Now Decatur was here as the commodore of one of two American
squadrons authorized by President James Madison and Congress to defeat Algiers and bring about peace without tribute.
In addition to the *Guerrière,* Decatur had nine ships under
his command, including the thirty-six-gun frigate *Constellation,* commanded by Charles Gordon, who had captained
one of the gunboats during the battles with Tripoli; the
thirty-eight-gun frigate *Macedonian,* commanded by Jacob
Jones; the eighteen-gun sloop-of-war *Epervier;* the sixteen-
gun sloop-of-war *Ontario;* the fourteen-gun brigs *Firefly,
Spark,* and *Flambeau;* and the twelve-gun schooners *Torch*
and *Spitfire.*

Decatur ordered the signal officer to send up a white flag and the Swedish flag, signifying that Decatur wished the Swedish consul, John Norderling, to repair aboard. Norderling had handled American affairs in Algiers since Lear had been dismissed. As the frigate anchored out of range of the Dey's guns, a boat left shore and arrived at the side of the warship carrying Norderling and the Dey's captain of the marine.

After they had been offered refreshments and taken seats in the great cabin, Decatur spoke. He told the captain of the marine that their admiral, Reis Hammida, was dead and his flagship, the pride of the Algerian navy, had been captured along with one of his brigs. Decatur handed the Algerian a letter from President James Madison, which was addressed to Omar Bashaw Dey. The message was straightforward: The United States had declared war on Algiers, and if the Algerians wished for peace, the United States was prepared to negotiate terms under the condition that no tribute would be paid.

The captain of the marine asked Decatur to come ashore under a flag of truce to discuss terms, but Decatur declined his offer. He remembered full well what had happened to Commodore Morris in Tunis and Captain Bainbridge in this very harbor. Negotiations would take place aboard the flagship. The captain of the marine then requested an amnesty so that any Algerian ships at sea could return while negotiations were under way. Again, Decatur refused. The United States and Algiers were at war. If any enemy ships appeared, he would destroy or capture them.

The captain of the marine accepted Decatur's terms. He had little choice, and by July 3, the United States and Algiers had signed a peace treaty in which Algiers renounced its right to annual tribute. The treaty broke the back of the strongest of the Barbary States. The war had finally been won.

Decatur sailed on for Tunis and Tripoli, where the Bey and Bashaw, respectively, signed lasting peace treaties with the United States. The Barbary States' reign of terror was over.

* * *

Decatur lived only six short years after the Algerians signed the peace treaty. On March 22, 1820, he was killed in a duel with Commodore James Barron in Bladensburg, Maryland. He was forty-one years old.

William Bainbridge was Decatur's second at the duel, and helped carry his friend home to his house on Lafayette Square. After the duel, Bainbridge continued to serve in the navy, commanding several naval yards. On July 28, 1833, he died at the age of fifty-nine.

Hamet was finally reunited with his family after word of Lear's secret treaty clause was leaked to the public. In 1809, Yusuf again awarded him the governorship of Derna, but Hamet fled to Egypt in 1811. No record exists of his death.

Of the men who assisted Hamet and Eaton in their quest, Leitensdorfer and O'Bannon fared well. After the evacuation from Derna, Leitensdorfer continued his wanderings until 1809, when he arrived in Salem, Massachusetts, and looked Eaton up. Leitensdorfer made his way to Washington, D.C., with Eaton's letters of recommendation and got a job with Jefferson's chief architect, Benjamin Henry Latrobe, as surveyor of public buildings. In 1833, for his part in the march to Derna, he received three hundred and twenty acres in Missouri, where he lived until his death in 1845.

After leaving Derna, Lieutenant Presley Neville O'Bannon continued to serve aboard the *Argus,* and retired from the Marine Corps on March 5, 1807. After the battle of Derna, the phrase "to the shores of Tripoli" was added to the Marine Corps' battle hymn, and the marine officer's sword, adopted in 1826, was modeled after the Mameluke scimitar given to Lieutenant O'Bannon in honor of his march on Derna.

O'Bannon and his wife emigrated to Kentucky in 1809, where his wife gave birth to a son, Eaton, who died at an early age. O'Bannon went on to serve in both houses of the Kentucky legislature. He died on September 12, 1850, at the age of seventy-four in Russellville. In Frankfort, Kentucky, there is a memorial to him with the inscription: "As Captain of the United States Marines, he was the First to Plant the American Flag on Foreign Soil."

After returning from the Mediterranean in 1804, Edward Preble was instrumental in designing and building gunboats and bomb ketches for the U.S. Navy. But his health never recovered, and on August 25, 1807, he passed away at the age of forty-six.

Of the many other naval officers who served in the war, three stand out. Midshipman Thomas Macdonough, Midshipman Charles Morris, and Lieutenant James Lawrence accompanied Decatur during the burning of the *Philadelphia*. Thomas Macdonough was the hero of the battle of Plattsburgh that was fought on Lake Champlain during the War of 1812. During the battle, Commodore Macdonough's forces captured four British warships: one frigate, one brig, and two sloops of war, dealing a decisive blow to the British navy. At the outbreak of the War of 1812, Charles Morris was a first lieutenant on the *Constitution* and played a heroic role in the action against H.M.S. *Guerrière*. He was promoted to captain after this action, and went on to command two of America's finest frigates, the *Adams* and the *Congress*. James Lawrence rose to even greater fame than either Morris or Macdonough. During the war, he commanded the *Hornet,* captured the H.M.S. *Peacock,* and was promoted to captain. On June 1, 1813, as commander of the forty-nine-gun frigate *Chesapeake,* he fought the H.M.S. *Shannon.* During the action he was mortally wounded, but told his men to keep fighting: "Tell the men to fire faster and not to give up the ship; fight her till she sinks!" In honor of Captain Lawrence, a group of women stitched the words "Don't Give Up The Ship" into a flag and presented it to Oliver Hazard Perry, commander of the U.S.S. *Lawrence,* named in the late captain's honor. The navy has since named many ships in his honor, and his words aboard the *Chesapeake* became the motto of the U.S. Navy.

Yusuf Karamanli remained on the throne until 1835. When war broke out between his two sons, Muhamed and Ali, over who would ascend to the throne, the British and

French consuls asked Turkey to intervene, and at the head of a fleet of twenty-two ships and six thousand men, Nejib Pasha took control of Tripoli and removed the Karamanli family from power. Yusuf died in Tripoli in 1837 and was buried with full honors.

ACKNOWLEDGMENTS

A book is the work of an individual, but an effort one cannot accomplish alone. I would like to thank the following people and institutions for their help: the Huntington Library, for providing me with access to the William Eaton Papers; and Professor Michael Johns, for allowing me to be a visiting scholar in the Department of Geography at the University of California, which opened up the rich resources of Berkeley's libraries. A special thanks to Professor Michael Watts, for his mentorship over the many years I spent at Berkeley, both as an undergraduate and a graduate student. And thanks to Professor Abe Peck, who helped me hone my writing skills at the Medill School of Journalism. I also have to go back through time and thank Deborah Doyle, my high school history teacher, who provided me with a deep appreciation for history.

This book would never have been published without the tireless effort of my agent, Agnes Birnbaum, Bleecker Street Associates, who found a home for this project and whose advice and counsel over the past five years have been invaluable. I would also like to thank Ron Doering, my editor at Presidio Press, who had faith in my ability and whose editorial skills are clearly evident.

As any writer knows, friends and family play a large role in an author's success. I would like to thank Bjarki, who never gets acknowledged for anything, and his wife, Kim, who puts up with him; my brother, Michael, for his creative inspiration; and my parents, who have always encouraged me to become a writer. I would especially like to thank my father, for his careful editing and proofreading. I am also grateful to my daughters, Emma and Margot, who are just now beginning to read, and allowed me some quiet time to write. Lastly, I want to thank my wife, Andrea, for her constant support and encouragement, and without whom I would have no stories to tell.

NOTES

Epigraph

v   "If the President": Edwards, p. ix.

Chapter I: The Thin Blue Line

1   It was April 27: United States, vol. V, p. 554.

Chapter II: Consul to Tunis

5   thirty-three days: United States, vol. I, p. 293.

5   At the top: Edwards, p. 67.

5   Eaton stood five feet, eight: Sparks, p. 356.

6   Eaton was born: Tucker, p. 348.

7   named Khair ad Din: Ibid., p. 50.

8   Each year, more than: Whipple, p. 25.

10   The streets were little: *National Geographic,* Feb. 1928, p. 223.

10   Eaton wondered if Bonaparte: United States, vol. I, p. 302.

10   seventy-two hours: Edwards, p. 68.

11   with his left hand: Ibid., p. 69.

11   addressed the Dey: Ibid., p. 68.

11   Ahead of them, the Plomb: United States, vol. I, p. 164.

12   As Eaton gazed toward Carthage: Ibid., vol. I, p. 579.

12   Barlow, based in Algiers: Rodd, p. 37.

12   generally exceeded ten percent: United States, vol. I, p. 269.

13   Finally, article twelve: Ibid., vol. I, p. 270.

13   Eaton was also authorized: Rodd, p. 39.

14   "To account for the extraordinary": United States, vol. I, p. 272.

14   Barlow had promised Famin, Felton, p. 190.

15   Eaton saw that all: Edwards, p. 70.

15   Famin welcomed Eaton: Ibid.

15　　Eaton was introduced: Ibid.
16　　He told Eaton that: Eaton, p. 62.
16　　who was openly hostile: Edwards, p. 70.
16　　On February 9, 1799: Wright, p. 38.
16　　While France had been weakened: Ibid.
17　　were expected at the Kasba: Ibid., p. 33.
18　　Is your vessel: Tucker, p. 113.
18　　The Bey responded that: Felton, p. 192.
19　　"It cost you but little": Wright, p. 33.
19　　The U.S. Navy was currently: Felton, p. 193.
19　　However, as they left: Ibid., p. 194.
19　　The engineer told Cathcart: Ibid., p. 195.
20　　Eaton replied that: Ibid., p. 199.
20　　Eaton remained firm: Ibid.
20　　"You will call the": Ibid., p. 200.
20　　Finally, as March ended: Ibid., p. 205.
20　　With regard to article twelve: Wright, p. 36.
21　　on the occasion of hoisting: United States, vol. I, p. 318.
21　　On April 2, the Bey: Felton, p. 206.
21　　Eaton brought linen: United States, vol. I, p. 314.
21　　"If you will not agree": Felton, p. 206.
22　　The value of such a present: United States, vol. I, p. 325.
22　　a perfidious scoundrel: United States, vol. I, p. 318.
23　　"It is hard to negotiate": Felton, p. 208.
23　　Eaton also knew that: Wright, p. 37.
24　　required $1,918.21 for repairs: United States, vol. I, p. 321.
25　　Aletti had been born: Edwards, p. 71.
25　　Eaton responded by asking: Felton, p. 210.
25　　A short time later: Ibid.
26　　"Consult your government": United States, vol. I, p. 325.
26　　"and let the Bashaws wreak": Wright, p. 47.
26　　He offered the Sapitapa $90,000: Felton, p. 211.
26　　would fetch more than: United States, vol. I, p. 326.
27　　Tunis had a hundred and twenty cruisers: Wright, p. 50.
27　　the cruising grounds of Corsica: United States, vol. I, p. 327.
27　　Venice had come under: Wright, p. 48.
27　　"Their long latteen yards": United States, vol. I, p. 327.
27　　Eaton had heard just how: United States, vol. I, p. 327.
28　　Under the pretext of sightseeing: Wright, p. 49.

28   If Congress do not consent: Ibid., p. 47.
28   On June 28: Felton, p. 212.
29   find a pretext for war: United States, vol. I, p. 328.
29   had been reduced to famine: Felton, p. 213.
29   Eaton understood that in order: United States, vol. I, p. 328.
29   the Portuguese and Sicilian ambassadors: Felton, p. 213.
29   "No sum whatever": United States, vol. I, p. 333.
30   "I have earnestly insisted": Ibid., vol. I, p. 328.
30   Toward the end of the month: Felton, p. 214.
31   The Bey, Eaton thought: Ibid.
31   Eaton climbed to the top: Wright, p. 53.
31   Eaton estimated three regiments: Ibid.
32   "Caution against Barbary Pirates": United States, vol. I, p. 336.
32   John Shaw, ship's doctor: Wright, p. 58.
32   instructed him to carry them: Felton, p. 215.
33   American ships would only stop: United States, vol. I, p. 337.
33   Famin had told the Sapitapa: Ibid.
34   "The importance of sending": Ibid., vol. I, p. 343.
34   "should our differences with France": Ibid.
35   "Do you take us for dupes?": Felton, p. 220.
35   "This looks a little more": Ibid., p. 222.
36   "To me," replied the Bey: Ibid., p. 223.
36   On April 12, 1800: United States, vol. I, p. 354.

Chapter III: Dark Clouds

37   It was May 25: United States, vol. I, p. 356.
38   "If further testimony be": Ibid., vol. I, p. 357.
39   Eaton spied an Arab: Wright, p. 70.
40   "I will send you out": Felton, p. 231.
40   "How!" said the Bey: Ibid., p. 232.
42   the Danish consul, Mr. Hammekin: Ibid., p. 226.
42   Eaton remarked that he could: Ibid., p. 227.
42   "That is past": Ibid.
43   reputation for cowardice: Wright, p. 72.
44   Famin had outbid him: United States, vol. I, p. 364.
44   He wrote to the Sapitapa: Ibid.
45   fired by President Adams: Wright, p. 63.
45   The date was September 17: Tucker, p. 19.
45   The *George Washington:* Ibid.

46   Over the course: Ibid., p. 20.

46   As they entered: Whipple, p. 55.

46   O'Brien, who was used: Tucker, p. 21.

46   The Dey told him: United States, vol. I, p. 376.

46   "You pay me tribute": Whipple, p. 56.

47   As the deck of the *Catherine:* United States, vol. I, p. 372.

47   laden with sugar, coffee: Ibid.

48   On October 15, Cathcart: Ibid., vol. I, p. 382.

48   "Consul, there is no": Ibid., vol. I, p. 383.

49   the only delinquent tributary: Ibid., vol. I, p. 397.

50   "What am I to deduce": Ibid.

51   Eaton asked the Bey: Ibid., vol. I, p. 398.

51   "Genius of My Country": Ibid.

53   "Gentlemen, I had the honor": Ibid., vol. I, p. 421.

Chapter IV: Tripoli Declares War

56   Jefferson stayed at: Schachner, p. 664.

56   Jefferson was deeply: Tucker, p. 40.

56   but he also knew: Ibid.

57   "Shall the squadron": Schachner, p. 685.

57   one hundred feet above: Chapelle, p. 498.

58   for seamen to climb: O'Brian, p. 23.

58   the one-hundred-and-seventy-five-foot frigate: Whipple, p. 69.

60   "Recent accounts received": United States, vol. I, p. 465.

60   "Should the Bey": Ibid.

61   It was June 27,: Ibid., vol. I, p. 491.

62   at 10 a.m., the lookout: Ibid.

62   On June 20, Eaton: Ibid.

63   Eaton argued that: Ibid., vol. I, p. 492.

64   On July 1, Commodore: Ibid., vol. I, p. 497.

64   She no longer looked: Tucker, p. 138.

66   In February The Bashaw: United States, vol. I, p. 451.

68   were well manned: Ibid., vol. I, p. 497.

68   the afternoon writing: Ibid.

68   Sir James Saumerez: Ibid.

70   He told Bainbridge: Ibid., vol. I, p. 500.

71   set of orders, which Barron: Ibid.

73   fourteenth of May: Ibid., vol. I, p. 459.

74   Hours later, he saw: Ibid., vol. I, p. 451.

75   latest post from London: Ibid., vol. I, p. 494.

75   "In my last letters": Ibid.
76   a long, blue coat: Ibid., vol. I, p. 251.
77   he had argued: Ibid., vol. I, p. 430.
79   appeared to be undergoing repairs: Ibid., vol. I, p. 491.

Chapter V: A Wily Enemy

82   eighty-nine crewmembers: United States, vol. I, p. 538.
82   on the gun deck: United States, vol. II, p. 84.
88   teach the Bashaw a lesson: United States, vol. 1, pp. 537, 538, 547, 553.
89   promised them three days': Ibid., vol. I, p. 543.
91   Gavino watched, powerless: Ibid., vol. 1, p. 544.
91   two Moroccan vessels: Ibid., vol. 1, pp. 543–544.
91   On September 1, a Greek: Ibid., vol. 1, p. 566.
91   "This would be an event": Ibid., vol. 1, pp. 566–568.
92   he would remain anxious: Ibid.
93   Hamet was the second: Tucker, p. 227.
93   After Hassan's death: Ibid., p. 228.
94   Yusuf did not forget: Ibid., p. 229.
94   "Sir, The inclosures": United States, vol. I, p. 569.
95   "The idea of dethroning": Ibid.
97   It was his favorite room: Colbert, p. 104.
98   He was a fighter: Tucker, p. 132.
98   He had "begged leave": United States, vol. II, p. 76.
98   Jefferson was well acquainted: Tucker, p. 153.
99   "You will see from": United States, vol. II, p. 116.
100   "The most effectual plan": Ibid., vol. II, p. 61.
100   Faithful Dick followed: Colbert, p. 104.

Chapter VI: A Badly Led War

101   At six o'clock on: United States, vol. II, p. 159.
101   Commodore Morris sat on: Ibid., vol. II, p. 274.
102   They had been held: Whipple, p. 85.
102   Then, Morris recounted: United States, vol. II, p. 162.
103   On May 24, Eaton received: Sparks, p. 267.
103   If the Bey of Tunis: Ibid., p. 268.
106   In 1773, at the age: Tucker, p. 154.
106   Eaton told him the history: United States, vol. II, p. 97.
106   Murray told Eaton that: Ibid., vol. II, p. 168.
106   Did not the principles: Ibid.
107   two enemy cruisers sailed: Ibid., vol. II, p. 169.

107 Captain Andrew Morris: Ibid., vol. II, p. 176.
108 in the Bay of Gibraltar: Ibid., vol. II, p. 236.
109 "Our operations of the": Ibid., vol. II, p. 248.
110 "I am constrained": Ibid., vol. II, p. 249.
110 offered Hamet the governorship: Ibid., vol. II, p. 247.
110 In Leghorn, Cathcart: United States, vol. II, p. 251.
111 "Sir, Not having your": Ibid., vol. II, p. 245.
112 "Although it does not": Ibid.
112 Then, on September 5: Ibid., vol. II, pp. 271–272.
112 Murray's letter indicated: Ibid.
113 Eaton covered his tracks: Ibid.
113 "Tell the American Consul": Ibid., vol. II, p. 272.
114 "But so long as he": Ibid.
114 Meanwhile, in Tangier: Ibid., vol. II, p. 283.
115 Murray had told Cathcart: Ibid., vol. II, p. 288.
115 calms and easterly winds: Ibid., vol. II, p. 296.
115 Cathcart told Morris: Ibid., vol. II, p. 291.
116 Cathcart knew: Ibid.
116 Yesterday, November 8: Ibid., vol. II, p. 312.
117 Malta on November 20: Ibid., vol. II, p. 348.
117 Morris handed him his: Ibid., vol. II, p. 349.
118 Jefferson awoke at five a.m.: Randall, p. 553.
118 America would soon need: Jefferson, p. 1.
118 "While other civilized": Ibid., p. 2.
119 "The nation claiming": Ibid.
119 He knew the west: Randall, p. 568.
119 At seven in the morning: United States, vol. II, p. 344.
121 "I should have": Ibid., vol. II, p. 346.
121 "Sir, I have this moment": Ibid., vol. II, p. 356.
122 Finally, on February 22: Ibid., vol. II, p. 351.
123 on February 27: Ibid., vol. II, p. 352.
123 Rather than return: Ibid.
125 nine o'clock on the morning: Ibid., vol. II, p. 353.
125 At eight a.m., Cathcart: Ibid., vol. II, p. 354.
127 "No. You have a good": Ibid.
128 Robert Livingston, the minister: Schachner, p. 735.
128 On April 11: Ibid., p. 738.
129 the French fleet sailing: Ibid., p. 737.
129 Monroe arrived in Paris: Ibid., p. 740.
129 he concluded that Commodore: Whipple, p. 95.
130 "I have not heard": United States, vol. II, p. 396.

130   on May 8, Jefferson: Whipple, p. 96.
131   Meriwether Lewis bade good-bye: Peterson, p. 762.

Chapter VII: Disaster

133   Bainbridge scanned the dark: United States, vol. II, p. 518.
133   Convinced that she: Ibid.
134   they had not detained: Ibid., vol. II, p. 519.
135   On August 6 he: Ibid., vol. II, p. 520.
136   The officer on duty: United States, vol. III, p. 24.
137   Preble was born in: Tucker, p. 190.
137   Captain Haskell had told: United States, vol. III, p. 18.
137   saw that one of them: McKee, p. 139.
138   Lear was a trusted: Tucker, p. 194.
138   Lear knew Simpson: United States, vol. III, p. 23.
139   The captain told Lear: Ibid.
140   At eight-thirty p.m.: McKee, p. 140.
141   As the deck cleared: Ibid., p. 42.
143   "At eleven at night": Ibid., p. 20.
143   On September 14: United States, vol. II, p. 271.
143   As rumors floated: Whipple, p. 113.
144   On September 9, Commodore Morris: Whipple, p. 100.
144   As they came within: United States, vol. III, p. 30.
144   "Sir, You will": Whipple, p. 100.
145   "Comrades: The result": Tucker, p. 205.
146   accompanied by Colonel Lear: McKee, p. 164.
146   silver teapots, silks, muslins: Ibid.
146   Simpson had gathered: Ibid.
146   To their right: Ibid.
147   wearing a woolen haik: United States, vol. III, p. 126.
147   "Are you not in fear": Tucker, p. 206.
147   The emperor continued: United States, vol. III, p. 126.
148   Bainbridge scanned the: United States, vol. III, p. 192.
148   The sound of two bells: United States, vol. III, p. 192.
149   sent Lieutenant David Porter: United States, vol. III, p. 189.
150   Bainbridge asked Porter: Ray, p. 81.
150   Porter responded that: Ibid.
150   ordered Porter to climb: United States, vol. III, p. 190.
150   she was stuck fast: Ibid., p. 193.
150   announced that nine gunboats: Ibid.
150   Meanwhile, the vessel: Ibid., vol. III, p. 190.
151   The answer was unanimous: Ray, p. 81.

151   The crash of shot: United States, vol. III, p. 193.
152   found that the guns: Ibid.
152   the carpenter, William Godby: Tucker, p. 216.
152   ordered Midshipman Daniel: Ibid.
152   Mr. Hodge, the boatswain: Ray, p. 81.
152   Bainbridge reflected on: United States, vol. III, p. 171.
153   Bainbridge knew that: Ibid.
153   He did not have: Ibid., p. 174.
153   The seaman at the ensign: Ray, p. 82.
153   everything of value was: Ray, p. 83.
154   As Cowdery watched: Cowdery, p. 5.
154   As the Tripolitan officers: Ibid., p. 6.
155   On the beach stood: Ray, p. 86.
155   He was overweight: Ibid.
156   He sat on thick, velvet: Ibid.
156   Dr. Cowdery stood on: Cowdery, p. 7.
157   Outside the prison: Ray, p. 88.
157   "with a frigate of": Ibid., p. 89.
157   On November 24: United States, vol. III, p. 256.
158   The British captain: McKee, p. 179.
158   Three days later, Preble: United States, vol. III, p. 256.
158   Preble concluded his note: Ibid., vol. III, p. 257.

Chapter VIII: Burning the *Philadelphia*
159   His grandfather had been: Tucker, p. 267.
159   She lay at anchor: Ibid., p. 275.
159   two enemy cruisers: Ibid.
160   the ketch carried: United States, vol. III, pp. 416, 423.
161   Decatur had first learned: Ibid., vol. III, p. 376.
161   He knew Charles well: Tucker, p. 268.
162   Decatur could read: United States, vol. III, pp. 253, 410.
162   Bainbridge wrote that: Ibid., vol. III, p. 253
163   fishing smack, the *Mastico:* Ibid., vol. III, p. 377.
163   capturing the fourteen-gun: Tucker, p. 267.
163   asking for sixty-two volunteers: United States, vol. III, p. 376.
163   Decatur selected James Lawrence: Ibid., vol. III, p. 423.
164   on February 3: Ibid., vol. III, p. 415.
165   cabin he would share: Tucker, p. 272.
165   Decatur ordered the spoiled: United States, vol. III, p. 418.
165   signaled the hour: Tucker, p. 270.

165	On February 7, 1804: Ibid., p. 271.
166	Catalano and Midshipman Charles: Ibid.
166	Stewart ordered his own: United States, vol. III, p. 415.
167	Finally, at four a.m.: Ibid.
167	wedged into a platform: Tucker, p. 272.
167	to the Gulf of Sidra: Ibid.
167	They reached Point Taguira: McKee, p. 194.
168	the two ships sailed: United States, vol. III, p. 416.
168	he held a council: Ibid., vol. III, p. 418.
168	Finally, the *Siren:* Ibid., vol. III, p. 416.
168	Dressed in loose Maltese: Tucker, p. 273.
169	The raiding party would: Ibid., p. 274.
169	Decatur divided his men: Ibid., p. 275.
170	a Tripolitan naval officer: Ibid.
170	they were the *Transfer:* Ibid., p. 276.
170	a mere twenty yards: Ibid.
171	the hour of ten p.m.: United States, vol. III, p. 417.
171	"Board, Captain, board": McKee, p. 197.
171	and nearly fell: Tucker, p. 276.
171	It was Morris: Whipple, p. 138.
173	the *Siren*'s Thomas Anderson: United States, vol. III, p. 418.
174	Twenty dead Tripolitans: Ibid., vol. III, p. 413.
174	"Board the Frigate": Ibid., vol. III, p. 376.
175	Midshipman Morris lit: Tucker, p. 278.
176	caught in the rigging: Ibid.
176	The ketch didn't budge: Ibid., p. 279.
177	shot through the *Intrepid*'s: United States, vol. III, p. 414.
177	emptying the entire broadside: Ibid.
177	Inside the Bashaw's prison: Ibid., vol. III, p. 282.
177	Dr. Cowdery was awakened: Cowdery, p. 13.
179	He instructed Eli: Edwards, p. 131.
180	discouragement supercedes resolution: Minnigerode, p. 70.
180	On May 16, Smith: McKee, p. 278.
181	If these ships, along with: Ibid., p. 280.
182	In June, Eaton finally: Minnigerode, p. 70.
182	staggering sum of $85: Edwards, p. 131.
184	Later that evening: McKee, p. 277.
184	Be assured, Sir: Ibid.
185	a lookout from the maintop: Ibid., p. 307.
185	It was Sunday afternoon: Ibid.
186	"Sir, the written orders": Tucker, pp. 351–352.

Chapter IX: Searching for Hamet

189   On November 25, 1804: United States, vol. V, p. 161.
189   Eaton scanned the harbor: Ibid., vol. V, p. 163.
189   it was under siege: Rodd, p. 164.
190   the pilot came aboard: United States, vol. V, p. 162.
190   The admiral returned: Ibid., vol. V, p. 164.
190   The Turkish viceroy, Muhammed: Rodd, p. 165.
190   Thrown into the fray: Rodd, p. 166.
191   personage of Monsieur Drovetti: Ibid.
191   Eaton had seen no: Tucker, p. 356.
191   On November 30: United States, vol. V, p. 167.
191   O'Bannon, who was a: Tucker, p. 356.
192   Misset, in true British: United States, vol. V, p. 171.
192   Eaton strode through the: Ibid.
193   "Excellency, I am the": United States, vol. V, p. 172.
193   At three p.m. the expedition: Ibid., vol. V, p. 186.
193   on the following day, Eaton: Ibid., vol. V, p. 174.
194   a party of Turks arrived: Ibid., vol. V, p. 186.
194   Their escort conveyed them: Ibid., vol. V, p. 178.
195   they came back with: Ibid., vol. V, p. 187.
195   confirmed what he had heard: Ibid., vol. V, p. 301.
195   Hamet's alliance with a: Ibid., vol. V, p. 187.
195   At eight o'clock on: Ibid., vol. V, p. 188.
195   At the gates, guards: Ibid.
196   The viceroy, speaking through: Ibid.
197   he would consider Hamet: Ibid., vol. V, p. 301.
197   He told the viceroy that: Ibid., vol. V, p. 189.
197   "Excellency, From Alexandria": Ibid., vol. V, p. 180.
198   word reached Eaton that: Ibid., vol. V, p. 301.
198   Money had exchanged hands: Ibid.
199   "Excellency, God ordained that": Ibid., vol. V, p. 197.
199   Eaton made four copies: Ibid., vol. V, p. 302.
199   One of the men he: Tucker, p. 362.
199   Lietensdorfer set off: Ibid.
199   Gervasso Prodasio Santuari: Ibid., p. 361.
201   He calculated that three hundred: United States, vol. V, p. 302.
201   Unguarded and unreserved: Ibid.
202   Hull sat in his cabin: Ibid., vol. V, p. 214.
202   Eaton read Hull's response: Ibid., vol. V, p. 229.
203   Yet the dangers were: Ibid., vol. V, p. 268.
203   He heard that Benghazi: Ibid., vol. V, p. 270.

203 "On this date I am": Ibid., vol. V, p. 252.
203 he and his entourage: Ibid., vol. V, p. 302.
204 he would not let him: Ibid., vol. V, p. 303.
205 The stench was terrible: Edwards, p. 163.
205 He complimented the man: United States, vol. V, p. 303.
205 The general was moved: Ibid., vol. V, p. 302.
206 First, he had shown contempt: Ibid., vol. V, p. 314.
206 The Turks provided the: United States, vol. V, p. 304.
206 His servant, Selim: Ibid., vol. V, p. 313.
207 messenger arrived from Alexandria: Ibid., vol. V, p. 317.
207 One evening, Eaton spied: Ibid., vol. V, p. 314.
208 Monsieur Thainville and Consul: Ibid., vol. V, p. 311.
208 "I believe the Bashaw": Ibid.
208 "I believe he would take": Ibid.
209 As they approached the: Ibid., vol. V, p. 349.
210 He had always felt: Ibid.
210 Eaton asked Hull to: Ibid.
210 Eaton also requested two: Ibid., vol. V, p. 353.
210 On February 12, a ketch: Ibid., vol. V, p. 349.
210 Later on he learned: Ibid., vol. V, p. 350.
211 he sent his secretary of state: Ibid., vol. V, p. 356.
211 The tower was actually: Rodd, p. 189.
211 "His Highness Hamet Bashaw": United States, vol. V, p. 369.

Chapter X: Across the Desert
213 Eaton examined the force: Rodd, pp. 191–192.
214 their departure was delayed: United States, vol. V, p. 388.
215 "Friend, you must have": Ibid., vol. V, p. 279.
215 Peck looked into: Ibid., vol. V, p. 362.
216 Eaton also learned: Ibid., vol. V, p. 396.
216 Peck was too thirsty: Ibid., vol. V, p. 362.
217 Eaton turned to Hamet: Ibid., vol. V, p. 405.
217 The sheik was unmoved: Ibid.
217 the army passed through: Ibid., vol. V, p. 410.
217 Hamet's entourage began: Ibid.
218 On March 18 they: Ibid., vol. V, p. 423.
219 Eaton tried to persuade: Ibid.
219 Eaton awoke and found: Ibid., vol. V, p. 425.
220 The pilgrim had seen: Ibid., vol. V, p. 433.
220 they had agreed to remain: Ibid.
220 saw at least fifty: Ibid., vol. V, p. 435.

221   Commodore Barron read: Ibid., vol. V, p. 438.
221   accompanied by the sloop: Ibid., vol. V, p. 446.
221   Barron was alarmed by: Ibid., vol. V, p. 439.
221   Through his minister: Ibid., vol. V, p. 417.
221   Only six days ago: Ibid.
222   "I have no doubt that": Ibid., vol. V, p. 438.
222   Dr. Cowdery had told: Ibid., vol. V, p. 443.
222   At three o'clock in the: Ibid., vol. V, p. 444.
222   Eaton had set up his tent: Ibid.
223   true deity was cash: Ibid., vol. V, p. 448.
223   Forty-seven tents: Ibid., vol. V, p. 454.
223   a messenger rode: Ibid., vol. V, p. 456.
224   Eaton was furious: Ibid.
224   He swore revenge against: Ibid., vol. V, p. 459.
224   arrived with a note: Ibid.
224   He had written that: Ibid.
224   Eaton preferred an open enemy: Ibid.
224   Eaton again ordered the army: Ibid.
225   the messenger returned with: Ibid.
225   "You see the influence I": Ibid.
225   Eaton responded that: Ibid.
225   Eaton saw that Hamet: Ibid., vol. V, p. 464.
225   Hamet sent an officer: Ibid., vol. V, p. 465.
226   he surveyed the landscape: Ibid., vol. V, p. 471.
226   they examined the lace: Ibid., vol. V, p. 472.
226   They thought all of this: Ibid.
227   As the Christians and baggage: Ibid.
227   Hamet told Eaton that: Ibid.
227   The journey from Alexandria: Ibid.
227   five sheiks came to: Ibid., vol. V, p. 475.
228   he could not live only: Ibid., vol. V, p. 476.
228   intended to compel: Ibid.
228   "Remember, you are in": Ibid.
228   "I have found you": Ibid.
228   Eaton that he was: Ibid.
228   fidelity to Hamet: Ibid.
229   one-hundred-and-eighty: Ibid., vol. V, p. 482.
229   estimated that they were: Ibid., vol. V, p. 483.
229   Eaton called for a halt: Ibid., vol. V, p. 490.
229   He responded that: Ibid.

230   preferred famine to fatigue: Ibid.
230   disaster was imminent: Ibid., vol. V, p. 491.
230   "The Christians are preparing": Ibid.
230   charged toward the thin: Ibid.
231   "For God's sake": Ibid.
231   One of the Arabs snapped: Ibid.
231   Eaton approached Hamet and: Ibid.
231   under one condition: Ibid.
232   two dead men floating: Ibid., vol. V, p. 495.
232   camped in a valley: Ibid., vol. V, p. 498.
232   only to use him: Ibid., vol. V, p. 499.
232   agreed with Hamet: Ibid.
233   At seven p.m. an officer told: Ibid.

Chapter XI: The Assault on Derna
235   afternoon of April 15: United States, vol. V, p. 512.
235   eaten in three days: Ibid., vol. V, p. 363.
235   past twenty-five days: Ibid., vol. V, p. 553.
235   shouts of "infidel" and: Ibid., vol. V, p. 512.
236   Hamet's Casnadar: Ibid.
236   he could hardly believe: Ibid., vol. V, p. 363.
237   defended by a battery: Ibid., vol. V, p. 527.
237   He left his cloak: Ibid., vol. V, p. 528.
238   covered with red cedars: Ibid., vol. V, p. 538.
238   led by Hassan Aga: Rodd, p. 238.
239   summit of Jebel Akdar: Tucker, p. 397.
239   northwest, were three districts: Rodd, p. 230.
239   ten-inch howitzer mounted: United States, vol. V, p. 541.
239   On the promontory: Rodd, p. 233.
240   Bu Mansur, was: Ibid., p. 234.
240   contained his palace and: Ibid., p. 233.
241   "Sir, I want no": United States, vol. V, p. 542.
241   "My head or yours": Ibid.
242   Volney, a traveler and writer who had described: Ibid., vol. V, p. 552.
242   Hamet now had: Ibid., vol. V, p. 551.
242   Muhammed el Layyas: Rodd, p. 231.
243   the chief difficulty was: United States, vol. V, p. 554.
243   some twenty feet high: Ibid., vol. V, p. 547.
243   200 bags: Ibid., vol. V, p. 542.

245   overlooking the town: Ibid., vol. V, p. 554.
247   wall of the battery: Ibid., vol. V, p. 547.
248   then to a Hiram: Ibid., vol. V, p. 555.

Chapter XII: Betrayed
249   Eaton also ordered: Rodd, p. 238.
249   On May 8, Eaton: United States, vol. VI, p. 6.
249   He had tried persuasion: Ibid., vol. VI, p. 5.
250   He told Eaton: Ibid.
250   The Christians no longer: Ibid., vol. VI, p. 11.
250   Eaton told the sheik: Ibid.
251   he was stirring up: Ibid.
251   It was probably this: Ibid., vol. VI, p. 14.
252   half past nine: Ibid., vol. VI, p. 20.
252   He could now: Ibid., vol. VI, p. 14.
253   the enemy, who had: Ibid.
253   "I have this day": Ibid., vol. VI, p. 13.
253   The man reported that: Ibid., vol. VI, p. 15.
254   deserters and spies told: Ibid.
255   He told Barron all: Ibid.
255   heavy winds and heavy gales: Ibid., vol. VI, p. 24.
255   the character of Hamet: Ibid., vol. VI, p. 22.
255   "I am of the opinion": Ibid.
256   "These factors and": Ibid.
256   At two bells: Ibid., vol. VI, p. 29.
257   He told Hull: Ibid., vol. VI, p. 28.
257   The wind began to: Ibid., vol. VI, p. 29.
258   an Arab chief who: Ibid., vol. VI, p. 43.
258   column of heated dust: Ibid., vol. VI, p. 45.
259   the sirocco continued: Ibid., vol. VI, p. 47.
259   news had just reached: Cowdery, p. 31.
259   power to make peace: Ibid.
260   Eaton remembered hearing: United States, vol. VI, p. 60.
260   "You would weep": Ibid., vol. VI, p. 61.
261   he had secured: Ibid., vol. VI, p. 81.
261   included a secret article: Ibid., vol. VI, p. 82.
261   Beaussier was demanding: Ibid., vol. VI, p. 88.
262   They had struck: Ibid., vol. VI, p. 60.
263   "In a few minutes": Ibid., vol. VI, p. 117.

Epilogue

265   Eaton also hoped: Rodd, p. 278.
265   "On Monday arrived": Whipple, p. 265.
265   "The arduous and dangerous": Rodd, p. 275.
266   At least, thought Eaton: Sparks, p. 335.
266   "I don't want your kind": Edwards, p. 240.
266   Later that month: Rodd, p. 277.
266   In January 1806: Ibid., p. 278.
266   in a 473-page report: Edwards, p. 245.
266   "However unpleasant the task": Whipple, p. 268.
267   Hamet was: Ibid., p. 269.
267   He calculated that he: Ibid., p. 267.
267   finally agreed to pay him: Ibid., p. 266.
267   he had been subpoenaed: Edwards, p. 251.
268   Eaton continued to make: Ibid., p. 248.
268   "Fortune has reversed her tables": Rodd, p. 293.
269   Decatur had nine ships: Tucker, p. 453.
270   Decatur ordered the signal: Ibid., p. 456.
271   the governorship of Derna: Ibid., p. 281.
271   After the evacuation: Tucker, p. 438.
271   his death in 1845: http://www.stlgs.org/efdb/d327.htm#P14176
271   After leaving Derna: Tucker, p. 439.
272   Preble was instrumental: McKee, p. 326.
272   Yusuf Karamanli remained: Rodd, p. 282.

BIBLIOGRAPHY

Adams, William Howard. *The Paris Years of Thomas Jefferson.* New Haven and London: Yale University Press, 1997.

Cathcart, James Leander. *The Captives: Eleven Years a Prisoner in Algiers.* La Porte, Ind.: Herald Print, 1899.

———. *Tripoli: First War with the United States.* La Porte, Ind.: Herald Print, 1901.

Chapelle, Howard I. *The History of the American Sailing Navy.* New York: Bonanza Books, 1949.

Cooper, J. Fenimore. *Lives of Distinguished American Naval Officers.* Philadelphia: Carey and Hart, 1846.

Cowdery, Jonathan. *American Captives or Dr. Jonathan Cowdery's Journal in Miniature Kept During His Late Captivity in Tripoli.* Boston: Belcher & Armstrong, 1806.

Eaton, William. *The Life of the Late Gen. William Eaton: Several Years an Officer in the United States' Army.* Brookfield, Mass.: E. Merriam & Co., 1813.

Edwards, Samuel. *Barbary General: The Life of William H. Eaton.* Englewood Cliffs, N.J.: Prentice-Hall, Inc., 1968.

Felton, Cornelius C. *Life of William Eaton.* In The Library of American Biography. New York: Harper & Brothers, 1848.

Fischer, Godrey. *Barbary Legend: War, Trade, and Piracy in North Africa, 1415–1830.* Oxford: Clarendon Press, 1957.

Foner, Philip S. *Basic Writings of Thomas Jefferson.* New York: Willey Book Company, 1944.

Foss, John. *A Journal of the Captivity and Suffering of John Foss, Several Years a Prisoner in Algiers.* Newburyport, Mass.: A. March, Middle-Street, 1798.

Gerson, Noel B. *Barbary General: The Life of William H. Eaton.* Englewood Cliffs, N.J.: Prentice-Hall, 1968.

Jefferson, Thomas. *Public and Private Papers.* New York: First Vintage Books, 1990.

————. Transcript of Jefferson's Secret Message to Congress Regarding the Lewis & Clark Expedition (1803). www.ourdocuments.gov. June 30, 2004.

Lewis, Charles L. *The Romantic Decatur.* Philadelphia: University of Pennsylvania Press, 1937.

Maclay, Edgar S. *Reminiscences of the Old Navy.* New York: Knickerbocker Press, 1898.

McKee, Christopher. *Edward Preble: A Naval Biography, 1761–1807.* Annapolis, Md.: Naval Institute Press, 1972.

Minnigerode, Meade. *Lives and Times: Four Informal American Biographies.* New York and London: G. P. Putnam's Sons, Knickerbocker Press, 1925.

Nash, Howard P., Jr. *The Forgotten Wars: The Role of the U.S. Navy in the Quasi War with France and the Barbary Wars 1798–1805.* New York: A. S. Barnes and Company, 1968.

O'Brian, Patrick. *Men-of-War: Life in Nelson's Navy.* New York: W.W. Norton & Company, 1995.

O'Neill, Richard, ed. *Patrick O'Brian's Navy: The Illustrated Companion to Jack Aubrey's World.* Philadelphia: Running Press Book Publishers, 2003.

Peterson, Merrill D. *Thomas Jefferson and the New Nation: A Biography.* New York: Oxford University Press, 1970.

Randall, Willard Sterne. *Thomas Jefferson: A Life.* New York: Henry Holt and Company, 1993.

Ray, William. "The American Tars in Tripolitan Slavery." *The Magazine of History,* no. 14. Troy, N.Y.: Oliver Lyon, 1808.

Rennell, Francis J. R. R. *General William Eaton: The Failure of an Idea.* New York: Minton, Balch and Company, 1932.

Schachner, Nathan. *Thomas Jefferson: A Biography.* New York and London: Thomas Yoseloff Ltd., 1951.

Sumner, Charles. *White Slavery in the Barbary States.* Boston: John P. Jewett and Company, 1853.

Tucker, Glenn. *Dawn Like Thunder: The Barbary Wars and the Birth of the U.S. Navy.* Indianapolis: The Bobbs-Merrill Company, Inc., 1963.

United States, Office of Naval Records and Library. Naval documents related to the United States Wars with the Barbary Powers, Vols. I–VI. Washington, D.C.: U.S. Government Printing Office, 1939–1944.

Wheelan, Joseph. *Jefferson's War: America's First War on Terror 1801–1805*. New York: Carroll & Graff Publishers, 2003.

Whipple, A.B.C. *To the Shores of Tripoli: The Birth of the U.S. Navy and Marines*. New York: William Morrow and Company, Inc., 1991.

Wright, Louis B., and Julia H. Macleod. *The First Americans in North Africa: William Eaton's Struggle for a Vigorous Policy Against the Barbary Pirates, 1799–1805*. Princeton, N.J.: Princeton University Press, 1945.

INDEX